W9-BZX-527

Far Above Rubies

By Lynda Coats

Revised by Robin Scarlata

Family Christian Academy

Proverbs 31:10-31

Who can find a virtuous woman? for her price is far above rubies.

The heart of her husband doth safely trust in her,

so that he shall have no need of spoil.

She will do him good and not evil all the days of her life.

She seeketh wool, and flax, and worketh willingly with her hands.

She is like the merchants' ships; she bringeth her food from afar.

She riseth also while it is yet night,

and giveth meat to her household, and a portion to her maidens.

She considereth a field, and buyeth it:

with the fruit of her hands she planteth a vineyard.

She girdeth her loins with strength, and strengtheneth her arms.

She perceiveth that her merchandise is good:

her candle goeth not out by night.

She layeth her hands to the spindle, and her hands hold the distaff.

She stretcheth out her hand to the poor; yea,

she reacheth forth her hands to the needy.

She is not afraid of the snow for her household:

for all her household are clothed with scarlet.

She maketh herself coverings of tapestry; her clothing is silk and purple.

Her husband is known in the gates,

when he sitteth among the elders of the land.

She maketh fine linen, and selleth it;

and delivereth girdles unto the merchant.

Strength and honour are her clothing; and she shall rejoice in time to come.

She openeth her mouth with wisdom;

and in her tongue is the law of kindness.

She looketh well to the ways of her household,

and eateth not the bread of idleness.

Her children arise up, and call her blessed;

her husband also, and he praiseth her.

Many daughters have done virtuously, but thou excellest them all.

Favour is deceitful, and beauty is vain:

but a woman that feareth the LORD, she shall be praised.

Family Christian Academy

Published by:
Family Christian Academy
487 Myatt Drive
Masison, TN 37115
(615) 860-3000
FAX (615) 860-9788

First Edition 1993© Lynda Coats
Second Edition, Revised1994© Family Christian Academy
Third Edition, Revised 1995© Family Christian Academy
All Rights Reserved. No portion of this book may be reproduced in any form without written

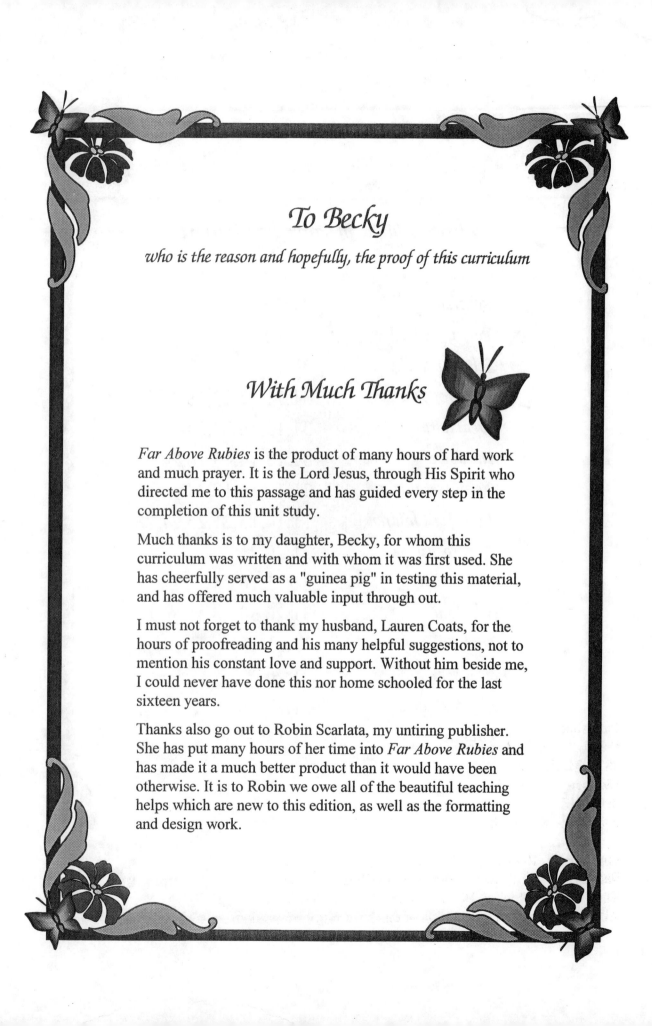

To Becky

who is the reason and hopefully, the proof of this curriculum

With Much Thanks

Far Above Rubies is the product of many hours of hard work and much prayer. It is the Lord Jesus, through His Spirit who directed me to this passage and has guided every step in the completion of this unit study.

Much thanks is to my daughter, Becky, for whom this curriculum was written and with whom it was first used. She has cheerfully served as a "guinea pig" in testing this material, and has offered much valuable input through out.

I must not forget to thank my husband, Lauren Coats, for the hours of proofreading and his many helpful suggestions, not to mention his constant love and support. Without him beside me, I could never have done this nor home schooled for the last sixteen years.

Thanks also go out to Robin Scarlata, my untiring publisher. She has put many hours of her time into *Far Above Rubies* and has made it a much better product than it would have been otherwise. It is to Robin we owe all of the beautiful teaching helps which are new to this edition, as well as the formatting and design work.

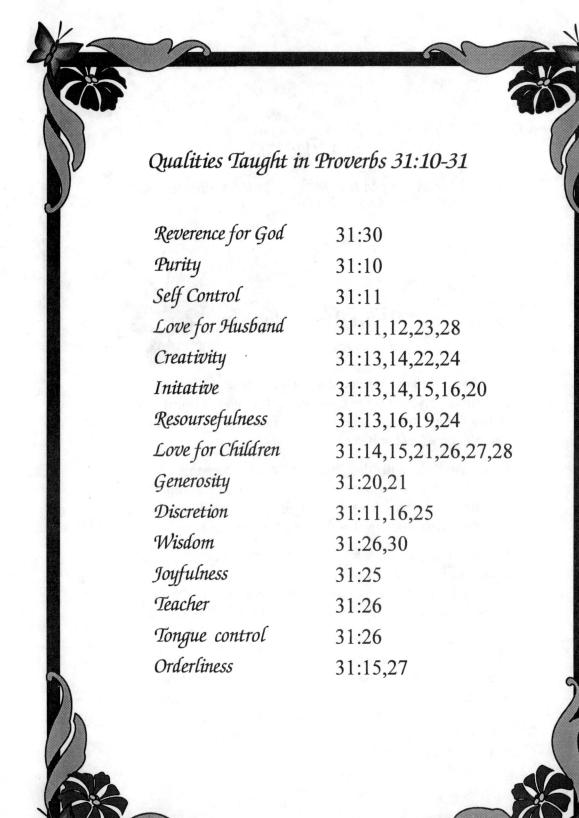

Qualities Taught in Proverbs 31:10-31

Reverence for God	31:30
Purity	31:10
Self Control	31:11
Love for Husband	31:11,12,23,28
Creativity	31:13,14,22,24
Initative	31:13,14,15,16,20
Resoursefulness	31:13,16,19,24
Love for Children	31:14,15,21,26,27,28
Generosity	31:20,21
Discretion	31:11,16,25
Wisdom	31:26,30
Joyfulness	31:25
Teacher	31:26
Tongue control	31:26
Orderliness	31:15,27

Table of Contents

To the Parent i

Essential Materials iii

How the Units Work iv

Goal Planning v

Lesson Planning and Record Keeping vii

Notebooks viii

Timeline ix

Units Divided Thematically x

Scope and Sequence xii

Unit One 1

Unit Two 17

Unit Three 31

Unit Four 43

Unit Five 57

Unit Six 75

Unit Seven 91

Unit Eight 105

Unit Nine 121

Unit Ten 133

Unit Eleven 147

Unit Twelve 159

Unit Thirteen 173

Unit Fourteen 187

Unit Fifteen 199

Unit Sixteen 215

Unit Seventeen 231

Unit Eighteen 245

Unit Nineteen 259

Unit Twenty 271

Appendix I 286

Appendix II 292

To the Parent

The *Far Above Rubies* unit study is designed to train girls to become the godly women our Lord wants them to be. It is based on Proverbs 31:10-31, and is designed to cover all subjects for a complete high school education, including many suggestions for expanding into specialized areas of interest. The main emphasis of this unit is on preparing our daughters for the life calling of wife and mother. Though we try to provide a well-rounded curriculum useful for college preparatory purposes as well as offering a number of business and vocational skills, our goal is to help Christian young ladies develop their skills and abilities for useful service within the family setting. We hope to help maturing Christian girls understand the importance of homemaking as a full-time profession, even for a woman who may have another profession or occupation. This curriculum stresses the importance of a woman making her family her number one earthly priority in terms of time and emotional commitment.

Each of the 20 units in the study is based on one or more verses from the passage under study. Each unit consists of activities related directly or indirectly to the target verse(s), and includes all the following areas:

1. **Bible and Christian Character**

2. **Cultural Studies** — history, geography, civics, general economics, law, etc.

3. **Reading and Literature**

4. **Composition**[1] — includes handwriting, spelling, grammar, vocabulary development, research, and related skills.

5. **Math**[2] **and Personal Finance** — basics, for those who need them, as well as algebra, geometry, consumer math, bookkeeping, and accounting.

6. **Science** — includes all areas of biological, physical, and earth science.

7. **Health and Physical Fitness** — exercise, nutrition, first aid and nursing skills, and general health.

8. **Practical Arts** — crafts of all kinds, homemaking, languages, woodworking, business, and vocational skills.

9. **Creative and Performing Arts** — music, art, drama, both in the performance and appreciation areas, and artistic expression.

Because this study is designed for young adults, materials are written directly to the student. Parents may work with students and should monitor and direct them as they see fit. There is enough material in each unit to provide for every type of learning style and a wide choice of activities, much more than any one student will ever need.

---

[1]A general knowledge of grammar is assumed for any of these activities. For additional or remedial grammar suggestions see the *Far Above Rubies Companion*.

[2]Math is practiced and strengthened in each unit. If you are using a separate math text, you may skip all or most of the math in each unit. However, do not skip the personal finances activities in the math section. See suggestions in the *Far Above Rubies Companion* for recommended or remedial math programs.

Parents are encouraged to work with their daughters to choose those items which are appropriate to their learning styles, family beliefs, and educational goals, being sure to adequately cover a variety of subject areas. It is important that parents and students do not become slaves to this material, but rather let it work for you and your daughter.

The units may be done in any order, except that we recommend starting with Unit 1 and ending with Unit 20 as these are a springboard and a wrap up unit, respectively. Regardless of the order in which the units are approached, we do suggest that you do all of your work within the same unit, but no one is expected to complete every part of any one unit or the entire manual. You may find that some long projects take more than the allotted time for a particular unit, for example, growing vegetables. In this event go on to the next unit and continue with the project until it is completed. There are some activities such as gardening, that you may not be able to do. DFeel free to skip any activities that do not fit your goals or lifestyle.

Since this course is offered to mature teenagers and is designed to produce well-trained Christian adults, we deal with some topics to which young Christian children should not be exposed. Some of these areas come under the general heading of "sex education." We believe this subject should be taught within the family and that each family should approach it from their own perspective. All materials we suggest for use in this area are written from a Christian perspective but may contain specific denominational or doctrinal leanings which would be unacceptable to some families. They are offered only as suggestions without endorsement from our company.

Other topics in this curriculum which may be controversial include millennial views, church government, secular psychology, vegetarianism, and the use of alcohol. We recognize differing opinions among sincere believers on these topics and try not to take a stand on issues on which Biblical teaching seems to leave room for us to disagree. This material also discusses abortion and evolution from a Christian perspective. We do not present them as acceptable, but try to familiarize the student with each area so she can have a reasonable understanding of the issues if and when she is confronted. Parents who feel uncomfortable with having their daughter learn about any of the above topics can easily skip those sections. They are not essential to the remainder of the material.

This unit need not be used as a whole, but may also be used in part and combined with other studies. Many activities are usable for younger students, girls who may have gaps in previous learning, and those with learning difficulties. The unit includes an extensive resource list for materials referenced. Our company can sell many of the books and other materials and can direct you to sources for others. Many lists and reviews are in *The Big Book of Home Learning* by Mary Pride and *Christian Home Educators Manual* by Cathy Duffy.

Essential Materials for this Course

This course cannot be taught without access to the following materials:

1. Bible - any version; literal translations are better than paraphrases
2. Concordance - should be designed for the Bible translation you are using
3. Dictionary - we recommend Webster's 1828 edition as well as a good modern one
4. Encyclopedia - the library is close enough for these as they aren't used all the time
5. One or more hymnbooks or Christian songbooks - you may be able to borrow from your church
6. English Grammar Handbook - we recommend **Writers INC**

Students may also find the following helpful throughout the course in addition to those books named in the curriculum:

1. Commentaries
2. Field guides of birds and animals
3. Several good cookbooks and/or nutrition guides
4. Word processor or typewriter
5. Record, cassette tape, or CD player
6. Medical encyclopedia or health care book
7. General history texts
8. General and consumer math texts
9. Thesaurus
10. Classic poetry anthology
11. Extensive short story anthology
12. Any good anthology of Shakespeare's plays
13. Recent World Almanac
14. Assortment of classical music
15. Book or collection of prints of famous paintings
16. A three hole paper punch

Some of these items may be listed in some units, but they may be helpful in some other places as well. It is advisable to keep each of these handy, if possible. Many of them are available in most public libraries, and that may be sufficient. Students are urged to use them whenever needed.

How the Units Work

Each unit is divided into 9 subjects:

1. Bible
2. Cultural Studies
3. Literature
4. Composition
5. Math
6. Science
7. Health
8. Practical Arts
9. Creative and Performing Arts

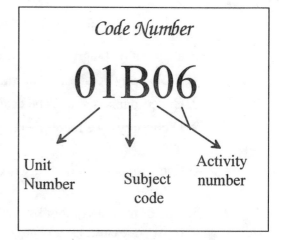

Code Number

01B06

Unit Number

Subject code

Activity number

Activities have a code number and the number of points for credit.

1B03. List the character traits of the ideal wife in Proverbs 31. B - 3 EG - 5

1B15. Complete *God's Priceless Woman* Bible Study course. B - 35

Each activity has a point value. Depending on the activities the student completes, she will receive points in one or more of the following 28 subjects listed below. Record keeping is easy. Just keep track of points earned using the record keeping system in the *Far Above Rubies Companion*.

Key to Credit Codes

A - Accounting & Bookkeeping

AA - Art Appreciation

B - Bible and Christian Doctrine

BE - Business Education

CE - Economics

CG - Government

CR - Practical Crafts

DR - Dramatic Arts

EC - English Composition

EG - English Grammar

FL - Foreign Language

G - Geography

H - History

HA - Human Anatomy

HE - Health Education

HF - Home and Family Life, Teacher Ed and Child Development

HM - Homemaking

L - Literature

M - Mathematics

MA - Music

PA - Practical Agriculture

PE - Physical Education

SB - Science: Biology

SC - Science: Chemistry

SE - Earth Science & Ecology

SP - Physical Science

VA - Visual Arts

WW - Woodworking

Goal Planning

Far Above Rubies is designed to be a four year high school study for grades 9-12 but can be adapted. See plans below:

Typical Four Year Plan

To complete 20 units in a four year period, plan on completing 5 units per year. To complete 5 units per year, plan on studying each unit for approximately seven weeks. Some units you may want to spend more or less time on. Keep track of points earned and points needed by filling out the record keeping form in the *Far Above Rubies Companion*.

Adapted Three Year Plan

If you only have three years of high school left you should already have credits from your previous year. You can still go through all 20 units, although you will need to chose fewer activities per unit. To complete 20 units in three years, plan on completing 7 units per year. You will study each unit for approximately 5 weeks.

Adapted Two Year Plan

If you only have two years of high school left you should already have credits from your previous years. You can still go through all 20 units, although you will need to chose fewer activities per unit or chose only the activities you need credit in. To complete 20 units in two years, plan on completing 10 units per year. You will study each unit for approximately 3½ weeks.

Adapted Five Year Plan

Many girls are mature enough and academically ready for the *Far Above Rubies* assignments as early as seventh or eighth grade. To complete 20 units in a five year period, plan on completing 4 units per year. To complete 4 units per year plan on studying each unit for approximately 9 weeks. Activities or reading assignments that are on a higher level can be postponed until the second or third year if necessary.

A Word About Points and Grades

Please understand the points are only a guideline. You decide how many points your student receives for each activity. For example, let's say you assign her a research paper that suggests 5 points in English composition. If she spends weeks at the library and gathers dozens of sources, you would give more points. Likewise, if she only thew together a few paragraphs or does much less than you were expecting, record the points accordingly. Count each 45 minutes to one hour as a point. One credit is equal to 135 points.

Some parents decide to give a letter grade "C" to a student that completes 135 hours in one subject and a higher grade for more points. Use what ever system works best for your student. Remember the goal is not a letter grade or passing a state test.

Our goal is to teach our daughters to love the Lord, to love to learn, and to develop the talents the Lord gave them to become godly young ladies, wives and mothers.

Goal Planning

A total of 135 points constitutes one high school credit. A credit may be earned in one single area or by combining two or more similar areas, for example, grammar and composition, two types of science, etc. You may name credits other than these categories if you see fit; our system is offered only as a guide line. School systems and colleges require any where from 18 to 28 credits at the high school level. If the student has already done some high school work, subtract those credits from the total required to find what your student needs for graduation. Certificates of completion will be issued upon receipt of parent's request and signed affidavit of credits completed. Below is a sample of Tennessee requirements and a goal planning sheet from the *Far Above Rubies Companion.*

Tennessee Requirements for graduation

College Preparatory		General	
Bible	3	Bible	3
Language Arts	4	Language Arts	4
Math - Algebra 1, Algebra 2, Geometry or Advanced Math	3	Math	2
Science - General Science, Biology, Chemistry, Physics	3	Science	2
Social Studies - US History, World History, American Government	3	Social Studies - US History, World History, American Government	3
Economics	½	Economics	½
Health	½	Health	½
Physical Education	1	Physical Education	1
Foreign Language	2	Foreign Language	
Visual Performance	1	Visual Performance	1
Elective		Elective	4½
Total Credits	**21**	**Total Credits**	**21**

Sample of Far Above Rubies Goal Planning Sheet from the *Far Above Rubies Companion.*

Bible	Bible	3
Language Arts	English Composition & English Grammar Combined	4
Math	Algebra 1, Algebra 2, Advanced Math - supplemental text	3
Science	Biology, Earth Science, Human Anatomy & Ecology Combined	3
Social Studies	Geography, Government & History Combined	3
Economics	Economics & Personal Finance Combined	1
Health	Health Education	1
Physical Education	Physical Education	1
Foreign Language	Foreign Language	1
Visual Performance	Visual Arts	1
Elective	Elective - Home and Family Life, Homemaking, Vocal Music	3
Total Credits		**24**

Lesson Planning and Record Keeping

The *Far Above Rubies Companion* includes enough of the following sheets for each unit:

1. *Lesson Planning* sheets
2. *Points Earned* sheet
3. *Total Points Earned This Unit* sheet

Lesson Planning

Activity #	Date Assigned	Date Due	Note or Materials Needed	
01B01	9-10-93	this week	Bible	4
01B02	9-10-93	9-14-93	Bible	4
01C01	9-16-93	2 weeks	Index Cards	
01C05	9-10-93	9-11-93	Streams of Civilization	4
01C16	9-10-93	Today	Encyclopedia	
01W01	9-16-93	9-20-93	Writers INC	4
01W05	9-16-93	each Friday	Misspelled word List	
01B06	9-16-93	10-10-93		
01S01	9-16-93	Today	Encyclopedia	4

Before each unit, decide which activities your student will be using. Fill out the *Lesson Planning* sheets (you decide—daily, weekly or for the entire unit). When an activity is completed, jot down the activity number and points earned in the proper column on the *Points Earned* sheet. Transfer the total number of points earned to the *Total Points Earned This Unit* sheet. At the end of the twenty units you will transfer all points from the *Total Points Earned This Unit* sheet to the *Credits Earned* sheet.

Points Earned

Note:
Some points will be listed in more than one subject.
Example:
Activity #01W01 give points in Bible and English Grammar.

Subject								
Bible	01B01	01B02	01B06	01B07	01B12	01B16	01R06	01W01
Points	3	10	20	15	25	20	1	1
History	01C01	01C05	01C11	01C14				
Points	1	2	3	3				
English Grammar	01W01	01W10	01W07	01W10	01W12			
Points	1	10	1	5	20			
Science, Earth	01S01	01S03	01S05	01W15				
	1	2	3	20				

Note Books

You'll need several notebooks through out this course. Preferably the 2 or 3 inch white notebook binder with see-thru pockets on the outside. You can use drawings, paintings or enlarged photos to decorate the covers. Notebooks demand management by the way of upkeep, rewrites, corrections, and regular improvement in the way of method and skills. All work should be quality, you should be proud of your work. Consistency is important to have a neat notebook. Determine whether you will use one or both sides of paper consistently throughout the notebook. Determine whether you will use print, cursive, or type through out the course. All errors should be completely erased or removed with white-out. Keep a set of colored pencils handy for illustrations and highlighting. Invest in a three hole paper punch so you can add card stock and other papers as needed. Divide your notebooks into categories in one of three ways: Unit Books, Subject Books or Theme Books.

Unit Book

A Unit Book will include all papers, notes, reports, essays, photos of projects, etc. in one unit. All papers should include the date and activity code number. You will have 20 Unit Books at the end of this course.

Subject Books

To keep your papers by subject, make 9 notebooks, one for each of the following:

1. Bible
2. Cultural Studies
3. Literature
4. Composition
5. Math

6. Science
7. Health
8. Practical Arts
9. Creative and Performing Arts

Theme Books

My favorite way is to keep a Theme Book for each topic. A Theme Book would include all notes, reports, essays, photos of projects, etc. on one topic. For example in Unit One you could have a Theme Book about *Life in Bible Times*, *Rocks and Gems*, or *The Virtuous Woman*. For Unit Two you would have three Theme Books, *Marriage and Courtship*, *Reproduction* and *Government* etc. You will need 3 to 6 notebooks a unit.

Other Notebooks

You will begin a geography note book in unit 1, see #01C04. You will add to this notebook in each unit. You will be including reports, pictures and maps of different countries in each unit. If you use a ***Book of the Centuries*** for your timeline you can choose to add your maps to it. You will begin a school journal in unit 1, see #01W03. Use a spiral notebook, looseleaf note book or store bought journal. You will need separate spiral notebooks for handwriting practice, vocabulary words, and frequently misspelled words. See unit 1, #01W01, #01W02, and #01W04. Make or buy an art portfolio to keep all drawings in.

Timeline

A time line is a "before and after" tool. It may be used before delving into a new study to emphasize relationships with other contemporary civilizations. After learning about a particular person, group, or event, a timeline is an abbreviated summary of the study. It is a reminder that recalls the whole. The most effective timeline for your student is one to which he has contributed or one he has made himself. Wall time lines are great and every family should have one! But an individual gains more from one that he creates, one that he can take with him, particularly as he grows older and his studies expand beyond what the family is doing. Instructions for making a timeline and timeline cards are listed in unit 1, see #01C01-01C03. You will add to the timeline through out the entire course. The timeline can be displayed on the wall, in a photo album or kept in an index file box.

The Book of the Centuries is a timeline book for students to record information in a sturdy nine ring notebook. These features help to organize the information: Pages begin with Creation, the Fall, and the Flood; The timeline is marked for each ten years from 3500 B.C. to A.D. 2000; There is twice as much space from A.D. 1600 to the present because of the proliferation of people, discoveries, and events; There are color pages separating B.C. from A.D.; Lined "Notes" pages are three-quarter cut so that the time line can be seen continuously; Plenty of area for drawing illustrations; Section for family tree; and pages for drawing maps.

What could be recorded in a Book of the Centuries?

⧗ Bible Events and Characters.

⧗ Dates for Books of the Bible.

⧗ Civilizations and Kingdoms.

⧗ Drawings of Period Housing, Dress, Weapons, etc.

⧗ Dates for Relatives from Your Family Tree.

⧗ Scientific Discoveries and Inventions.

⧗ Styles of Art and Artists; Music and Musicians.

⧗ Time/Setting for Biographies and Historical Novels.

⧗ ...And Elaborate with More Information in the "Notes."

Units Divided Thematically

Unit	Verse	Theme
1	Who can find a virtuous woman? for her price *is* far above rubies.	The Virtuous Woman Life In Bible Times Rubies, Rocks and Minerals
2	The heart of her husband doth safely trust in her, so that he shall have no need of spoil. She will do him good and not evil all the days of her life.	Marriage and Courtship Government Human Body: Reproduction Systems Personal Economics
3	She seeketh wool, and flax, and worketh willingly with her hands.	Shepherd and Sheep Diligent Work Fabric and Sewing Textile Industry
4	She is like the merchants' ships; she bringeth her food from afar.	Vikings Bible Travelers Ships Birds Oceans
5	She riseth also while it is yet night, and giveth meat to her household, and a portion to her maidens.	Ancient Egypt Civil War Human Body: The Digestive System Slavery
6	She considereth a field, and buyeth it: with the fruit of her hands she planteth a vineyard.	Botany Gardening Agriculture Real Estate
7	She girdeth her loins with strength, and strengtheneth her arms.	Ancient Greece Sports Exercise Human Body: Skeletal and Muscular System
8	She perceiveth that her merchandise *is* good: her candle goeth not out by night.	Astronomy Light and Energy Banking Human Body: Eyes
9	She layeth her hands to the spindle, and her hands hold the distaff.	Industrial Revolution Machines Interior Design Human Body: General
10	She stretcheth out her hand to the poor; yea, she reacheth forth her hands to the needy.	Great Depression Economics Charity Environment

Unit	Verse		Theme
11	She is not afraid of the snow for her household: for all her household *are* clothed with scarlet.		Weather Atmosphere Human Body: Respiratory System
12	She maketh herself coverings of tapestry; her clothing *is* silk and purple.		Renaissance/Reformation Architecture Fashion Interior Design Human Body: The Skin
13	Her husband is known in the gates, when he sitteth among the elders of the land.		Early America Marriage Federal Government Politics Exterior Design- Building Repair Health: Stress
14	She maketh fine linen, and selleth *it*; and delivereth girdles unto the merchant.		Ancient Rome Business Home Industries Animals
15	Strength and honour *are* her clothing; and she shall rejoice in time to come.		Diligence Middle Ages Future Medicine
16	She openeth her mouth with wisdom; and in her tongue *is* the law of kindness.		Wisdom Home Education Human Body: The Brain Child Training
17	She looketh well to the ways of her household, and eateth not the bread of idleness.		Westward Movement Homemaking Local Government
18	Her children arise up, and call her blessed;		Child Birth Parenting
19	Her husband *also*, and he praiseth her. Many daughters have done virtuously, but thou excellest them all. Favour *is* deceitful, and beauty *is* vain: *but* a woman *that* feareth the LORD, she shall be praised.		Godly Wives Beauty Human Body: The Heart
20	Give her of the fruit of her hands; and let her own works praise her in the gates.		Spiritual Fruit Concluding Activities Graduation

Far Above Rubies Scope and Sequence

	Verse	Bible	Cultural Studies	Reading and Literature	Composition	Mathematics and Personal Finance	Science	Health and Fitness	Practical Arts	Decorative and Performing Arts
1	31:10 Who can find a virtuous woman? for her price is far above rubies.	Good Christian character, standards of behavior for the Christian, and study of women of the Bible.	History of Old Testament times, church history, timelines, and geography.	Book reports, independent reading, historical novels, and biographies of Christian women.	Literary composition skills, writing a résumé, and creative writing.	Economics, appraisals, measurements, and basic math.	Gems, rocks and minerals, mining, crystals, atoms, molecules, periodic table of elements, chemistry introduction.	Medical technology, nutrition.	Drawing, painting, jewelry making, typing or word processing.	Music, art appreciation, and drama.
2	31:11 The heart of her husband doth safely trust in her, so that he shall have no need of spoil.	Marriage relationships, proper role of a wife, loyalty, dependability and submission to authority.	God's ordained system of government, family's correct role in church and community, civil governments, family lifestyles in different cultures and times in history.	Book reports, independent reading, historical novels, Shakespeare, and biographies of America's First Ladies.	Handwriting, literary composition skills, essays, poems, and other creative writing.	Budgeting, investing, careful shopping, consumer awareness, decimals, percents, interest rates and reading contracts.	Scientists, anatomy, human reproduction, animals reproduction, mating and gestation.	Prenatal care, birth control, and sexually transmitted diseases.	Coupons, home finance and record keeping, needlework, tax returns, wills, insurance, and clothing care.	Calligraphy, drawing or painting, art appreciation, music appreciation, and play writing.
3	31:13 She seeketh wool, and flax, and worketh willingly with her hands.	God as our shepherd, relationship of sheep to the master, diligence, and Psalms of David.	History and origins of textiles, Industrial Revolution, and native Americans.	Novels about shepherds and sheep ranches, book reports, independent reading, and Christian biographies.	Handwriting practice, literary composition skills, and creative writing.	Graphs, problem solving, decimals, percents, ratios and proportions.	Wool industry, cotton industry, plant life cycles, fabrics, farming, insects, and synthetic fabrics.	Skin care, chemical reactions, arthritis, agility.	Wardrobe planning, fabric care, and needle work.	Calligraphy, drawing, painting, art appreciation, and music appreciation.
4	31:14 She is like the merchants' ships; she bringeth her food from afar.	Paul's travels, Abraham's journeys, Israelites routes during the Exodus, Old Testament food laws, Passover and Hebrew excile.	Vikings, map reading, country reporting, Crusades, history of Christianity, major explorers, import and export laws, food co-ops, and immigration laws.	Biographies, letters and diaries of explorers, poetry, historical novels, and stories of American immigrants.	Journaling, handwriting, vocabulary, spelling, creative writing, proof reading, corrections, and book reports.	Ratios, portions, percentages, graphs, compare prices, coupons, distance, radius, circumference, diameter and areas.	Sea life, floatation, plants, plant life cycles, bird migration, magnetism, gravity, compasses, aviation, aerodynamics, flight, and food transport.	Herbs used for medicinal and therapeutic uses, diseases--causes and prevention, preserving food, nutrition, safety, and exercise.	Menu planning, grocery shopping, maps, globes and charts, jelly making, vegetable canning, fruit drying, studying a foreign language, and cooking.	Art appreciation and music appreciation.
5	31:15 She riseth also while it is yet night, and giveth meat to her household, and a portion to her maidens.	Diligence, organization, Biblical laws concerning slavery, Daniel, Hagar, and Joseph.	Ancient Egypt, Slavery throughout history from Biblical times to the Civil War, and Civil Rights Movement.	Biographies and novels about people during Biblical times, the Civil War, and the Civil Rights Movement.	Book reports, journaling, vocabulary, creative writing, speech writing, and essay writing about slavery.	Graphs, percent, ratio, and portions.	Human and animal digestive systems, anatomy, enzymes, hormones, excretory system, bacteria and fungi.	Food allergies, dental problems, diseases of digestive system, vitamins, and general nutrition.	Meal planning, cooking, nutrition, hospitality, and entertaining.	Calligraphy, drawing, print making or other graphic arts to prepare projects reinforcing this unit.

Far Above Rubies Scope and Sequence

	Verse	Bible	Cultural Studies	Reading and Literature	Composition	Mathematics and Personal Finance	Science	Health and Fitness	Practical Arts	Decorative and Performing Arts
6	31:16 She considereth a field, and buyeth it: with the fruit of her hands she planteth a vineyard.	Biblical principles for buying, selling and owning property, and parables about plants.	Topography, geology, agriculture, real estate, taxes, insurance, and loans.	Books on gardening, landscaping, poetry, and Christian biographies.	Book reports, journaling, vocabulary, creative writing, and poetry about gardening.	Geometry, measurements, and basic trigonometry.	Types of soil, soil erosion, organic and chemically treated gardening, insects, general botany.	Nutritional value of fruits and vegetables, first aid, insect born diseases, and pollen allergies.	Soil testing, compost, fertilizers, landscaping, lawn care, gardening, and farming.	Song writing, calligraphy, drawing, and painting.
7	31:17 She girdeth her loins with strength, and strengtheneth her arms.	God's commands concerning the care of our bodies, whole armor, readiness, alertness, and perseverance.	Ancient Greece, sports through history, athletic traditions in other countries, and the Olympic games.	Greeek mythology, biographies of Christian athletics.	Book reports, journaling, vocabulary, creative writing, speech writing, and essay writing about sports and the Olympics.	Charts, percentages, graphs, ratios and proportions.	Human anatomy- the skeletal and muscular systems.	Exercise and nutritious diet.	First aid, water safety, typing, and CPR training.	Drawing, painting, and music appreciation.
8	31:18 She perceiveth that her merchandise is good: her candle goeth not out by night.	Preparedness, readiness, attentiveness to duty, vigilance, Biblical references to lamp and light, and parables.	Natural and artificial light, animal and vegetable oils, electricity, inventors, scientist, whaling, stock market.	Biographies of scientists, inventors, biographies of blind people, and those in the Federal Reserve.	Book reports, journaling, vocabulary, creative writing, and essay writing about inventors, scientists or the blind.	Interest rates, graphs, percent, ratio, and proportions.	Electricity, fuel, environment, human eye, solar system, astronomy, the eye and Christian scientists.	Diseases and disorders of the eye and prevention (blindness, cataracts, glaucoma).	Household inventory, asset management, electric generator, candle making, and house electrical repairs.	Model of solar system, college, Bible verses in calligraphy, and stained glass.
9	31:19 She layeth her hands to the spindle, and her hands hold the distaff.	Diligence of a godly women and commitment to hard work, sewing and needle work in the Bible.	Textile industry, Industrial Revolution, and history of the labor union.	Classics written during the Industrial Revolution, manuals about spinning and weaving, and biographies of inventors.	Writing plays, essays, and speeches about the Industrial Revolution.	Units of liner measurement in English and metric conversions.	Simple Machines, The eye.	Perception, eye-hand co-ordination.	Handicraft such as: embroidery, crochet, needlepoint, sewing, knitting, smocking, and weaving.	Fabric crafts.
10	31:20 She stretcheth out her hand to the poor; yea, she reacheth forth her hands to the needy.	Biblical concepts about stewardship, tithing, charity and serving others.	History of domestic and foreign aid and social programs; The Great Depression, inflation, and recession.	Biographies of Christians who devoted their lives to helping the needy.	Book reports, journaling, vocabulary, creative writing, and essay writing about charity.	Graphs, budgeting, tithing, and percentages.	Environmental problems from poverty, water treatment, and hybrids.	Health hazards, health clinics, malnutrition, and diseases caused by poor sanitation.	Volunteer work such as: nursing home, soup kitchen, shelter, relief organization, etc.	Craft making to give to a shelter, mission church, etc.

Far Above Rubies Scope and Sequence

	Verse	Bible	Cultural Studies	Reading and Literature	Composition	Mathematics and Personal Finance	Science	Health and Fitness	Practical Arts	Decorative and Performing Arts
11	31:21 She is not afraid of the snow for her household: for all her household are clothed with scarlet.	God's control over weather, miracles, parables about weather.	Climate zones, geography, history of Arctic and Antarctic exploration, and timeline.	Short stories, biographies and novels about countries and explorers studied in this unit.	Journaling, vocabulary, creative writing, book reports and weather reports.	Graphs, mean and median, percent, ratio and proportion.	Weather—hurricanes, tornadoes, blizzards, clouds, precipitation, wind, the respiratory system, and forecasting.	Illness and health problems during cold weather, the respiratory system, first aid, and safety precautions.	Fabrics, weather maps, home heating, automotive care in cold weather, and typing.	Calligraphy, drawing, or poetry to prepare projects reinforcing this unit.
12	31:22 She maketh herself coverings of tapestry; her clothing is silk and purple.	*Covering* and *tapestry*, the tabernacle appropriate modes of dress, symbolism, colors, and head coverings.	Renaissance and Reformation, ashion and architecture through history.	Biographies of craftsmen, artisans, designers, or architects, how to books on knitting, quilting and weaving.	Book reports, journaling, vocabulary, creative writing, and poetry about fashion.	Perimeters, areas, and measuring.	The skin, sound waves, chemical processes, upholstery, carpet, pigment and paint.	Health factors relating to sleep, vertebraes, nails and hair.	Sewing, quilting, appliqué, weaving, and other needle work to make coverings for bedding, windows, tables, etc.	Calligraphy, drawing, print making or other graphic arts to prepare projects reinforcing this unit.
13	31:23 Her husband is known in the gates, when he sitteth among the elders of the land.	Godly woman's support of her husband and Christian leadership.	America's Christian heritage, civil government, local, state, national politics, and geography.	Christian biographies about persons in United States history, American Presidents and First Ladies, Kings and Queens.	Essays, letters, vocabulary, and poems about government.	Area, perimeter, percentages, and charts.	Simple machines, and inventors who were involved in politics.	Stress, high blood pressure, ulcers, diet, and exercise.	Volunteer to work in a political campaign.	Draw and design political flyers, calligraphy, and political cartoons.
14	31:24 She maketh fine linen, and selleth it; and delivereth girdles unto the merchant.	Business skills women can have and use in the home and Biblical teachings that apply to business transactions.	Ancient Rome, trades and crafts through out history, taxes, licensing, and zoning laws.	Novels and stories during Ancient Rome, biographies of Christian business men and entrepreneurs.	Book reports, journaling, vocabulary, creative writing, resume and proposal writing.	Graphs, profit and loss, income tax forms, and book keeping for a real or pretend business.	Anatomy of animals used for leather or fur-bearing, physical and chemical process of taxidermy.	Health related businesses, home health care, and midwifery.	Market needle work, crafts, and run a home business.	Designing a logo, business card or flyers for advertisement.
15	31:25 Strength and honour are her clothing; and she shall rejoice in time to come.	Dignity and the lives of Christian women who displayed great strength and dignity during times of adversity.	Middle Ages, Women in history who triumphed in the face of great odds, and major wars in history.	Biographies of those who overcame handicaps and of Christian women who maintained a ministry after widowhood.	Handwriting practice, term papers, letter writing, proof reading and corrections, vocabulary, and creative writing.	Investments and insurance.	The endocrine system, insects, animals that hibernate, global warming, acid rain, ecology, natural resources, and conservation.	Serious illness and preventive measures, major causes of death and disabilities.	Canning, drying and smoking foods, generators, life insurance, wills, and conservation.	Card making, plans for building projects, and music.

Far Above Rubies Scope and Sequence

	Verse	Bible	Cultural Studies	Reading and Literature	Composition	Mathematics and Personal Finance	Science	Health and Fitness	Practical Arts	Decorative and Performing Arts
16	31:26 She openeth her mouth with wisdom; and in her tongue is the law of kindness.	Biblical wisdom, knowledge and obedience, importance of regular Bible study, role of women in the NT church.	History of American education, home education, purpose of public schools, Constitutional law, home schooling, and the Bill of Rights.	Books on home schooling, child training, biographies of famous persons who were home taught.	Outlining books read in this unit, writing a biblical analysis, writing critiques, and other creative writing.	Graphs, ratios, proportions, mode and median, bell curve and basic algebra.	The brain and nervous system, evolution with Biblical evidence that refutes it, science lessons for children.	Learning styles, recreation, handicaps, learning disabilities, and herbs.	Home educating children. Organizing and teaching a Bible study and Bible object lesson, preparing a unit study and lesson plans.	Song writing, drawing, calligraphy, creating visual aids for Bible study.
17	31:27 She looketh well to the ways of her household, and eateth not the bread of idleness.	All aspects of homemaking, family life, need for consistent Bible study, prayer, diligence and dangers of laziness.	The Westward movement, gold Rush, building codes, deed restrictions, government services, public offices, lobbying, and state laws.	Books about homemaking, organization, family and household repairs.	Letter writing to legislators and other officials, handwriting, term papers, vocabulary and other creative writing.	Percentages, graphs, bill paying, and budgeting.	General anatomy, the cell, deases, genes, tissue, common household chemicals, plumbing, appliances, insulation, recycling, ecology, and physics.	Prescription drugs, allergies, immunizations, first aid, homeopathy, nutrition and exercise.	Cleaning and maintaining appliances, repair or recover upholstery, care of paneling, wood floors, and furniture, clothing repair, and organizing.	Calligraphy, drawing, illustrating and planning a skit.
18	31:28a Her children arise up, and call her blessed.	What the Bible says about children, mothers in the Bible.	State regulations of home-birth and midwifery, child abuse laws, Roe v. Wade and other Supreme Court decisions, lobbying, history and social effects of abortion in history.	Biographies of women who "mothered" orphaned children, classics about family life, books on Christian parenting, midwifery and abortion.	Book reports, journaling, vocabulary, creative writing, speech writing, and essay writing about mothers and children.	Mean, mode, median, comparisons, graphs, percentages and proportions.	Anatomical and physical development of babies from conception to birth, infant and child development, maternal instinct, nurturing, and birth.	Physical and emotional effects of abortion on the mother, prenatal care, midwifery and obstetricians, drugs used during labor and the effects, and childhood nutrition.	Childcare, first aid, making baby food, sewing baby clothes.	Designing and painting a mural or painting for a nursery, and music appreciation.
19	31:28b & 30 her husband also, and he praiseth her. Many daughters have done virtuously, but thou excellest them all.	Praise as it applies to God and the accomplishments of others, fearing the Lord, husband/wife relationships, and godly women of the Bible,	Women and wives from different historical periods compared to Biblical standards, missionaries, and Christian martyrs.	Biographies of Christian women, composers, painters, women who held high political offices.	Book reports, journaling, vocabulary, creative writing, speech writing, and essay writing about women.	Mean, mode, median, comparisons, graphs, percentages and proportions.	The Heart and circulatory system and scientific evidence of the effects of praise.	Psychological findings of Pavlov concerning praise and conditioning, self esteem, humility.	Play writing, and creating puppet shows.	Drama, art and music appreciation.
20	31:31 Give her of the fruit of her hands; and let her own works praise her in the gates.	Fruit of the Spirit, sharing the gospel, analyzing and evaluating progress throughout this unit.	Reformation, and The Great Awakening. Christian heritage of America, missionary efforts, origins and history of church denominations, life and ministry of preachers.	Books that show fruits produced through ministry, novels of Christian families, and biographies of leaders of the Reformation movement.	Book reports, journaling, vocabulary, creative writing, speech writing, and essay writing about this course and its effects.	Graph, record keeping, and averaging.	Fruit trees and the production of fruit, plant parables, personality types.	Nutrition, health care, first aid, and exercise.	Preparing a resume, plant and care for trees, preparing a hope chest, and preparing a transcript of high school work.	Designing personal graduation announcements, certificate, planning a ceremony, and planning a recital.

Unit 1

"Who can find a virtuous woman?
For her price is far above rubies."

Proverbs 31:10

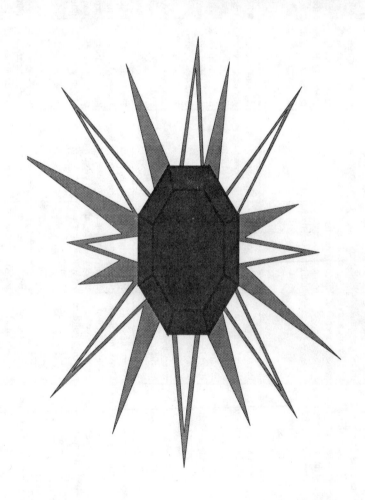

Introduction to Unit 1

In this unit you will set up your timeline and notebooks you'll be using for the entire course. You'll get familiar with the "writing to learn" philosophy and study the writing process.

In this unit, you will study life during Mesopotamia[1] and early Bible history. You'll do a large portion of Bible reading. This Bible reading will cover history from Adam to Moses. We are praying that it will also create in you a hunger for spiritual food and get you into the habit of daily Bible reading. This unit encourages the study of many women from the Bible and throughout history, scrutinizing them by the standards of this Proverbs 31:10-31.

Literary composition skills activities include writing essays, poems, reports, stories and articles, as well as summarizing and outlining materials relating to the subject matter of the unit. The topic of this verse allows us to investigate minerals, crystals, and precious and semi-precious stones. You will delve into rudimentary geology and some elemental chemistry. If you wish to expand on these, you may use this study as a springboard for a full course in either subject.

In the area of economics, this unit deals with the value of work and with appraisals and measurement of gems and jewelry. There is a little basic math involved in the determination of the value of various stones and the value of work performed by a homemaker. Ample opportunity is provided for work in ratios, proportions, percent, decimals, fractions, and making graphs. Geometry is also introduced in relation to crystalline shapes. You and your parents may wish to expand this by going into a complete geometry course.

Practical arts in this unit include typing, working with children, meal planning, and several crafts. You'll have a chance to make jewelry, polish rocks, and create a collage. Creative abilities are also encouraged in the areas of drama, musical composition, singing, playing musical instruments, and drawing or painting. There are also experiences in art and music appreciation.

Some activities started in this unit will be continued throughout the entire study. These activities are marked by this symbol ⊕.

---

[1] Mesopotamia is studied further with farming in Unit 6.

Bible

During this course you will read through the entire Bible. We want you to develop the habit of daily Bible reading. You can read the Bible through, each year, by reading three chapters each day or by following the *Daily Bible Reading Schedule* (page 1693) in **The Narrated Bible.** We recommend **The Narrated Bible** for history study because it rearranges the Scriptures chronologically in the order the Bible events occurred. It is neither a translation nor a paraphrase. The central text is composed entirely of scripture, using the NIV. Narrative commentary notes are included to give the story background. **The Narrated Bible** is an excellent history text that reads like a beautiful, exciting story. The *Daily Bible Reading Schedule* in the back of the book is divided into 365 easily readable sections. On the average, each reading is less than 5 pages. For in depth Bible Study we recommend the King James Version with access to Hebrew and Greek Lexicon.

		Points
01B01	Because this unit researches life in early Bible times you need to read the Pentateuch or Torah (the first five books of the Bible). You may use the King James Version or any other literal translation which your belief allows. If you use **The Narrated Bible** you will need to complete approximately 6 pages per day for this unit.	B - 25 Reading Genesis through Deuteronomy or 1-295 in the Narrated Bible.
01B02	List all skills and character traits of the ideal wife named in Prov 31. This describes the long-range goals of this curriculum.	B - 3 EG - 5
01B03	Study the major woman in the Bible, their character traits, and how you can apply the appropriate character traits in your life by completing **God's Priceless Women Bible Study** Course.	B - 50
01B04	Using a concordance or the book **Women of the Bible** to identify and study a woman in Scripture who possessed each trait or skill in #1B02.	B - 20
01B05	Read how each of the women showed exemplary behavior in the following verses: *Abigail*: I Sam 25:1-41. *Jael*: Judges 4:8-22 and 5:24-27. *Rahab*: Josh 2:1-16, 6:23, Heb 11:31 and James 2:25. *Tabitha*: Acts 9:36. *The wise woman*: II Sam 20:14-22; *Zipporah*: Exod 4:24-26. Write a summary paragraph about each woman.	B - 20 EC - 10
01B06	Read the poetic response of the following women: *Deborah's song*: Judges 5:1-31; *Hannah's prayer:* I Sam 2:1-10; *Mary's song*: Luke 1:46; and *Miriam's song*: Exod 15:21. Paraphrase each song or prayer in present day language.	B - 10 EC - 10

	Points

01B07   Write a summary about how the following women worshipped in the Old Testament. *Hannah*: I Sam 1:10-20. *Rachael*: Gen 30:6 & 22. *Rebekah*: Gen 25:21-23. Refer to *Summary Writing* (180-182) in **Writers INC.**   B - 5   EC - 5

01B08   Throughout this year, complete books 1-4 of the Bible Log Series. Written as a personal travelogue, these books guide you through a whirlwind journey of the places, character and events of the greatest book of all time. This series can take you through the Old Testament in one year by following the provided lesson plans completing one session per week. **Book 1: The Saga Begins**— Genesis to Ruth. ☺   B-30

01B09   Write a paper comparing the women in the Old testament and in the early church using #01B08 and #01B09.   B - 10   EC - 10

01B10   Write a summary about the women in the following parables that Jesus told: *Parable of the lost coin*: Luke 15:8, *Parable of the persistent widow*: Luke 18:1-8. *Parable of the ten virgins*: Matt 25:1-13. *Parable of yeast and flour*: Matt 13:33.   B - 10   EC - 10

01B11   Write a paragraph, on each topic, showing what Jesus' taught about women in the following verses: *Marriage*: Mark 10:2-12. *Honoring parents*: Mark 7:9-13. *Members of the Kingdom*: Mark 12:49, 3:34, Luke 8:21. *Crippled woman*: Luke 13:10-17. *Generous widow*: Mark 12:41-43. *Martha*: John 11:21-27. *Mary, mother of Jesus*: John 2:1-5. *Samaritan woman*: John 4:4-30. *A sick woman*: Mark 5:25-34. *Woman who anointed Jesus*: Mark 14:3-9 and Luke 7:36-50.   B - 10   EC - 10

01B12   Use **Women of the Bible** to find names of women for #01B03-01B04 but study each woman from the actual Bible passage.   B - 20

01B13   Study **Christian Character: A Course for Training Young People**. This workbook provides an examination of the character that should be found in the lives of young people. List twenty-eight character traits, student exercises, personal evaluations, and goal settings.   B - 30

01B14   Study the book of Genesis and list each godly woman found there, with a verse to show why you consider her godly.   B - 20

01B15   Study the women of the book of Joshua, listing all godly women as in #1B14.   B - 15

		Points
01B16	Study the book of Judges, listing all godly women as in #1B14.	B - 15
01B17	Repeat #1B14 with I & II Samuel.	B - 15
01B18	Repeat #1B14 with I & II Kings.	B - 25
01B19	Repeat #1B14 with I & II Chronicles.	B - 25
01B20	Scan through the entire New Testament and list all women named there. Find and list a Scripture passage to show whether each woman was godly or ungodly.	B - 25
01B21	Make a chart showing a Scripture which commands or teaches each item in #1B02.	B - 6
01B22	Study and memorize Galatians 5:19-23.	B - 3
01B23	Study and memorize Proverbs 31:10-31.	B - 10
01B24	Listen to, outline, and discuss with your parents the tape series *Ethics Course: Personal Holiness* by Greg Bahnsen.	½ credit
01B25	Using the following verses, write a summary about how the women worshipped in the Early Church. *Received the Spirit of God*: Acts 2:17. *Became a part of the believers*: Acts 1:12-14, 5:14, 8:5 & 12, 17:1 & 4, 17: 10-12. *Workers in the church*: Rom 16:1, Acts 9:36, I Tim 5:3-16. *Host to believers*: Acts 12:12, 16:15, Rom 16:3-5, I Cor 16:19 and Col 4:15. *Prophesied*: Acts 21:9 and I Cor 11. *Served fellow workers*: Rom 16:3 and Phil 4:2.	B - 5 EC - 5
01B26	Read *Origins of the Bible* on page 12-13 in **Mysteries of the Bible.**	B - 1

Cultural Studies

		Points
01C01	Make timeline cards. As you study people or events in this unit, write each item on a colored 3 x 5 card with dates or time period and an appropriate illustration. Assign a different color card for each specific region of the world. For example: North, South and Central America: blue, Asia: yellow, Europe: orange, etc. You will add to this timeline (or one below) in each unit. ◔	H - 1 VA - 1 For each card
01C02	Make a timeline. Hang twine, masking tape, or string across a long wall (eg. down a staircase or along a hallway). Attach the above cards to the timeline in chronological order. If you can't put up a timeline due to space, make the cards as above and file in chronological order from front to back in a file box (include card dividers indicating time periods) or place in a photo album (use a three ring binder photo album adding pages as needed). ◔	Same as above no extra credit for making timeline
01C03	Use the **Book of the Centuries** to make a timeline book. Sketch or glue illustrations in the blank pages below the timeline. Include drawings of the dress, housing, weapons, inventions, etc. for each time period. Include notes on the provided lined pages. ◔	Same as above
01C04	Start a geography notebook. Write a 1-3 page report on any country studied in this unit. Include countries studied in #01C19. Include pictures and maps. You will add to this notebook in each unit. ◔	G - 2 EC - 1 each
01C05	Use **World History Dates** (4-10), and/or **Kingfisher's Illustrated History of the World** (24-37) to read about people and events during Bible times.	H - 1 each
01C06	Study the lives and homes during Bible times by reading chapters 1-3, 8, & 10 of **Manners and Customs of Bible Lands.**	H - 2 B - 2
01C07	To further understand this period from a secular perspective, read **The Jewish Wars** and/or the **Antiquities of the Jews** both by Josephus.	H - 30
01C08	Read pages 28-80 in **Streams of Civilization.**	H - 5
01C09	Use the **Time Traveler** series by Usborne to read about homes and family life at different times in history.	H - 3 each book
01C10	Make a room box or diorama of a typical home in Bible times.	H - 5 VA - 5
01C11	Read and outline The Pentateuch (16-95) in **Mysteries of the Bible.**	H - 5

	Points

01C12 List and discuss ways that location, terrain, climate, and other geographical factors would affect the activities pursued by the diligent homemaker. — **G - 2**

01C13 List ways in which women served their country during each of our nation's wars, including ways in which they had to alter their daily lives and that of their families. — **H -3**

01C14 Study the geography of Palestine and surrounding areas from Bible times until today using **Baker Bible Atlas** and the accompanying study guide. — **G - 50**

01C15 Locate on a national map all major mining areas in your country, using some symbol to show what is mined in each area. — **G - 2**

01C16 Listen to and discuss tapes 1 *Creation to the Destruction of Assyria* in the series **What in the World is Going on Here? A Judeo Christian Primer of World History**. These tapes start with Creation and take you on a whirlwind tour through the ancient civilizations and show their relationship to the Old Testament. These tapes will give you an excellent chronological foundation of God's unfolding plan, through history, that we will build on throughout the units. — **H - 2 each**

01C17 Do research about the development of the written language called cuneiform. Write a letter only using pictures and symbols. — **H - 2**

01C18 Mark on a world map all countries which are major sources of gems and minerals. — **G - 2**

01C19 Read what the Bible says about learning history: Deut 7:17-19; Psalm 78:4-6; 2 Chron 20:6-13; and 1 Cor 10:11. — **B - 1**

01C20 Sumer is an ancient country of western Asia, corresponding approximately to Babylonia of biblical times. Do research and make a list of the scientific and technological contributions made by the Sumerians. — **H - 3** **S - 1**

01C21 Mesopotamia, one of the earliest centers of urban civilization, in the area of modern Iraq and eastern Syria, lay between two rivers, the Tigris and the Euphrates. The name Mesopotamia is a Greek word meaning "between the rivers." Do a report on Mesopotamia. Include a map of the Fertile Crescent. — **H - 3**

01C22 The Code of Hammurabi is a collection of the laws and edicts of the Babylonian King Hammurabi. Make a comparison chart between The Code of Hammurabi and Biblical law. — **H - 2**

01C23 Read and outline *Cities in the River Valleys* (20-28) in **Everyday Life Through the Ages** by Reader's Digest. — **H - 2**

Reading and Literature

		Points
01R01	Read the biography, **Abigail Adams**, who was the second First Lady and President John Adams partner. A born-again Christian, her whole life was guided by His Word. She was steadfast through fortune and misfortune.	H- 5
01R02	Read 3 - 10 Christian novels dealing with romance, marriage, and/or family life and observe how characters follow or violate the principles in Proverbs 31.	L - 3 B - 1 each book
01R03	Read the Christian view about the years of transition from childhood to womanhood that are filled with wonderful interest and promise in **Beautiful Girlhood.**	L - 5
01R04	Read three classics compare the main female character in each to the ideal set forth in Prov. 31.	L - 4 B - 1 each
01R05	Find and memorize one poem (10 line minimum) dealing with each of the fruits of the Spirit listed in Gal. 5:22-23.	L - 1 each
01R06	Read 1-3 fictionalized biographies of Biblical figures checking each story with the Biblical account for accuracy.	L - 1 B - 3 each
01R07	Read 3 or more biographies or fact-based novels about godly women from history. Compare each to Prov. 31.	B - 1 H - 3 each
01R08	Read **Unlocking the Mysteries of Creation**. This book gives an overview of the many issues associated with Genesis presenting a case for a young earth and a literal flood. .	H - 2 L - 2 SE - 2
01R09	Read 3-6 historical novels about women during different periods of history and analyze the major characters as in # 01C02.	L - 2 each
01R10	Read several short stories about daily life, home, and families in other parts of the world.	L - 1 each
01R11	Study how God's Word differs from the worlds view of the humanist on the issue of women and the church by reading **Woman and the Church: Earthly Images of the Heavenly Bride.**	B - 5
01R12	Read **Adam and His Kin**. An interesting reflection of how the events of Genesis chapters 1-11 could have happened.	L - 2 B - 2

		Points

01R13   Read about the character traits of the King's daughter in ***Dear Princess***. It is a "how to" book written to lead a young Christian girl to victorious living—that happiest, most satisfying and joyous life that our heavenly Father has planned His children to have.   **L - 4**

01R14   Read biographies of any of the people mentioned in the history tapes or readings in this unit.   **H - 4** each

01R15   Read historical fiction set in the time periods studied in this unit.   **H - 4** each

01R16   Start a Reading Log and add to it in each unit. Refer to *The Reading Log* (257-261) in ***Writers INC***.   **EC - 1** each entry

01R17   Read about gems through history in ***The Golden Gem of the Ages***[1] by Patty Rice. It starts with history during the Sumerian civilizations in Mesopotamia. It also includes: archaeology, geology, mythology and jewelry.   **SE - 2** / **H - 2**

01R18   Read ***Minerals, Resources and the Destinies of Nations*** by Walter Youngquist. This book explains the importance of minerals in motivating exploration, war, and industrialized specialization.   **SE - 2** / **H - 2**

01R19   Read ***Sumer and the Sumerians*** by Harriet Crawford. It is an illustrated synthesis of recent and archaeological historical research.   **H - 4**

01R20   Read ***History Begins at Sumer: 39 First in Mans recorded history***. by Samual Kramer.   **H -4**

01R21   Read ***Mesopotamia*** by Julian Reade or another book about Mesopotamia.   **H - 4**

01R22   Read ***Cradle of Civilization*** by Samual Kramer from the Great Ages of Man series.   **H - 4**

01R23   Read ***Everyday Life in Babylonia and Assyria*** by H.F. Sagg.   **H - 4**

01R24   Read *In the Fertile Crescent, Ur of the Chaldees*, and *Digging Up the Flood* in ***The Bible as History***.   **H - 2**

---

[1]   Books from #01R17 to #01R24 should be available in your library or through inter-library loan.

Composition

	Points

01W01 For handwriting practice, write every Bible verse you study or memorize in a spiral notebook or journal. This will be a record of all verses studied, as well as handwriting practice throughout this entire course. You may use cursive, Italic or another form of calligraphy. ☺
    EG - 1
B - 1 each page

01W02 In a spiral notebook, list in alphabetical order (two or three pages per letter) all new words from your reading and/or studies and their definitions. Learn at least 10 new words per week. This will be a record of vocabulary words throughout this entire course. Read *Improving Vocabulary Skills* (443-444) in **Writers INC**. ☺
    EG - 1
per 10 words

01W03 Keep a journal of each school day's activities throughout this entire course. Read *Journal Writing* (470-471) in **Writers INC**. ☺
    EC - 1 each week

01W04 In a spiral notebook, keep a record of frequently misspelled words. List words in alphabetical order (two or three pages per letter). You will add misspelled words in each unit. Proofread and correct spelling errors in all written work in this unit. Refer to *Steps to Become a Better Speller* and *Spelling Rules* (713-714) in **Writers INC**. ☺
    EG - 1 per corrected paper

01W05 You will be asked to write in each unit. "Writing to learn" is an approach that will help you personalize learning so you can understand course work better and retain what you have learned longer. Writing is thinking on paper. You will discover connections, describe processes, express understandings, raise questions and find answers. Read and discuss *Writing to Learn* (469) in **Writers INC**. This will help you understand the writing assignments in each unit. Do not skip this activity.
    EC - 3

01W06 Read and outline *The Writing Process* (002-030) in **Writers INC**. Refer to *The Outline* (110-112) in **Writers INC**. Do not skip this activity.
    EC - 3

01W07 Have someone dictate several paragraphs to you, using passages from books used in this unit. Proofread and correct the paragraphs.
    EC - 3 per 3 paragraphs

01W08 Have someone dictate several Bible verses, to you, using verses you have studied in this unit. Proofread and correct the verses.
    EC - 2 per 3 verses

01W09 Write a newspaper ad looking for a godly wife. Use the standards of Proverbs 31.
    EC - 1

01W10 Write a job description for a godly wife based on the standards of Proverbs 31 and the basic format used in industry.
    EC - 1

		Points
01W11	Write a résumé for a woman who fits the Proverbs 31 ideal, relating each skill to an appropriate area of the job market. Refer to *Writing Résumés* (422-424) in **Writers INC**.	EC - 2
01W12	Write a diary as it may have been kept by one of the women studied in this unit. Refer to *Journal Writing* (470) in **Writers INC.**	EC - 5 5-8 entries
01W13	Write at least one book report or review each month, using books from this unit or the reading list. Refer to *Writing About Literature* (250-261) in **Writers INC**.	EG - 1 per paper
01W14	Write a formal research paper (5-8 pages) on one of the women in this unit, using *Writing the Research Paper* in **Writers INC** as a guide. Include footnotes, bibliography, etc.	EC - 20
01W15	As an alternative to cursive writing, you may study Italic handwriting using the workbook **Write Now**.	EG - 20 VA -20
01W16	Write and deliver before an audience a speech on *"The Value of the Full-Time Homemaker to Today's Family."* Refer to *Speech Skills* (490-524) in **Writers INC**.	EC - 20
01W17	Using a thesaurus, list as many synonyms as possible for each item on the list you made in # 01B03 of the Bible section of this unit. Refer to *Using the Thesaurus* (201) in **Writers INC**.	EG - 3
01W18	Prepare a booklet on gems and minerals. Include types and descriptions of gems; how they are made, identified, and used; methods of mining; data on crystalline structure, etc.	EC - 10 SE - 20
01W19	Dalton was regarded as the founder of atomic theory. Do research and write an essay on his findings. Include illustrations.	EC - 4 each SP - 2
01W20	Proofread and correct all grammar and punctuation errors in all written work. Refer to *Proofreaders Guide* (600-714) in **Writers INC**.	EG - 1 per paper
01W21	Write a paper on the scientific and technological advances made by the Sumerians.	EC - 1
01W22	To encourage attentiveness to the preaching of the Word, take notes on all sermons you attend, or listened to by tape or radio.	EC - 3 each
01W24	Write a fictional short story about a Christian family living in any chosen period of history. Tie into some historical event of the time or a real person. Try to accurately show the living conditions and daily struggles of that time. Refer to *Writing the Short Story* (218-227) in **Writers INC**.	EC - 10 H - 10

Math and Personal Economics

		Points
01M01	List jobs usually done by a godly wife and mother. Using average pay for each job and estimated time per week spent in it, compute the weekly pay she would get for each one. Add all jobs and multiply by 52 to get the annual value of a good wife's work. (Due to some overlap, total hours worked may total more than actual hours in a week.)	HF - 2 M - 5
01M02	Find what percentage of a homemaker's time is spent in each activity above out of a 168-hour week. (Remember overlap.)	M - 2
01M03	Show the above information in ratios and/or proportions as appropriate.	M - 2
01M04	Make a pie graph using the above data.	M - 3
01M05	Prepare a line and/or bar graph showing the number and percentages of women of different ages in the work force.	M - 3
01M06	Prepare a graph to compare the number of mothers in the work force in different years of our nation's history.	M - 3
01M07	Use data from the above graphs to practice proportions and ratios as needed.	parent's judgment
01M08	Use data from the above graphs to review percent, decimals, or fractions.	parent's judgment
01M09	Ask a jeweler for the current per-carat value of rubies. Multiply by the number of carats equal to your weight to decide your value if you are, indeed, "worth more than rubies," as the Proverbs 31 woman would be.	M - 2
01M10	Identify the geometric shape of each type of crystal studied. Learn the formulas for perimeter, area, and volume of each.	M - 3
01M11	Further investigate geometric shapes by playing *Oh, Euclid*.	M - 1-5 per time
01M12	Take a full geometry course if you wish, using a text book from the resource list.	M - 1 credit
01M13	Complete the geometry workbook from *Old Fashioned Crafts*.	M - ½ credit

Science

		Points
01S01	Research and list the names of as many naturally-occurring gems as possible.	SE - 1
01S02	Research each stone to determine its rarity, relative value, common locations, and methods of mining and/or production. Value depends on rarity; its hardness and toughness; and the skill with which it has been cut and polished	SE - 3
01S03	Examine the various synthetic gemstones and the processes by which they are made. Synthetic rubies were first produced in 1837 by fusing alum and chromium-oxide pigment at a high temperature.	SC - 2
01S04	Study various methods of mining gems and the effect of each on the environment.	SE - 3
01S05	Get a geological map of your state or locality and learn what minerals and/or gems are available there.	SE - 3
01S06	Instead of #01S01-01S05 above, study a complete geology course using any good text.	SE - ½ Credit
01S07	Tour a diamond (or other gemstone) mine or processing facility if possible.	SE - 2
01S08	Draw models of several elements showing the protons, neutrons and electrons in orbit.	SC - 2
01S09	Look up each word in an encyclopedia: quark, lepton, isotope, element, molecule, chemical bond, ionic bond, ion, ionic compound, covalent compound. Write a summary about each.	SP - 2 each
01S10	Write at least 10 structural formula for several compounds that demonstrate bonding. For example H-O-H for water shows the oxygen atom sharing bond with hydrogen.	SC - 1
01S11	Study physical chemistry in Usborne's *Dictionary of Chemistry* or *An Introduction to Chemistry.*	SC - 10
01S12	Use *The Geode Kit* and its companion book or any other kit to make geode shells and grow crystals.	SC - 3
01S13	Use the *Gem Hunter's Kit* and its accompanying book to mine, identify and display various gems.	SC - 3
01S14	Study the periodic table of elements. See section 960 in *Writers INC.* Explain how the elements are arranged and why.	SC - 2
01S15	In 1913 Niels Bohr developed a hypothesis known as the Bohr theory of the atom. Do research a write a report on his theory.	SC - 2

Health and Physical Fitness

		Points
01H01	Do research and make a list of the essential minerals vitamins for complete nutrition.	HE - 2
01H02	Study the effects of various mining methods on the health of the workers and the steps taken over the years to reduce the risk or treat the health problem.	SB - 3
01H03	Study the use of gems and crystals in surgery and medical technology.	SP - 2
01H04	Study and make a booklet about the "minerals" needed for a healthy body and the foods that contain them.	HE - 3
01H05	Study specific disorders caused by lack or shortage of the above "minerals."	HE - 2
01H06	Study the various methods of prevention and treatment of the above disorders and deficiencies.	HE - 2
01H07	Analyze your family's meals for one week to discover the levels of needed minerals you are getting. Alter or supplement your meals to correct any shortages.	HE - 7
01H08	Use **Physician's Desk Reference** or another source to study the makeup, uses, and side effects (if any) of various prescribed and/or over-the-counter "mineral" supplements.	HE - 5

Practical Arts

		Points
01P01	Decorate the notebook or journal you are keeping from #01W01.	VA - 1
01P02	Teach a child the song *"Love is One of the Fruits of God's Spirit"* and/or *"The Fruit of the Spirit is Not a Banana."*	TE - 2
01P03	Prepare a poster using drawing, painting, collage, or other desired medium to illustrate the variety of the activities performed by a full time homemaker.	VA - 1
01P04	Type all written work using either a typewriter or word processor. If you do not know how to type, now is the time to learn.	BE - 1 each page
01P05	Take a course or follow a tutorial or correspondence course in typing or word processing if needed and/or desired.	BE - 50
01P06	Put into practice any changes, in your family's diet, needed to achieve proper mineral consumption.	HM - 3
01P07	Using a kit or actual rocks or gems on hand, create one or more attractive pieces of jewelry.	CR - 1
01P08	Secure a rock polisher and use it to produce beauty from common minerals and rocks.	CR - 1
01P09	Learn to correctly polish and clean various types of jewelry.	CR - 1
01P10	Geologists use the knowledge gained in other fields of science such as physics, chemistry, and biology. Look up and define each of the following geological fields: geophysics, geochemistry, geochronology, and paleontology.	SE - 1
01P11	Attend the ***Institute in Basic Life Principles*** by Bill Gothard with the Advanced Training Institute International.	HF - 25 B-10
01P12	Attend the ***Advanced Institute in Basic Life Principles*** by Bill Gothard with the Advanced Training Institute of America.	HF - 25 B - 10
01P13	Listen to the tape ***The Scriptural Role of a Godly Wife*** by Jonathan Lindvall. as a guide along the path toward Christian womanhood.	HF - 3
01P14	Research methods to make marbleized paper. Make wrapping paper.	VA - 3

Creative and Performing Arts

		Points
01A01	Prepare and perform a dramatized song, dance, finger play, musical dramatization or other audio-visual presentation of Proverbs 31:10-31.	MA - 5 or DR - 5
01A02	Set Proverbs 31:10-31 to music, using an original tune or an existing one.	MA - 5
01A03	Sing and/or play the above song from the passage in public.	VA - 3
01A04	Draw, paint, or otherwise create a mural depicting a day in the life of a godly homemaker in one of the time periods studied.	VA - 5
01A05	Design a poster of Proverbs 31:10-31 in calligraphy. Include illustrations in a medium of your choice.	VA - 5
01A06	The ancient Mesopotamians developed writing on clay tablets. Clay was also used for pottery and terra-cotta sculpture. Use clay to make your own tablet, pottery, or sculpture.	H - 1 VA - 1
01A07	Listen to a large number of songs of different types about wives and mothers. Compare the woman described in each to the lady of Proverbs 31.	MA - 3
01A09	Compose a song (words and music) in any style approved by your parents which praises or encourages one or more of the attributes of the woman described in Proverbs 31.	MA - 5
01A10	Use clay or salt dough to make a relief map of the Fertile Crescent.	G - 2 VA - 1
10A12	Sumerians made baskets. Attend a basket weaving class. Weave at least one basket.	VA - 50
01A11	Designs are cut in precious or semiprecious stones either as cameos, or as intaglios. Intaglios were formerly often used as seals for making impressions on wax or damp clay. Intaglio cutting probably started in Mesopotamia, during the Sumerian civilizations. Use wax or clay to make a design similar to a cameo or intaglios.	VA - 2
01A12	Create a book with one of the following titles: *The Virtuous Woman; Life in Bible Times; Women in Bible Times*; *Mesopotamia; Gemstones, Rocks and Minerals;* or *Geology*. This can be a simple notebook that includes all the reports and art work during this unit or a bound story book written as a nonfiction book. You may include text and illustrations as you desire. Points will depend on the amount of time spent on this project. Share the book with someone.	Parents discretion

Unit 2 ❦

> "The heart of her husband doth safely trust in her so that he will have no need of spoil. She will do him good and not evil all the days of her life."
>
> Proverbs 31:11

Introduction to Unit 2

This unit explores the marriage relationship and the proper role of the wife within the family. In it, you will study the concepts of loyalty, honesty, dependability, and submission to authority as taught in Scripture.

We will examine all aspects of marriage, including physical intimacy and procreation. You and your parents are encouraged to discuss these topics and determine how they wish you to proceed with this study in a way which suits the values and beliefs of your family. This unit includes the study of male and female anatomy and the physiology of sexual intercourse and childbirth. Opportunity is given to expand this into a study of midwifery for the girl whose interests lean that way. We attempt to recommend resources which treat these topics from a Christian perspective whenever possible.

Cultural studies will center on God's ordained system of government and order within the family and the family's correct role within the church and community. We will investigate the many realms in which civil governments tend to operate and seek to determine which of these areas should be the jurisdiction of the family and/or the church as outlined in Scripture. You will compare family lifestyles in different cultures and at different times in history, and look at famous women in history who "did their husbands good and not evil."

Budgeting, investing, careful shopping, consumer awareness, and other methods by which a stay-at-home wife may increase the family's spendable income are covered in this unit. We will study or review decimals, percents, and interest rates, and how to read contracts.

This unit offers a wide variety of opportunities for you to express yourself in art, instrumental and vocal music, drama, and many crafts. Writing activities abound, as do lessons in vocabulary, grammar, and other specific writing skills.

Practical arts include financial management skills, sewing, home management, and clothing care. Typing and word processing skills introduced in the last unit continue in relation to the written work of this one.

Bible

		Points
02B01	Read your Bible daily as started in #01B01. You can read the Bible through each year by reading three chapters each day or follow the *Daily Bible Reading Schedule* in *The Narrated Bible.* ☺	B - 1 per 7 chapters
02B02	Read Eph 5, I Peter 3, and I Cor 7 and summarize the teachings about marriage in a report or essay. Use commentaries and other references only after studying the Scriptures for yourself.	B - 5 EC - 2
02B03	Write a summary about how the wife is to respect her husband, based on 1Cor 11:3, Eph 5:22 & 33, Col 3:18, Titus 2:3-5, I Pet 3:1-6.	B - 5 EC - 2
02B04	Read Matt 10:2-12 to see what Jesus said about the sanctity of marriage.	B - 2
02B05	Use a concordance to find all Scriptures related to the duties of wives or the marital relationship. Study these carefully.	B - 8
02B06	Read Genesis 1-3 to understand the effects of the fall upon the family.	B - ¼
02B07	Read and paraphrase the Song of Solomon.	B - 8
02B08	Study *The Christian Family*, looking up all relevant Scriptures, and taking notes on the role of a Christian wife as described therein.	B - 5 HF - 5
02B09	Complete the *Apple Tree Personal Study Guide* a devotional guide about Christian family lifestyles to be used with *Under the Apple Tree.* It includes a wealth of information about marraige, natural childbirth, natural family planning, breastfeeding and parenting.	HF - 5
02B10	Draw a chart to show the relationship of the godly woman to her family, church, and society. Provide a reference verse for each relationship.	B - 2
02B11	Study all Biblical references to Aquila and Priscilla and try to describe their relationship.	B - 1
02B12	Study the Biblical accounts of Jezebel, Delilah, and other women who were curses, and not blessings, to their husbands. Determine where each of them went wrong.	B - 1 each
02B13	Study *Rejoicing in Truth,* the Looking Glass Bible study guide on honesty.	B - 2

02B14	Read Acts 5:1-11 as an example of when a wife should not obey her husband.	B - ¼
02B15	Listen to and discuss with parents the cassette tape *Godly Homes in America* by Martin Freed. Available free of charge from Pilgrim Tape Ministry.	B - 3
02B16	Listen to the tape series *Passion and Purity* by Elisabeth Elliot and discuss it in light of the Scripture passages in this unit. Compare to the book of the same name in Reading and Literature section.	B - 10
02B17	Read Elisabeth Elliot's book *The Shaping of a Christian Family* as an example of how to put the principles of this unit into practice.	HF - 5
02B18	Complete *Pursuing Christian Womanhood* Bible study tape series.	B - 35
02B19	Read the following verses: Exod 22:28; Prov 25:6,7; Rom 13:1-7, Titus 3:1,2; ! Pet 2:12-20; 1 Sam 24:6,7; 26:8-11 and Acts 23:2-5. Write a summary explaining what the Bible says about government and government officials are to be treated. Refer to *Writing Summaries* (180-182) in *Writer's INC*.	B - 1 EC - 2
02B20	Find out if you should be obedient to if government and God's law conflicts. Refer to Acts 4:18-20; and 5:28-33.	B - ¼
02B21	Find out what can we do for our leaders. Refer to Jerm 29:7 and 1 Tim 1:1-2.	B - ¼
02B22	Find out what God expects from leaders. Refer to Exod 32; Num 11:1-3,12, 14:1-4,20-35;16:1-35, 41-50, 21:4-9; 27:12-14; Deut 17:12, 21:18-21 and Jude 6,7.	B - 1
02B23	Write a summary about the high demands and requirements placed on those who are in leadership positions. Read the following verses: Matt 23:1-4;5-15;14,15;16-24;25-28;29-35; 1 Tim 3:1-7; 3:8-13; Exod 18:21,22; and Acts 6:3. Refer to *Writing Summaries* (180-182) in *Writer's INC*.	B - 1 EC - 2
02B24	Write a summary about the importance of family relationships to a leader. Use the following verses: Gen 2:18; Deut 17:14-20; 1 Tim 3:2-12; Titus 1:7.	B - 1 EC - 2

Cultural Studies

		Points
02C01	Continue adding to the timeline started in Unit 1. Prepare an entry for each person or event studied in this unit. Include entries for each king and/or queen studied in this unit and for all major events during the reign of each. ☺	H - 1 VA - 1 each
02C02	Prepare timeline entries for the term of office of each United States President and all major events during each administration.	VA - 1 H - 1 each
02C03	Continue adding reports to the geography notebook started in #01C04. Write a 1-3 page report on any country studied this unit. ☺	G - 2 EC - 1 each
02C04	Study chapters 1 and 2 in volume 1 of *God and Government* dealing with self and family government. Do all questions and activities at the end of each chapter.	CG - 8 each chapter
02C05	Study the lives of all the First Ladies of our nation, noting especially the ways each "did her husband good."	H - 10
02C06	Study church history from the time of the Apostles to the 20th century using *Sketches of Church History*.	H - 15
02C07	Study Narcissa Whitman, Elisabeth Elliot, Edith Schaeffer, and other wives who were involved in their husbands' ministries.	H - 2 each
02C08	Read about Queens through history (38-39, 53-56, 80, 123, 147, 188, 380) in *Streams of Civilization*. Write a summary of each.	H - 3
02C09	Study the American temperance movement of the 1800's and decide whether the women involved were examples of this passage.	H - 2
02C10	Study the women's suffrage movement in this country and decide whether the women involved were examples of this passage.	H - 2
02C11	Study the marriage laws of your state and compare to the vows used in the marriage ceremony as conducted in your church.	CG - 1
02C12	Study marriage and courtship customs in other countries and present in a report or booklet.	G - 1 each country
02C13	Use *World History Dates* or *Kingfisher's Illustrated History of the World* to prepare timeline entries for all events in the lifetime of each woman studied in this unit.	VA - 1 H - 1 each
02C14	Study the history of courtship and dating. See #02P01 and 02P02.	H - 3
02C15	Look at the lives of typical families in different countries and periods in history. Compare on a poster or chart.	G - 2 each family

Reading and Literature

		Points
02R01	Read the story about the courtship of Jim and Elizabeth Elliot in *Passion and Purity*.	L - 5 HF - 2
02R02	Read *Christy* by Catherine Marshall.	L - 4
02R03	Study both husband's and wife's scriptural roles, responsibilities, and life together in oneness of spirit in *Becoming Heirs Together of the Grace of Life: A Study on Christian Marriage* by Jeff Barth.	HF - 4 B - 2
02R04	Read any articles written by Jonathan Lindvall with regards to dating and courtship. Discuss your family's position with your parents.	L - 2 HF - 2 each
02R05	Read any articles written by Jeff Barth with regards to dating and courtship (see *Home School Digest*).	L - 2 HF - 2 each
02R06	Study *The Taming of the Shrew* and compare the couple's personalities and their relationship at the beginning and end.	L - 3
02R07	Read and outline *What's a Smart Woman Like You Doing in a Place Like This?* Refer to *The Outline* (110-112) in *Writers INC*.	HM - 2 L - 2
02R08	Read the *Wedding Covenant* from ATIA.	HF - 2
02R09	Read and outline each chapter of *Creative Counterpart*. Refer to *The Outline* (110-112) in *Writers INC*.	HF - 5 EC - 3
02R10	Read any or all of Josh McDowell's books on sexuality, written for young people.	L - 3 HF - 2
02R11	Read 3-5 novels which deal with family life. Make reports analyzing the family's relationships. Include books written from a Christian perspective.	L - 3 EC - 1 per book
02R12	Read *What is a Family?* and other books written by Edith Schaeffer.	L - 3 HF - 2 each
02R13	Read *Aquila and Priscilla*.	B - 4
02R14	Read biographies of any or all of America's First Ladies.	H - 4 each
02R15	Study Shakespeare's *MacBeth*, paying close attention to how Lady MacBeth's "help" for her husband really did him evil.	L - 3

Composition

		Points
02W01	Continue making entries in your handwriting notebook started in #01W01. Include every Bible verse studied or memorized from this unit. ☺	EG - 1 B - 1 each page
02W02	Continue placing vocabulary words in the notebook you started in #01W02. Add at least 10 new words per week. ☺	EG - 1 per 10 words
02W03	Continue adding to your school journal started in #01W03. Review *Journal Writing* (470-471) and (031-033) in ***Writers INC.*** ☺	EC - 1 per week
02W04	Have someone dictate several paragraphs to you, using passages from books used in this unit. Proofread and correct the paragraphs.	EC - 1 per 3 paragraphs
02W05	Have someone dictate several Bible verses, to you, using verses you have studied in this unit. Proofread and correct the verses.	EC - 1 per 3 verses
02W06	Outline one or more of the books in the cultural studies section as needed to improve your outlining skills. Refer to *The Outline* (110-112) in ***Writers INC.***	EC - 5 each
02W07	Write a summary of both husband's and wife's scriptural roles and responsibilities. Refer to *Writing Summaries* (180-182) in ***Writer's INC.***	EC - 1 each B - 1 each
02W08	Write one book report per week on a book related to this unit or another approved by parents. Refer to *Writing About Literature* (250-256) in ***Writers INC.***	EC - 2 each book
02W09	Write a complete analysis of the theology and/or exegesis used in one of the books read for the Bible section of this unit.	B - 2 EC - 2
02W10	Write a story about Samson and Delilah as if she had been a godly wife. Refer to *Writing the Short Story* (218-227) in ***Writers INC.***	EC - 2
02W11	Read several articles from women's magazines on topics related to marriage and family life and write an essay on each analyzing it in light of Scripture. Refer to *Writing Essays* (105-118) in ***Writers INC.***	L - 1 E - 1 B - 1 each
02W12	Write an essay on *What it Means to be a Helpmate*. Use Scripture references. Refer to *Writing Essays* (105-118) in ***Writers INC.***	EC - 2 B - 1
02W13	Proofread and correct all grammar and punctuation errors in all written work. Refer to *Proofreader's Guide* (600-714) in ***Writers INC.***	EG - 1 each page
02W14	Proofread and correct spelling errors in all written work. Add any misspelled words to your spelling notebook.	EG - 1

Far Above Rubies © 1995

02W15 Write a paper giving your view of proper conduct for young people with regard to courtship and/or dating. Draw upon reading and studies in this unit and defend all statements with Scripture. For organization and clarifying ideas refer to *Writing to Persuade* (125) in **Writers INC**.

B - 2
EC - 2
HF - 2

02W16 Take a spelling test using words from your spelling notebook. Look up the spelling rule for each word spelled incorrectly.

EG - 1 per 10

02W17 Write an essay on the saying "Behind every successful man is a supportive woman." Review *The Writing Process* (002-023) in **Writers INC**.

EC - 2

02W18 Write reports on any or all of the women in this unit. Critique your paper using the checklist (029) in **Writers INC**.

EC - 3 each

02W19 Look up any prefixes, suffixes, and roots of new vocabulary words. Refer to section 446-448 in **Writers INC**.

EG - 1 per 10 words

02W20 Choose one of the papers you've written in this section. Circle any example of deadwood, jargon, flowery language clichés or euphemisms. Refer to *Concise and Natural* (067) in **Writers INC**. Rewrite any sentences with a circle in it, using fresh language.

EC - 1

02W21 Read the description *Parts of a Book* (200) in **Writers INC**. Using a book you've read in this section, find the following: copyright date, ISBN number, publisher, index and table of context.

EC - 1

02W22 Write one book report per week on a book related to this unit or another approved by parents. Refer to *Writing About Literature* (250-256) in **Writers INC**.

EC - ½ each book

Math and Personal Economics

		Points
02M01	Study and use as much as possible the *Financial Management Calendar* available from your county Agricultural Extension Office.	A - 5
02M02	Study *Get a Grip on Your Money* financial management course, completing all activities satisfactorily.	A - 1 Credit
02M03	Read *What Ever Happened to Penny Candy?*	A - 5
02M04	Study and complete all activities in the workbook *A Banker's Confession* In this book the principles of dept free living are presented in Christian Perspective. A study guide is available. This will show you how, with just $1 a day, the normal home owner can save $44,671 in interest.	A - 20
02M05	Using real income and expense figures prepare a workable budget for your family.	A - 5 M - 2
02M06	Prepare your family's income tax return, including schedule A.	A - 5 M - 5
02M07	Sort and organize appropriate coupons for a particular shopping trip Compare prices and use coupons when advantageous. Keep a record of your savings.	M - 2 each time
02M08	Study or review all math operations with decimals (money) and percents.	M - 2 per hour
02M09	Study interest rates and learn to compute simple and compounded interest.	M - 3
02M10	Study various investment opportunities available for your family and their rates of risk and return to determine which is best for you.	CE - 2
02M11	Use the tax codes and forms of your state and nation to find and compare in proportion the tax rates of a single person, married filing separately, and married filing jointly.	M - 2 A - 1
02M12	Fill out a 1040A tax form on the same real or imaginary income as if the taxpayer was single, married filing separately, or married filing jointly. Compare the differences in tax paid.	A - 10
02M13	Fill out a state income tax form on the same real or imaginary income for a taxpayer who is single, married filing separately, and married filing jointly. Compare differences in tax paid.	A - 10

Science

		Points
02S01	Study the spiritual aspects of human childbirth by reading **Born in Zion**. Includes dozes of birth stories as told by a Christian midwife.	HA - 3
02S02	Study **The Joy of Natural Childbirth** with your parents. Includes: physical and spiritual aspects of childbirth, common fears and misconceptions, prenatal nutrition, preparation, contemporary birthing practices, breast feeding advice, family centered child care, husbands role in pregnancy, birth and parenting, childbirth through the ages, childbirth in the Bible, and extensive bibliography.	HA - 20

NOTE TO PARENTS: This book presents very frank information about human sexuality and childbirth. It is presented with a tone of reverence and awe for God's creation, through a dialogue between a Christian couple, and their Pastor, Christian doctor and midwife. However "to everything there is a season," and the book should be read by Christian young people only after they have reached an appropriate level of personal and spiritual maturity that can only be judged by the young person's parents. Be sure to review this book to assess its suitability for your child.

		Points
02S03	Write an essay on *Childbirth Through the Ages* using **The Joy of Natural Childbirth** chapter 17 or other references.	HA - 2 EC - 2
02S04	Write a few paragraphs comparing childbirth in Bible days and today. Include hospital and home birth using **The Joy of Natural Childbirth** chapter 18 or other references.	HA - 2 EC - 2
02S05	Study the life and work of Pierre and Marie Curie. Study their discoveries in as much detail as possible.	SC - 2
02S06	Study uranium and other radioactive substances in relation to the work of the Curies.	SC - 3
02S07	Color and study *The Reproductive Organs* (122-127) in **Gray's Anatomy Coloring Book.**	HA - 2 each section completed
02S08	Study the mating habits of a variety of animals and birds, listing those which mate for life.	SB - 2
02S09	Study the various methods of reproduction among animals and one specific example of each type.	SB - 2
02S10	Study and list gestation periods for a variety of different mammals, comparing them for length and development of the baby at birth.	SB - 2

Health and Physical Fitness

		Points
02H01	Study the Christian sexuality course **Choices and Consequences**.	HE - 20
02H02	Learn about prenatal care recommendations and the importance of exercise, proper diet and other facets of care.	HE - 2
02H03	Study the various forms of birth control available and your family's beliefs about the acceptability of any or all of them. (This is entirely your parents' decision, as this training belongs in the family.)	HE - 2
02H04	Read and discuss with your parents **The Bible and Birth Control** and/or **Letting God Plan Your Family**.	HE - 5 each
02H05	Learn about sexually transmitted diseases and the necessity of abstinence and monogamy in preventing them.	HE - 2
02H06	Study **What Every Christian Should Know About the Aids Epidemic** or another book which discusses this topic from a Christian perspective.	HE - 4
02H07	Study health problems which are common in men and research possible steps a wife might take to prevent or alleviate each.	HE - 2
02H08	Read and discuss with your parents the **Full Quiver: Family Planning and the Lordship of Christ.** Write a summary paragraph on each of the following chapters: *Where Do Babies Come From, Guess Who's Not Coming to Dinner, and Showers of Blessings.* Refer to *Writing Summaries* (180-182) in **Writer's INC**.	HE - 5 EC - 1
02H09	Read **Under the Apple Tree.** It includes a wealth of information about marriage, natural childbirth, natural family planning, breastfeeding and parenting from a Christian perspective.	HE - 2 HA - 2 HF - 2
02H10	Read the **Apple Tree Guide for Expectant Parents.** This guide is to be used with a notebook, a Bible, a copy of Under the Apple Tree and The Joy of Natural Childbirth. Its purpose is to guide the reader into a deeper relationship with Jesus Christ in all areas of her life as she prepares for the birth of a child.	HE - 1 HA -1 B - 1

Practical Arts

		Points
02P01	Listen to the tape by Jonathan Lindvall, ***Preparing for Romance***.	HF - 5
02P02	Listen to the tape by Jonathan Lindvall, ***A Talk to Godly Teens About Sex and Romance.***	HF - 5
02P03	Read articles about birth stories in the ***Appletree Ministries Newsletter***.	HF - 1 each
02P04	Prepare and use a simple coupon file.	HM - 2
02P05	Prepare and keep up a home finance file.	A - 2
02P06	Learn to write checks and balance a checkbook.	A - 5
02P07	Type any or all papers written during the study of this unit.	BE - 1 each page
02P08	Create an original cross stitch, needle-point or similar project showing some aspect of the husband /wife relationship or extolling the value of a wife. Give as a wedding or anniversary gift or save for your hope chest.	HM - 5 VA - 3
02P09	Prepare a basic joint income tax return, including itemized deductions, and learn what records to keep for that purpose.	A - 3
02P10	Conduct and keep records of a home inventory, filing receipts, photos, written appraisals, and other evidences of your belongings.	HM - 5
02P11	Learn as much as you can about various kinds of life insurance policies and choose the best one for your family.	CE - 3
02P12	Study wills and practice making one using a common will kit.	CE - 3
02P13	Learn to sew one or more items of men's clothing.	HM - 10 each item
02P14	Learn the proper way to clean and care for suits, lined trousers, ties, and other clothing worn predominately by men.	HM - 1 each type
02P16	Listen to the tape ***The Scriptural Role of a Godly Wife*** by Jonathan Lindvall.	HF - 5
02P17	Attend ***The Bold Christian Youth Seminar*** (or listen to all 6 tapes) by Jonathan Lindvall. The seminar includes *Scriptural Patterns for Romance, Home Schooling College, Financial Freedom* and *Selecting a Spouse*.	HF - 30
02P18	Read the article ***Youthful Romance: Scriptural Patterns*** by Jonathan Lindvall. You can request a free copy (see Appendix for address).	HF - 1

Creative and Performing Arts

		Points
02A01	Examine words to a large variety of songs about wives, women, and marriage. Make a list and listen to, if possible, several samples of different types of music with words which boost and support marriage and wifely responsibility.	MA - 3
02A02	If you play an instrument, learn to play one or more of the above songs.	IM - 3 each
02A03	Learn to sing one or more of the wedding songs commonly used in your church.	M - 3 each
02A04	Write words and music for a song which would be appropriate to use in a Christian wedding.	MC - 6
02A05	Write and produce a play or puppet show on the lives of Aquila and Priscilla, Abraham and Sarah, or any other Biblical couple who exemplified these verses.	DR - 5 EC - 5
02A06	Use calligraphy, drawing, painting, or other art media to produce anniversary cards for various couples. Use Scripture in each.	VA - 2 each
02A07	Make a card for a bride-to-be using the ideas taught in this unit.	VA - 2
02A08	Tour an art gallery and observe various ways in which artists depict the marital relationship, courtship, weddings, and family life in general. (Parents may want to check exhibits beforehand to be sure they are not morally objectionable.)	AA - 2

Unit 3 🍎

"She seeketh wool and flax and worketh with her hands in delight."

Proverbs 31:13

Introduction to Unit 3

This unit allows us to explore the Biblical concept of God as our Shepherd and the relationship of the sheep to the master. We will also examine the Christian virtue of diligence, and study the beautiful Psalms of David, the shepherd.

On the practical side, we will study textiles, including their history and origins. We will learn about the history of the textile industry and those who have worked in it and how the Industrial Revolution changed the lives of ordinary people. We will examine and learn a variety of handcrafts made by women in various places at different periods of history, and even learn some of the crafts common in earlier days which have been mostly lost to this generation. We will study farming in a variety of contexts, concentrating on the production of wool, flax, and cotton and the difficulties associated with each crop. We will investigate the various chemical and physical processes that take place to produce a certain fabric from its parent fiber as well as the chemical production of synthetic fabrics.

This unit offers a wide range of suggested reading and composition activities related to any or all of the topics covered herein. The unit's mathematics, likewise, is related to the topics of farming and textiles. We will continue to work with graphs, percent, ratio, and proportion, as well as figuring total output of various phases of the textile industry. We will also work with price comparisons.

Bible

		Points
03B01	Read your Bible daily as started in #01B01. You can read the Bible through each year by reading three chapters each day or by following the Daily Bible Reading Schedule in *The Narrated Bible.* ☺	B - 1 per 7 chapters
03B02	Use a concordance to find and study all scripture references to wool or flax and/or the fabrics made from them.	B - 8
03B03	Use a concordance to find all scripture references calling Jesus "the Shepherd."	B - 10
03B04	Write a paper comparing the righteous to sheep. Use the following verses: Ps 78:52, Ez 34:11-31, Matt 25:31-40, John 10:1-16, and 21:16-17.	B - 8 EC - 3
03B05	Look up and study all references to working with one's hands.	B - 3
03B06	Write a paper showing how faith results in works. Use the following verses: Matt 7:16-20, 12:33, Luke 3:8-9, 6:43-45, Rom 2:11, 3:30-31, Titus 3:8-14, Heb 6:9-12, James 2:14-26 and Rev 22:12-14.	B - 15 EC - 5
03B07	Study *Willingness to Work*, the Looking Glass book on diligence and contentment.	B - 5
03B08	Study godly men and their character traits from "Little Bear" Wheeler's republished classic *Gaining Favor With God and Man*.	B - 20
03B09	Study and memorize John 10:1-18.	B - 7
03B10	Study the Psalms of David which were written while he was a shepherd.	B - 3
03B11	Study the stories of Jacob, Joseph, Moses, and David and how shepherding effected each of their lives.	B - 4
03B12	Study and memorize Psalm 23 (if you have not already done so.)	B - 2
03B13	Memorize one or more other Psalms which refer to us as God's sheep or Him as our shepherd.	B - 2 each
03B14	Use a concordance to investigate Scripture verses which explain the role of sheep in Old Testament Hebrew worship and why that was done away with by the death of Christ.	B - 3

Cultural Studies

		Points
03C01	Continue adding to the timeline started in Unit 1. Prepare an entry for each person or event studied in this unit. ⊕	H - 1 each VA - 1 each
03C02	Continue adding reports to the geography notebook started in #01C04. Write a 1-3 page report on any country studied this unit. ⊕	G - 2 EC - 1 each
03C03	On a world map, label and color regions, countries, and states that are major producers of flax, wool, cotton, silk, and cloth from these materials.	G - 2
03C04	Prepare a chart of different fabrics and the purposes for which they were used at different times in history.	SB - 1 H - 1
03C05	Compare in a chart or report the types and qualities of textiles produced and used in different countries.	SB - 1 G - 1
03C06	Study the cotton gin and its impact on the textile industry.	H - 2 SP - 2
03C07	Study Daniel Pratt, Eli Whitney, and others who built the textile industry.	H - 2 each
03C08	Study the major Native American groups and the textile fibers which they used.	H - 3
03C09	Study the history of cotton to discover where its use in textiles originated.	H - 3
03C10	Investigate the economic impact of the textile industry in your state or region.	CE - 2
03C11	Study the role played by cotton and the cotton gin in the development of the plantation system and slavery in the American South.	H - 3
03C12	Determine the part played by cotton in the causes of the War Between the States.	H - 3
03C13	Use **Kingfisher's Illustrated Book of History** to look up clothing in each time period: Ancient Egypt, Sumerian, Chinese, Roman, Viking, Middle Ages, Renaissance, Elizabethan, 17th Century, 18th Century, 20th Century. See pages: 36-37, 116-117, 217, 276-278, 357, 375, 434, 602, 677-691.	H - 3
03C14	Study the economic impact of cotton, flax, and wool production on the areas in which each is a major industry. Include India and the United States,	CE - 2

Reading and Literature

		Points
03R01	Read a poem, short story, or other writing from each of the countries studied in this unit.	L - 1 each
03R02	Read biographies of the inventors of the machines covered above and others involved in the development of the textile industry.	H - 4 each
03R03	Read, outline, and study *A Shepherd Looks at Psalm 23*. Refer to *The Outline* (110-112) in *Writers INC*.	B - 3 EC - 2
03R04	Memorize a poem (20-25 lines) about diligence.	L - 2
03R05	Memorize 25-30 lines of poetry about finding joy in your work.	L - 2
03R06	Read sections of *The Foxfire Book* relating to crafts at which a pioneer woman "worked with her hands in delight."	HM - 2
03R07	Read biographies of David, Moses, and other Biblical figures or church leaders who spent a part of their lives as shepherds.	B - 2 H - 2 each
03R08	Read biographies or historical novels set on sheep ranches and/or written about sheep or shepherds.	L - 4 each
03R09	Memorize 20-25 lines of poetry about sheep, shepherds, or a rural lifestyle.	L - 2
03R10	Read and write a book report on *Lessons from a Sheep Dog*. Refer to *Writing About Literature* (250-256) in *Writers INC*.	B - 3 EC - 2

Composition

		Points
03W01	Continue making entries in your handwriting notebook started in #01W01. Include every Bible verse studied or memorized from this unit. ☺	EG - 1 B - 1 each page
03W02	Continue placing vocabulary words in the vocabulary notebook you started in #01W02. Add at least 10 new words per week. ☺	EG - 1 per 10 words
03W03	Continue your school journal started in #01W03. Review *Guidelines to Journal Writing* (470-471) and (031-033) in **Writers INC**. ☺	EC - 1 per week
03W04	Have someone dictate several paragraphs to you using passages from books used in this unit. Proofread and correct the paragraphs using **Writers INC**.	EC - 1 per 3 paragraphs
03W05	Have someone dictate several Bible verses, to you, using verses you have studied this unit. Proofread and correct the verses.	EC - 1 per 3 verses
03W06	Take a spelling test using words from your spelling notebook. Look up the spelling rule for each word spelled incorrectly.	EG - 1 per 10
03W07	Write one book report per week on a book related to this unit or another approved by parents. Refer to *Writing About Literature* (250-256) in **Writers INC**.	EC - 2
03W08	Write an essay which tells us to "Work heartily as unto the Lord."	EC - 2
03W09	Write an essay defending or refuting the saying "Idle hands are the Devil's workshop." Use evidences from Scripture. Refer to *Writing an Essay* (105-118) in **Writers INC**.	EC - 2 B - 1
03W10	Write a fictional story set on a sheep, flax, or cotton farm. Refer to *Writing the Short Story* (218-227) in **Writers INC**.	EC - 4
03W11	Write thank you notes for all field trips and other help given during this unit.	EC - 1 each
03W12	Write reports or news articles on all field trips. Refer to *Writing Guidelines* (119-125) in **Writers INC**.	EC - 2 each
03W13	Proofread and correct all grammar and punctuation errors in all written work. Refer to *Proofreader's Guide* (600-714) in **Writers INC**.	EG - 1 each paper
03W14	Proofread and correct spelling errors in all written work. Add any misspelled words to your spelling notebook.	EG - 1 each paper

		Points

03W15 Write a fictional "how to" manual for one of the machines studied in this unit.

H - 1 each
SP - 2 each

03W16 Write reports on one or more of the inventors in this unit. Refer to *Writing About a Person* (119) in **Writers INC**.

H - 3 each

03W17 After studying the suggested Scriptures and other materials on that topic, write a paper explaining the importance of diligence in the life of a Christian. Follow each step of the writing process in section (004-024) in **Writers INC**. Also refer to *Writing an Explanation* and *Writing to Persuade* (124-125).

EC - 5

03W18 Write a brief report on the life of one of the inventors studied in this unit, emphasizing the importance of diligence and hard work in helping him achieve his accomplishments. Refer to *Writing About a Person* (119) in **Writers INC**.

EC - 3
H - 1

03W19 Write a poem about sheep. Refer to *Writing the Poem* (205-216) in **Writers INC**.

EC - 2

03W20 List and learn to spell names of all fabrics found in a trip to a store. Add the words to your vocabulary notebook.

EG - 1

03W21 Write a sonnet about a shepherds relationship to his sheep. Refer to *Sonnet* (360) in **Writers INC.**

EC - 1

03W22 Look up the word "diligence" in Webster's 1828 dictionary and in a contemporary one.

EG - 1

03W23 Write an essay to compare the two definitions of 'diligence' and analyze both in light of spiritual uses of the word. Follow directions from *Steps in the Essay Process* (108) in **Writers INC**.

EC - 3

03W24 Write reports on one or more of the men who made their fortunes in the textile industry. Refer to *Writing About a Person* (119) in **Writers INC**.

H - 3 each

03W25 Write several pages of a daily dairy as if you were a shepherd. Browse through the section *Writing with Style* (050-082) in **Writers INC**. Make the style clearly different from your own.

EC - 1 for each 3 pages

03W26 Review some of your writings with your parents. Find occurrences that lack detail or examples. Read *Showing Verses Telling* (051) in **Writers INC**. Rewrite these sentences into paragraphs adding substance and depth.

EC - ½ per paragraph

Math and Personal Economics

		Points
03M01	Prepare a bar graph showing production of flax by various nations and regions.	M - 3
03M02	Make a pie graph showing the above information in terms of percentages.	M - 3
03M03	Prepare a graph as in #03M01 to show wool production.	M - 3
03M04	Prepare a graph as in #03M02 to show wool production.	M - 3
03M05	Prepare graphs as in #03M01 and #03M02 for cotton production.	M - 3 each
03M06	Prepare graphs as in #03M01 and #03M2 for the production of silk.	M - 3 each
03M07	Use information from any or all of the above graphs to practice making and solving problems with percent, ratio, and proportion. (This will be review for many students, but some may need to learn the concepts first.)	M - 3
03M08	Using your best guess or figures from within the industry, determine how much wool one sheep produces annually and how much thread that will be produced once spun. Use these figures to determine the number of sheep needed to provide a given amount of wool thread.	M - 1
03M09	Investigate and chart the rise and fall of cotton, wool, or flax prices (only one) in your area or the nearest market.	M - 1
03M10	Use information from any or all of the above graphs to determine the gross income a farmer would make from a certain amount of the specified product at a given time.	M - 1
03M11	Check prices and find the cost of the wardrobe in #03P04.	M - 2

Science

		Points
03S01	Prepare a poster or flow chart showing wool production from sheep to finished garment.	SB - 3
03S02	Visit a sheep farm at shearing time to see how the wool is processed.	PA - 1
03S03	Prepare a poster or flow chart tracing cotton from plant to fabric as in #03S01.	SB - 2
03S04	Observe the planting, cultivation, harvesting, and baling of cotton and learn how it grows.	PA - 2
03S05	Tour a cotton gin, observe the processes, ask questions and take notes.	SP - 2
03S06	Prepare a poster or flow chart tracing flax from plant to fabric as in #03S01.	SB - 3
03S07	Tour a flax farm and/or talk to a flax farmer about growing and harvesting the crop.	PA - 3
03S08	Draw a poster or flow chart to show the processes used in the production of silk.	SB - 3
03S09	Study the anatomy, physiology, growth patterns, and life cycles of all plants and animals connected with textiles, including harmful insects.	SB - 4
03S10	Examine chemical and physical properties of various fabrics by subjecting each to: moisture, fire, boiling, bleach. Pull out fibers and examine under a microscope. Record results and compare.	SC - 3
03S11	Study or review the basics of organic chemistry as it relates to the above natural fibers.	SC - 10
03S12	Investigate and report on how various synthetic fabrics are made.	SC - 2
03S13	Watch a video about sheep farming or sheep dogs.	H - 2

Health and Physical Fitness

		Points
03H01	Study dermatitis and other conditions which could be caused by contact with certain fabrics.	HE - 3
03H02	Study the skin and proper care of it.	HE - 3
03H03	Learn about the various chemical finishes sometimes used in clothing and the effects each may have on conditions of the skin.	HE - 1 SC - 2
03H04	Study and catalog the flammability of various fabrics and fabric finishes.	SC - 2
03H05	Investigate various laundry detergents to see what possible skin irritants different ones contain.	SC - 2
03H06	Study arthritis and other conditions which affect one's ability to work with her hands. Learn how to prevent and treat each condition.	HE - 3
03H07	Learn and practice exercises to strengthen your grip.	PE - 3
03H08	Learn and practice exercises to strengthen and improve the agility of your wrists and/or fingers.	PE - 3
03H09	Study carpal tunnel syndrome, its causes, cures, and preventive measures.	HE -3

Practical Arts

		Points
03P01	Collect and mount samples of various types of fabrics. Label each with name, fiber content, origin, recommended uses, and care needed.	HM - 2
03P02	Visit a local fabric store and list all fabrics available which are made from wool, flax, or cotton. Note differences and similarities of each.	HM - 1
03P03	Visit a clothing store to see the variety of fabrics used for different types of clothing. Compare the texture and weight of natural and synthetic fibers. See how the prices of all natural garments compare to those of synthetics, and compare woven fabrics to knits.	HM - 1
03P04	Plan a wardrobe for each season for a real or hypothetical person living a certain lifestyle in a particular area.	HM - 4
03P05	Become fully competent in doing your family's laundry, sort by color and fabric type, and learning the type of care each fabric needs.	HM - 4
03P06	Type all major papers written for this unit.	BE - 1 each page
03P07	Observe and/or try sheep shearing.	PA - 2
03P08	Learn to do as many as possible of the "Early American" handcrafts from *The Foxfire Book* series or similar reference.	HM - 2 each
03P09	Tie dye, paint, or otherwise decorate a T- shirt or other article of clothing.	HM - 3 VA - 1
03P10	Take a course in smocking or tatting or other handwork of an earlier day.	HM - 5
03P11	Develop a hobby from one of the above crafts or another at which you can work with your hands. Develop the habit of taking your craft along so you can work on it in idle moments.	HM - 2 per week
03P12	Create a book with one of the following titles: *Shepherd and His Sheep, The Textile Industry, Diligence,* or *Life During the Industrial Revolution.* This can be a simple notebook that includes all the reports and art work during this unit or a bound story book written as a nonfiction book. You may include text and illustrations as you desire. Points will depend on the amount of time spent on this project. Share the book with someone.	Parents discretion

Creative and Performing Arts

		Points
03A01	Draw a picture of each field trip.	VA - 3 each
03A02	Use swatches, scraps, and samples of various types of cloth to make a picture or collage.	VA - 3
03A03	Make a poster or plaque of Psalm 23 using calligraphy and original illustrations.	VA - 3 B - 1
03A04	Set one or more of the Psalms, studied in this unit, to original tunes.	MA - 5 B - 2
03A05	Learn to sing one or more Christian songs about Jesus as the shepherd.	M - 2 each
03A06	Draw or paint pictures of your choice on velvet or similar fabric. Frame and hang.	VA - 3 each
03A07	Find and listen to a variety of songs about sheep, shepherds, cotton farming, and textiles. Compare styles and messages.	MA - 5
03A08	Tour an exhibit of fabric arts and notice the varied types and styles of work.	AA - 3
03A09	Tour an art exhibit and look for paintings of sheep, cotton, flax or similar farm scenes. Study each work and its artist. Compare time periods and styles.	AA - 3
03A10	Draw or paint your own illustration of one of the Psalms of David.	VA - 5
03A11	Draw or paint a pastoral scene showing a sheep or a cotton field.	VA - 5

Unit 4 ❦

*"She is like the merchants' ships;
she bringeth her food from afar."*

Proverbs 31:14

Introduction to Unit 4

This unit investigates shipping, ship building, trade, and travel from the beginning of time until the present day. We will look at the lives and travels of Old Testament patriarchs, New Testament apostles and missionaries, ancient seafarers, early European explorers, and other important travelers, ending with the astronauts of the twentieth century. This will include a look at different modes of travel throughout history and around the world. We will study cartography, map-reading, and world geography, including an investigation of other people and cultures.

This is the point at which you should learn a foreign language, if you wish to do so. We will look at the economic issues surrounding world trade, and the United States laws dealing with imports, exports, customs, tariffs, and immigration. We will study the origins and cultivation of various foods, concentrating on the animal or plant origins and the geographic regions in which each grows. We will discuss the uses of various herbs and spices in a variety of ethnic foods and reasons for each developing where it did.

We will study water, sea life, and the ocean floor. We will investigate the physical science principles involved in the building and use of boats and airplanes. We will learn to make and use compasses and sextants as early seafarers did and then examine the equipment used by modern-day pilots of sea and air. We will study magnetism, gravity, and the rotation and revolution of the Earth as well as its relation to other planets in the solar system.

We will investigate the literature, art, and music of a wide variety of countries and center on those American and British authors who wrote extensively about other parts of the world. Our literature will include mythology and stories from early civilizations, especially those of the Greeks, Romans, and Norsemen.

Practical skills taught in this unit include grocery shopping, model building, and food preservation and preparation. Music and visual art will be offered in relation to several different topics.

Bible

		Points
04B01	Read your Bible daily as started in #01B01. You can read the Bible through each year by reading three chapters each day or by following the Daily Bible Reading Schedule in *The Narrated Bible*. ☻	B - 1 per 7 chapters
04B02	Study Acts to I Corthinthians by completing the study/workbook *The Church Hits the Road.*	B - 45
04B03	Use a concordance to study all Bible references to trade or travel.	B - 5
04B04	Study Paul's travels from the book of Acts and trace on a map of the times.	B - 5 G - 2
04B05	Read each of Paul's epistles and study the history of the cities to which he wrote.	B - 15 G - 10
04B06	Study the journeys of Abraham and each of the other patriarchs from the book of Genesis.	B - 8
04B07	Study the routes traveled and events encountered by the Israelites during the Exodus.	B - 10
04B08	Study all Old Testament food laws from Leviticus 11, 17, and 19, and determine what food items that you eat today that would not be served in an Orthodox Hebrew home.	B - 5
04B09	Study the Passover as instituted by God through Moses. Learn how it is observed and the spiritual significance of each part of the observance.	B - 5
04B10	The New Testament teaches that the Jewish feasts are a "shadow of things to come" Col 2:16-17 and Heb 10:1. Study one or more of the Jewish feasts and discuss the symbolism with your parents.	B - 3 each
04B11	Study the Hebrew exile and return as told in Ezra, Nehemiah, Daniel, and Ezekiel.	B - 3 each
04B12	Study the book of Hebrews and discuss how it changes the "Kosher" laws of #04B08.	B - 8
04B13	Use *The Messianic Passover Haggadah* as a guide to prepare and observe the Passover with your family.	B - 15
04B14	Memorize a blessing in Hebrew from the tape *Messianic Music and Blessings Tape*.	B - 4

Cultural Studies

		Points
04C01	Continue adding to the timeline started in Unit 1. Prepare an entry for each person or event studied in this unit. ☺	H - 1 VA - 1 each
04C02	Continue adding reports to the geography notebook started in #01C04. Write a 1-3 page report on any country studied this unit. Refer to world map in section 961 in *Writers INC*. ☺	G - 2 EC - 1 each
04C03	Study explorers and their voyages in chapter 17 of *Streams of Civilization.* Answer the questions on page 369.	H - 4
04C04	Listen to Richard "Little Bear" Wheeler's *American Heritage Tapes*, Volume 1, the history from Wycliffe and Tyndale to Columbus.	H - 10
04C05	Find out Columbus' real motive for exploration by listening to the tape *Motives for Exploring* in the *America 350 Years* series.	H - 3
04C06	Find out what Cortez's mission was to the pagan Aztec society by listening to the lecture #2 from the *America 350 Years* series.	H - 3
04C07	Use maps of Bible times and maps of today to trace the journeys of Abraham.	B - 1 G - 2
04C08	Trace the Exodus on ancient and modern maps.	B - 1 G - 2
04C09	Trace the missionary journeys of Paul. Use ancient (found in most Bibles) and modern maps.	B - 1 G - 2
04C10	Compare the ancient and modern names of each city on the above maps. Study each city, regardless of whether or not they still exist.	G - 3
04C11	Write reports on the countries included on the above maps, being sure to include their Biblical history and any name changes.	G - 3 each country
04C12	Study the travels mentioned above using *Baker's Bible Atlas* and its study guide.	G - 3 each set
04C13	Study the forms of travel available to people when the Proverbs were written.	B - 1 H - 1
04C14	Study ancient and modern trade routes in various parts of the world and trace on map.	G - 5
04C15	Watch a travel video about one of the countries studied in this unit.	G - 3 each country
04C16	Play the geography board game *Where in the World*. You may recieve points each time you play through out this entire course. ☺	G - 2 each game

		Points
04C17	Research and list all major explorers who discovered new lands or made other important discoveries while seeking new trade routes.	H - 5
04C18	Complete all activities in the Good Apple workbook *Explorers*.	H - 5
04C19	Play the computer game *Sea Explorers* as often as possible and necessary.	H - 2 each time
04C20	Study the native country and sponsoring nation of each explorer in the unit.	G - 2 each country
04C21	Mark on a map the country of origin of each of our spices and common foods.	G - 2
04C22	Tour a United States customs office to learn about import/export laws, quotas, tariffs, and duties. (Offices are at international airports and major seaports, as well as borders.)	CG - 2
04C23	Interview an importer/ exporter. Discuss daily operations, applicable laws, and common problems.	CE - 2
04C24	Interview someone in a food co-op to better understand how it works.	CE - 2
04C25	Play *Global Pursuit* or *On Assignment* often.	G - 2 each time
04C26	Play the computer or board game *Where in the World is Carmen Sandiego?*	G - 2 each time
04C27	Study your country's immigration laws.	CE - 2
04C28	Study patterns of immigration in your nation's history, charting the trends of increase and decrease in new residents from specific countries.	H - 2
04C29	Play *Spices of the World* and memorize the sources of the common spices.	G - 2 each time
04C30	Research the history of trade and how traders helped spread Christianity.	H - 5
04C31	Study the travels of the Vikings and mark routes and major discoveries on a map.	H - 5 G - 2
04C32	Study the lives and travels of the Phoenicians, Greeks, and Romans of Bible times.	G - 4

		Points
04C33	Study Usborne's book *The Ancient World* or the individual volumes contained therein to further investigate the various cultures in this unit.	H - 5
04C34	Listen to, take notes on, and discuss tapes 3-6 in the series *World History: A Christian Survey.*	H - 8
04C35	Listen to and discuss the second volume in the Christian History tape series from Liberty Home Bible Institute.	H - 10
04C36	Complete timeline entries for all significant developments, events, or people mentioned in any of the above history tapes.	VA - 1 H - 1 each
04C37	Read Usborne's *Picture World History*.	H - 5
04C38	Study the Crusades and their effect on trade.	H - 5
04C39	Use *World History Dates* or *Kingfisher's Illustrated History of the World* to read about people and events studied in this unit.	H - 1
04C40	Trace sailing from its origins to the present day by reading *Sailor Through History* (heavily illustrated).	H - 1
04C41	Use *Kingfisher's Illustrated History of the World* to read about ships and boats through history: Minoan (39), Vikings (204, 216, 218), Middle Ages (261, 283), explorers (289, 306-308, 338, 341,) paddle steamer, (501) slave ship (544) steamship (548) clipper (625), 19th century warship (632-633).	H - ¼ each

Reading and Literature

		Points
04R01	Read and outline letters, diaries or other personal writings of Christopher Columbus, Marco Polo, Lief Erickson or other explorers.	H - 3 each
04R02	Read Usborne's **Explorers from Columbus to Armstrong**.	H - 5
04R03	Read the story about Eric the Lief, his son, Lief the Lucky, and the first Vikings to reach the new world in **The Vikings**.	H - 5
04R04	Read about Columbus' faith in the republished book based on the actual journals of Columbus, **Columbus and the New World**.	H - 5
04R05	Read about the tools of navigation, the craft of ship building, sailing routines and maps Columbus used in **Christopher Columbus: How He Did it.**	H - 5
04R06	Read the Sower Series biography, **Christopher Columbus.**	H - 5
04R07	Read Usborne's **Seas and Oceans**.	G - 3
04R08	Read the Viking story that draws on the heroic traditions of the Icelandic sagas, **The Story of Rolf and the Viking Bow**.	L - 5 H - 2
04R09	Read historical novels set in any of the time periods or about any of the groups of people in this unit.	H - 2 L - 2 each
04R10	Read the Sower Series biography **Issac Newton**.	SP - 5
04R11	Read novels or other works by Robert Lewis Stevenson, Rudyard Kipling, Earnest Hemingway, Jack London, and other authors that traveled extensively.	L - 4 each
04R12	Briefly study the life of an author whose work you have read in this unit.	L - 2 each
04R13	Read one or more stories of the life of American immigrants in the late 19th and 20th centuries.	H - 2 L - 2 each
04R14	Read biographies of well known explorers.	H - 3 each
04R15	Read short stories from and about other countries. Compare the styles of different authors and cultures.	L - 2

Composition

		Points

04W01   Continue making entries in your handwriting notebook started in #01W01. Include every Bible verse studied or memorized from this unit. ☺

     EG - 1
     B - 1 each page

04W02   Continue placing vocabulary words in the vocabulary notebook you started in #01W02. Learn at least 10 new words per week. ☺

     EG - 1 per 10 words

04W03   Continue your school journal started in #01W03. Review *Journal Writing* (470-471) in **Writers INC.** ☺

     EC - 1 per week

04W04   Have someone dictate several paragraphs to you, using passages from books used in this unit. Proofread and correct the paragraphs.

     EC - 2 per 3 paragraphs

04W05   Have someone dictate several Bible verses to you, using verses you have studied in this unit. Proofread and correct the verses.

     EC - 1 per 3 verses

04W06   Write 3 - 5 letters a sailor might send home from various ports of call on one of the ancient trade routes.

     EC - 1
     H - 1

04W07   Write a report on the major sources of export for each spice or food in #04C21.

     EC - 2
     G - 2 each

04W08   Write a paper explaining the symbolism in the Passover. *Blood applied to the door*: Ex 12:13,23,27 and Heb 9:22. *Sacrifice the male lamb*: Ex 12:25, 27, Heb 4:15, and I Cor 5:7. *Eating of the lamb*: I Cor 10:16-17, 11:24-26. *Unleavened bread*: Ex 12:8, 13:7, Mat 16:6, and Mark 8:15.

     B - 5
     EC - 5

04W09   Write a research paper about Columbus' real motives in exploration using #04C04 or 04R05. Refer to *Writing the Research Paper* (135-173) in **Writers INC.**

     EC - 3
     H - 3

04W10   Write a first person story or journal of a crew member of an explorer in this unit. Refer to *Writing the Short Story* (218-227) in **Writers INC**.

     EC - 3
     H - 2

04W11   Write a transcript of an interview with Paul, Abraham, or another Bible traveler.

     EC - 2
     B- 1

04W12   Write a script for a radio interview or discussion involving one or more early explorers. Refer to *Interviewing* (238 and 240) in **Writers INC**.

     EC - 1
     H - 1

04W13   Write an article that might have been submitted by a war correspondent covering the Crusades. Refer to *Writing the News Story* (230-247) in **Writers INC.**

     EC - 2
     H - 2

		Points
04W14	Write a poem about the sea or seafaring. Refer to *Writing the Poem* (205-216) in **Writers INC**.	EC - 2
04W15	Chose one explorer of the "New World" and write a paper analyzing the "morality" of his dealings with the natives he encountered. (#04C05 includes material needed). Refer to *Writing an Explanation* (124) in **Writers INC**.	EC - 2 H - 2
04W16	Write a story or play about a family migrating to America around the turn of the century. Try to be historically accurate about conditions they left, travel conditions, and the life they found when they arrived. Refer to *Establishing a Timetable* (140-141) in **Writers INC**.	EC - 10
04W17	Write a speech that might have been given by a native chief as he welcomed Columbus or another explorer to his land. Refer to *Speech Skills* (490-495) in **Writers INC**.	EC - 2 H - 2
04W18	Write a one page report on any of the explorers in this unit. Refer to *Writing About a Person* (119) in **Writers INC**.	H - 2 each
04W19	Write reports on all field trips. Refer to *Writing About a Place* (120) in **Writers INC**.	EC - 2 each
04W20	Outline appropriate books or sections of books from this units assigned reading. Refer to *The Outline* (110-112) in **Writers INC**.	EG - 3 each book
04W21	Take a spelling test using words from your spelling notebook. Look up the spelling rule for each word spelled incorrectly.	EG - 1 per 10
04W22	Write a poem about traveling. Refer to *Writing a Poem* (212) in **Writers INC**.	EC - 2
04W23	Proofread all written work and correct any errors in grammar, punctuation, etc. Refer to *A Proofreader's Guide* (600-714) in **Writers INC**.	EG - 1 each page
04W24	Proofread and correct spelling errors in all written work. Add any misspelled words to your spelling notebook.	EG - 2 per paper
04W25	Write thank you notes to hosts and tour guides of all field trips.	EC - 1 each
04W26	Write a summary of one or more of the assigned books or chapters of books. Refer to *Writing Summaries* (180-182) in **Writers INC**.	EC - 1
04W27	Write one book report per week on a book related to this unit or another approved by parents. Refer to *Writing About Literature* (250-256) in **Writers INC**.	EC - 2 each

Math and Personal Economics

		Points
04M01	Use an atlas or other source to find distances traveled by various explorers on their voyages. Use this information to make and work various calculations of distance, time, and rate. (D/T=R)	M - 3 H - 2 G - 1
04M02	Use the study of the earth, to learn about radius, circumference, diameter, area and volume of circles, ellipsoids and spears.	M - 2
04M03	Visit a farmer's market or co-op. View the products offered, compare prices, and talk with vendors.	M - 2 CE - 2
04M04	Prepare a line graph showing the nutritional value of various brands of a particular food.	M - 2
04M05	Copy and use information from food labels to practice ratios, proportions, percents and ratios.	M- 2
04M06	Use nutritional information to plan meals for a day that will provide 100% RDA of all essential nutrients.	M - 2 HM - 2
04M07	Keep track of and graph all of your own savings in various food categories through the use of coupons.	M - 2
04M08	Compare prices on several different size packages of food of the same product and decide which is the lowest price per unit.	M - 1 HM - 1
04M09	Compare prices on various foods listed in store flyers to decide where to shop for each item on a particular grocery list.	M - 1 HM - 1
04M10	Use advertisements and coupons to buy groceries for three meals giving 100% of a day's nutritional needs at the lowest possible price. Try this several times, trying to improve each time.	M- 1 HM- 2 HE - 2 each time

Science

		Points
04S01	Use an encyclopedia or book to study water and sea life.	SP - 5
04S02	Study the design of boats, what makes them float, and methods of powering them.	SP - 2
04S03	Study magnetism, gravity, and compasses.	SP - 10
04S04	Read Usborne's *Magnetism and Electricity*.	SP - 10
04S05	List all the spices and seasonings used in your home. Find out where each grows, what part of the plant it is, how it is grown or gathered.	SB - 5
04S06	Tour an herb or spice garden to learn how many varieties grow.	SB - 2
04S07	Determine what common food items grow abundantly in your area and why.	SB - 1
04S08	Play the computer game *SIMFarm* several times. Each time try farming a different crop in a different climate.	SB - 1 per hour
04S09	Study the life cycle, physiology and flight patterns of various migratory birds.	SB - 5
04S10	Use the Usborne *Spotter's Guide Birds of North America*, or an *Audubon Bird Field Guide* to identify birds found in your yard and determine which are and are not migratory.	SB - 1 each type
04S11	Study aviation, aerodynamics, and flight.	SP - 10
04S12	Read Usbornes's *Ornithology.*	SP - 10
04S13	Tour the air traffic control tower of your local airport.	SP - 2
04S14	Tour the food transport and storage area of a train yard including the grain elevators if possible.	SB - 2
04S15	Learn to: Use binoculars, identify bird species, build backyard birdhouses, recognize and imitate bird calls, make feather displays, navigate as owls do, create bird mask and games, draw birds, photograph birds, and feed birds in *Bird Watching for All Ages.*	Parents discretion
04S16	Tour a major port to see how foods are shipped and stored in transit.	SB - 2
04S17	Visit the warehouse of a grocery chain or food distributor to see how they handle products.	SB - 2

                    Far Above Rubies © 1995

Health and Physical Fitness

		Points
04H01	Study the medical and therapeutic uses of herbs and other natural foods.	HE - 5
04H02	Investigate the health benefits, if any, of each of the herbs and spices used in the *Spices of the World* game.	HE - 5
04H03	Study rickets and other diseases common to sailors. Find out the causes, prevention, and treatment.	HE - 2
04H04	Learn about various methods of storing and preserving foods and how each method keeps food fresh and safe for shipping and storage.	HE - 3
04H05	Study the nutrients needed by the human body and which foods provide which ones.	HE - 8
04H06	Investigate the purity and safety of various vitamins and food supplements on the market. Try to determine which, if any, you and your family should take.	HE -2
04H07	Study the causes, effects, treatment, and prevention of motion related illness.	HE -2
04H08	Study and try to apply safety rules for all forms of travel.	HE - 5
04H09	Investigate the safety and purity of your local water supply. Discover where it is obtained, how it is processed, and what chemicals are added to it.	HE - 3 SP - 3
04H10	Use medical books or health text to study the importance of water in our diet and its effects on health.	HE - 3

Practical Arts

		Points
04P01	Read ***Once a Month Cooking***. Shop, prepare, and freeze meals for a month.	HM - 50
04P02	Learn to bake a yeast bread (without a bread machine).	HM - 10
04P03	Shop for your family for one full week, making menu plans beforehand, checking for sales, using a list, and redeeming coupons.	HM - 10
04P04	Learn to read grocery labels and compare nutritive value of similar products.	M - 2
04P05	Use materials and tools of your choice to make a "seaworthy" boat.	CR - 5
04P06	Put together model kits of one or more boats from various periods of history.	CR - 2 each
04P07	Learn to use a compass.	SP - 2
04P08	Buy and prepare a full meal from products grown in your area and sold by farmers.	HM - 5
04P09	Can one or more types of fruits or acidic vegetables, using the water bath method.	HM - 5 each
04P10	Make and can one or more types of jelly, jam or preserves.	HM - 5 each
04P11	Can one or more types of vegetables using a pressure canner.	HM - 5 each
04P12	Prepare one or more types of fruit or vegetable for freezer storage.	HM - 5 each
04P13	Dry one or more types of fruit for long term storage.	HM - 5 each
04P14	This is the time to learn a classical or foreign language, if you plan on including it in your studies.	1 credit
04P15	Make one or more bird feeders or bird houses.	CR - 5 each
04P16	Learn to cook one or more dishes which originated in each of the countries you studied in this unit.	HM - 3 each dish
04P17	Clean and dress one or more animals (such as a chicken) for your family to eat, performing dissection as part of your procedure.	HM - 5 each

Creative and Performing Arts

		Points
04A01	Listen and learn several seafaring songs from various time periods. Vary the types of music.	MA - 3
04A02	Watch and /or listen to tapes of **Ring of the Nebulung** while studying the Vikings.	MA -10
04A03	Using the techniques in **Sailing Ships and How to Draw Them** or a similar book, draw a variety of sailboats, old and modern ones.	VA - 5
04A04	Create a mural or wall scene made of different types of ships you have learned to draw.	VA - 5
04A05	Draw posters or pictures of all field trips.	VA - 3 each
04A06	Draw or paint an attractive seascape.	VA - 5
04A07	Write lyrics and music for one or more songs about sailing or traveling in general.	MA - 10
04A08	Listen to and learn to sing one or more songs from each of the countries studied in this unit.	MA - 2 each
04A09	Listen to and learn to sing one or more songs in the second language you are learning.	MA - 2 each
04A10	View artwork from a wide variety of countries and compare themes and the styles of work.	AA - 3
04A11	Make a model of a Viking settlement using Usborne's **Make this Viking Settlement** or your own materials.	VA - 3 H - 3
04A12	Create a book with one of the following titles: *Vikings, Oceans, Ships, Birds,* or *Explorers.* This can be a simple notebook that includes all the reports and art work during this unit or a bound story book written as a nonfiction book. You may include text and illustrations as you desire. Points will depend on the subject you choose the amount of time spent on this project. Share the book with someone.	Parents discretion

Unit 5

She riseth also while it is yet night, and giveth meat to her household, and a portion to her maidens.

Proverbs 31:15

Introduction to Unit 5

This unit examines which we have already examined, such as diligence and organization. We will also look at Biblical teaching concerning nutrition and food. We will take mention of her "maidens" as a chance to look at the Bible's teachings about slavery and servitude and to study the lives of some well-known Biblical slaves.

We will look at slavery throughout history, from Ancient Egypt and ending with the War Between the States and the role slavery played in it. In studying that war and the period in which it occurred, we will read writings of several famous people of that time and a variety of literature about the period. We will also examine other causes of the war and the after effects of it in various parts of the country. We will read novels and biographies about people and places on both sides of that war as well as slaves and former slaves. We will take a brief look at other important moves this country has made in the area of racial equality and civil rights, including the tumultuous Civil Rights movement of the 1950's and 1960's. We will take a look at indenture, penal servitude, and similar institutions as they compare to slavery.

We will study nutrition, meal planning, and food safety, as well as the anatomy and physiology of digestion (including the roles played by the endocrine and excretory systems). We will look at diseases of the digestive tract, eating disorders, and food-related allergies or illnesses and their treatment and prevention. In this context, we will learn about bacteria and other microscopic organisms, both harmful and benevolent. We will take a look at nursing procedures used for combating the above ailments. Opportunity is given for more detailed study in the field of nursing.

We will learn to cook a wide variety of dishes and develop other skills relating to food service, hospitality, and entertaining. We will also examine techniques for counting and controlling calories, fat, cholesterol, and other things we need to restrict in our diets. We will study positive and negative claims made in these areas and seek evidence to substantiate or refute such claims.

Bible

05B01	Read your Bible daily as started in #01B01. You can read the Bible through each year by reading three chapters each day or by following the *Daily Bible Reading Schedule* in **The Narrated Bible.** ☺	B - 1 per 7 chapters
05B02	Use a Bible dictionary, concordance, and/or other references to find and read all Biblical references to slavery.	B - 15
05B03	Identify and list all slaves mentioned by name in the Bible.	B - 10
05B04	Read the story of Hagar.	B - 2
05B05	Study Joseph's life as a slave in Egypt and his rise to power.	B - 3
05B06	Read and paraphrase the book of Philemon.	B - 2
05B07	Study the slavery of the Israelites and God's deliverance of them in the books of Exodus through Deuteronomy.	B - 10
05B08	Study Daniel's period of captivity in exile. Contrast and compare it to examples of slavery in other verses.	B - 5
05B09	Read Rom 1:1, Gal 1:10, Col 3:23, and I Thess 1:9. What do these verses teach about our relationship to Christ?	B - 3
05B10	Look up all the verses that teach about being a slave to sin and what we can do to escape that slavery: I Kings 8:46, 20, Ps 14:3, 130:3, 143:2, Pro 20:9, Eccles 7:20, Jer 13:23, John 8:34, Rom 3:9-18,23, 6:6, 16 & 17, 11:32, Gal 3:22, and Eph 2:3.	B - 10
05B11	Learn to share the gospel with others from the standpoint of our being freed from slavery to sin.	B - 2
05B12	Use a concordance to find and study other verses in Proverbs which extol the virtues of rising early. Determine what you believe to be the principle taught in these verses.	B - 5
05B13	Study Biblical teaching which supports or refutes the necessity of Christians being vegetarians.	B - 1
05B14	Study the Biblical laws in Leviticus and Deuteronomy governing the taking and treatment of slaves.	B - 1
05B15	Find and memorize the verse that shows Jesus "arose a great while before the day."	B - ½

Cultural Studies

		Points
05C01	Continue adding to the timeline started in Unit 1. Prepare an entry for each person or event studied in this unit. ☺	H - 1 each VA - 1 each
05C02	Continue adding reports to the geography notebook started in #01C04. Write a 1-3 page report on Egypt, Liberia and any other country studied this unit. ☺	G - 2 EC - 1 each
05C03	Read about the struggle of freedom of God's people from Moses and the children of Israel, to the founding of our nation in "Little Bear" Wheeler's republished book, *The Price of Liberty*.	H - 25
05C04	Study slavery in Ancient Egypt using the *Greenleaf Study Guide to Ancient Egypt*.	H - 20
05C05	Read about the history of Egypt in *The Pharaohs of Ancient Egypt*.	H - 4
05C06	Trace the development of slavery in the Roman Empire and the treatment of slaves.	H - 5
05C07	Read about Ancient Egypt (54-60) in *Kingfisher's World History Dates*.	H - 3
05C08	Study and chart the history of slavery in the British Empire.	H - 3
05C09	Study the indentured service as used in England and its colonies. Compare and contrast to the slavery of Bible times and that used in early America.	H - 5
05C10	Study the English debtors' prison system and compare to slavery and to indenture.	H - 3
05C11	Study the founding of the Commonwealth of Australia and its use as a penal colony.	H - 3
05C12	Identify, mark on a map, and study the countries which have been heavily involved in slave trade over the years.	G - 3
05C13	Study the economic impact of the slave trade on each of the countries above.	C - 1 each country
05C14	Study the founding of Georgia and its connection to the debtors' prison system.	H - 3
05C15	Study Clara Barton and her work during the Civil War.	H - 5
05C16	Read about Harriet Tubman, a slave who escaped to the underground railroad.	H - 5

		Points
05C18	Study about slavery and abolitionism by listening to lecture #30, *The Coming of the War* from the **America 350 Years** series. (This includes the anti-slavery movement in the south and the theological tensions between the Calvinist and the Anti-Calvinist.)	H - 15
05C19	Study the consequences of the Civil War and the reconstruction period by listening to Lecture #32, *The War and its Aftermath* from the **America 350 Years** series.	H - 15
05C20	Tour one or more battlefields, museums, or other historic sites connected with the War Between the States.	H - 2 each
05C21	Study the underground railroad and those who ran it.	H - 5
05C22	Study the lives of former slaves who made important contributions to our nation.	H - 2 each
05C23	Tour Tuskegee University or other educational institution started by former slaves for their own people.	H - 2
05C24	Watch documentaries about the Civil War (try the local video store).	H - 3 each
05C25	Study the history of slavery in the United States.	H - 5
05C26	Study all laws, rules, and court decisions in your country related to slavery. Compare to Biblical slavery laws.	H - 5 B - 3
05C27	Study the abolitionist movement and the lives of some famous leaders in it.	H - 3
05C28	Mark on United States map the states which allowed slavery at what periods.	G - 2 H - 2
05C29	Study the War Between the States and list factors other than slavery, which contributed to the start of the War.	H - 10
05C30	Study the relationship between cotton and slavery in the American South.	H - 2
05C31	Mark on a United States map those states which fought on each side in the Civil War, heavily embattled border states, and those which remained uninvolved or were not states at the time.	G - 2 H - 2
05C32	Study the lives of famous lawmakers and politicians immediately preceding and during the War Between the States.	H - 2 each

Far Above Rubies © 1995

		Points
05C33	Read and study *Facts the Historians Leave Out: A Confederate Primer*. Compare it to other material studied in this unit. Try to substantiate this information from other sources.	H - 5
05C34	Study the Civil Rights movement in the United States in the 1950's and '60's and the lives of some of its leaders.	H - 5
05C35	Tour the Martin Luther King museum in Atlanta, Georgia; King Memorial Baptist Church in Montgomery, Alabama; and/or other memorials to King or other civil rights leaders.	H - 2 each place
05C36	Watch the movie *The Long Walk Home* and discuss the events shown there and their impact on the Civil Rights movement.	H - 3
05C37	Study socialism, fascism, and other totalitarian systems which enslave their citizens.	CG - 10
05C38	Read about the Civil War (557, 558, 560, 582-585, 625, 632-633) in *Kingfisher's Illustrated History of the World*.	H - 3
05C39	Read *War, Terrible War*. Abraham Lincoln, John Brown, Harriet Tubman, soldiers on both sides, slave owners, abolitionist and the average citizens—all were affected by the horror of the war during this tragic and dramatic period. Reviewed as *"Best Story of the Civil War for Young Readers."* Book 6 in the *History of US* series.	H - 20
05C40	Read *Reconstruction and Reform*. America began to rebuild after the devastation of the Civil War. Urban areas grew, the plains and westward farmlands became settled, the woman and labor movement begin, and exciting new inventions such as the telephone, telegraph, and electric light began to appear. Book 7 of the *History of US* series.	H - 20
05C41	Create a book with one of the following titles: *Ancient Egypt, Civil War*, or *Slavery*. This can be a simple notebook that includes all the reports and art work during this unit or a bound story book written as a nonfiction book. You may include text and illustrations as you desire. Points will depend on the subject you choose and the amount of time spent on this project. Share the book with someone.	Parents Discretion
05C42	Read about events and people in Ancient Egypt (10-11) in *Word History Dates*.	H - 1
05C43	Read about the Civil War (92, 97, 99) in *Word History Dates*.	H - 1

Reading and Literature

		Points
05R01	Read the story of a slave girl in Ancient Egypt, *Mara, Daughter of the Nile*.	L - 4
05R02	Read about a young boy in Ancient Egypt, *The Golden Goblet*.	L - 4
05R03	Read *Ben Hur*, *The Robe*, or other novels of slavery set in the Roman Empire.	L - 5 each
05R04	Read *Spartacus*.	L - 4
05R05	Read fiction stories about *Hagar* and/or *Miriam*.	B - 3 L - 1
05R06	Read the fiction novel about *Joseph*.	L - 4
05R07	Read biographies of well-known abolitionists in the United States or elsewhere.	H - 4 each
05R08	Read one or more biographies of military leaders during the War Between the States.	H - 4 each
05R09	Read and discuss *Red Badge of Courage*.	L - 4
05R10	Study the poem *John Brown's Body* and memorize 100 or more lines of it.	L - 10
05R11	Read *Up From Slavery*.	H - 4
05R12	Read one or more of the books in Bruce Catton's series on the Civil War.	H - 4 each book
05R13	Read biographies of Sojourner Truth, George Washington Carver, and/or other famous slaves.	H - 4 each
05R14	Read *Uncle Tom's Cabin*.	L - 5
05R15	Read the biography *Abraham Lincoln.*	H - 4
05R16	Read a biography of Jefferson Davis.	H - 4
05R17	Read sermons, essays, and other writings of the abolitionists.	H - 1 per item
05R18	Read and discuss *Roots* or watch the video series.	H - 5

		Points
05R19	Read **Devil on Deck,** the biography of John Newton, ex-slave trader and pastor.	H - 4
05R20	Read **Little Dorrit.**	L - 5
05R21	Read the sections of **The Hidden Art of Homemaking** on cooking or serving food.	HM - 2
05R22	Read the cooking and nutrition sections of **How to Live on Practically Nothing and Have Plenty**.	HM - 2
05R23	Read the biography **Robert E. Lee**.	H - 5
05R24	Read the biography **Stonewall Jackson**.	H - 5
05R25	Read **Christ in the Camp** which describes the spiritual life of the Confederate Army.	H - 4
05R26	Read the **Confederate Trilogy for Young Readers.**	H - 6
05R27	Read and discuss **Killer Angels.**	H - 5
05R28	Read **Gone with the Wind** and **Scarlett**.	L - 3 each
05R29	Add book reviews to the Reading Log started in Unit 1. Refer to *The Reading Log* (257-261) in **Writers INC**.	EC - 1 each book entry

Composition

		Points
05W01	Continue making entries in your handwriting notebook started in #01W01. Include every Bible verse studied or memorized from this unit. ☺	EG - 1 B - 1 each page
05W02	Continue placing vocabulary words in the spiral notebook you started in #01W02. Learn at least 10 new words per week. ☺	EG - 1 per 10 words
05W03	Continue adding to your school journal started in #01W03. Review *Journal Writing* (470-471) in ***Writers INC***. ☺	EC - 1 per week
05W04	Have someone dictate several paragraphs to you, using passages from books used in this unit. Proofread and correct the paragraphs.	EC - 1 per 3 paragraphs
05W05	Have someone dictate several Bible verses to you, using verses you have studied this unit. Proofread and correct the verses.	EC - 1 per 3 verses
05W06	Rewrite in first person form the story of Joseph, from Genesis. Fill in some of the events you think may have occurred during the times for which the Bible is silent. Also, try to capture his feelings at the time of the major turning points mentioned in Scripture.	EC - 5 B - 5
05W07	Write a series of 8-10 journal entries for a hypothetical Hebrew slave leaving Egypt with Moses and Aaron.	H - 3 B - 3
05W08	Write an essay to compare and contrast slavery as practiced by Old Testament Hebrews and that in the United States in the 1700's and 1800's. Refer to *Writing Essays* (105-118) in ***Writers INC***.	H - 5 EC - 3
05W09	Write a paper comparing indentured service to each of the above types of slavery.	H - 5 EC - 3
05W10	Write an extensive research paper on one of the people studied in the cultural studies section of this unit. Refer to *Research Papers* (135-173) in ***Writers INC.***	H - 5 EC - 10
05W11	Draw upon books, videos, and other materials in this unit to write a paper on the major causes of the Civil War, giving both sides of each issue. Document your sources. See section 151-167 in ***Writers INC***.	EC - 5 H - 5
05W12	Choose one of the issues which was a factor in causing the Civil War and prepare one side of a debate, taking the position you believe. If possible, present debate with a sister or friend taking the other side.	EC - 5
05W13	Write and give a speech or demonstration on some aspect of nutrition or cooking. Refer to *Speech Skills* (490-524) in ***Writers INC***.	EC - 3 HM - 2

 Far Above Rubies © 1995

05W14 Write a paper comparing a slave to sin and a servant of Christ, using results from #05B08 and #05B09.

B - 10
EC - 2

05W15 Prepare Biblical arguments for both sides of a debate on vegetarianism.

B - 2
HM - 2

05W16 Prepare a booklet on nutrition, devoting one or more pages to each major nutrient; each common nutrition or food-related disease; and the dangers of caffeine, sugar, chemical additives, and artificial sweeteners.

HM - 5
HE - 5
SB - 5

05W17 Outline appropriate books or sections of books from this unit's assigned reading.

EG - 3 each book

05W18 Prepare a written report on one or more of the health hazards studied in this unit. Show your research sources.

EC - 2
HE - 2

05W19 Write one book report per week on a book related to this unit or another approved by parents. Refer to *Writing About Literature* (250-256) in **Writers INC**.

EC - 2 each

05W20 Take a spelling test using words from your spelling notebook. Look up the spelling rule for each word spelled incorrectly.

EG - 1 per 10

05W21 Proofread and correct all grammar and punctuation errors in all written work. Refer to *Proofreader's Guide* (600-714) in **Writers INC**.

EG - 1 each page

05W22 Proofread and correct spelling errors in all written work. Add any misspelled words to your spelling notebook.

EG - 2 per paper

05W23 Write thank you notes to hosts and tour guides of all field trips.

EC - 1 each

05W24 Write reports on all field trips. Refer to *Writing Guidelines* (119-125) in **Writers INC**.

EC - 2 each

05W25 Read the creative essay *Why Did Kamal Die?* (117) in **Writers Inc.** Rewrite the essay as if it were told by Kamal's parents.

EC - 3

05W26 Write reports on two or more of the conductors for the underground railroad.

H - 3 each

05W27 Paraphrase *The Debate is Over* and/or other abolitionist literature to relate it to the abortion issue of today.

EC - 1
CE - 1 each

05W28 Write a fictional story of a slave who gained his/her freedom with the Emancipation Proclamation. Refer to *Writing the Short Story* (218-227) in **Writers INC**.

EC - 5

Math and Personal Economics

05M01	Make one or more graphs comparing the fat and/or calorie content of various foods.	M - 4
05M02	Keep a record of the calorie, fat, and protein content of foods eaten by your family over a period of several days.	M - 5
05M03	Make percent, ratio, and proportion problems from the above graphs.	M - 5
05M04	Use your mastered skills in mathematics and basic algebra to alter sizes and portions of your recipes as needed.	M - 3-5 parent's own judgment
05M05	Tally costs of the meals your family eats for one full week. Try to provide menu plans containing the same amounts of nutrients at a lower cost.	M - 5
05M06	Using statistics from history books and other material from archives departments and such, make a bar graph showing the populations of the various slave states in the United States comparing the numbers of free citizens to slaves.	M - 4 H - 3
05M07	Perform the calculations necessary to show the data in # 05M06 as percentages, ratios, and proportions.	M - 5
05M08	Make a pie graph to show the data in # 05M06.	M - 4

Science

		Points
05S01	Read ***Fearfully and Wonderfully Made*** and/or ***In His Image*** by renowned surgeon Paul Brand and award winning writer Philip Yancey. This book studies biology and relates the human body to the body of Christ. Dr. Ed Wheat said, "*Finest medical presentation of the structures and functions of the human body that I have ever seen.*" about this book.	HA - 5 B - 3 each
05S02	Read and outline *The Digestive System* (232-257) in ***ABC's of the Human Body*** by Reader's Digest.	HA - 5
05S03	Study the anatomy and working of the teeth, gums, and tongue, using cross-section pictures or a cut-away model.	HA - 3
05S04	Study the enzymes, hormones, and other "juices" which play a part in digestion and the organs which produce them.	HA - 3
05S05	Study the excretory system, how it works, and its connection to digestion.	HA - 5
05S06	Use felt cut-outs, transparency overlays, or cut away diagrams as visual aids for studying the above systems and organs.	No extra points
05S07	Study the digestive systems of one or more animals representative of a genus or class, using dissection, a plastic cut-away model, videos, or transparencies.	SB - 5 each
05S08	Learn about the chemical processes involved in digestion and the chemical makeup of the various digestive juices.	HA - 3
05S09	Experiment to observe the effect of saliva on various food substances.	HA - 2
05S10	Subject a variety of foods to common chemical tests for salt, sugar, acidity, etc. and record your findings.	SC - 3
05S11	Study the Usborne book ***Food, Fitness, and Health***, doing all of the projects and experiments.	HA - 3 HE - 3
05S12	Study the effects of temperature, humidity, and other environmental factors on the quality, safety, and taste of various food products.	SC - 2 HE - 2
05S13	Study bacteria, fungi, and other organisms which affect food and may cause illness.	SB - 2 HE - 2
05S14	Color and study all systems and organs related to the digestive system in ***Gray's Anatomy Coloring Book***.	HA - 2 each section completed

Health and Physical Fitness

		Points
05H01	Listen to the set of tapes *Walking in Divine Health*.	HE - ½ credit
05H02	Interview a dentist. Refer to Interviewing (238) in *Writers INC.*	HA - 5
05H03	Discuss your dental records with your dentist and find out what they show him.	HE - 2
05H04	Tour a dental office and lab and learn as much as you can about how a dentist and his staff do their work.	HE - 2
05H05	Learn about food allergies and other health problems connected with specific foods or types of foods and their symptoms, prevention, and treatment.	HE - 4
05H06	Study a complete nutrition course using a textbook or material from 4-H, county extension office, or other sources.	HE - 10 HM - 10
05H07	Prepare a poster on the "Four Basic Food" groups or the USDA's nutritional pyramid. For each food group show main nutrients offered, amounts, and primary sources.	HE - 2 HM - 3
05H08	Study and compare the pros and cons of these common sweeteners: saccharin, sugar, honey, Nutrasweet, powdered fructose.	HE - 2
05H09	Study the negative health effects of caffeine, tannin, and other natural or artificial stimulants.	HE - 2
05H10	Compare various sources of required nutrients and learn to consistently choose those lowest in fat, cholesterol, and/or calories.	HE - 5
05H11	Study cholesterol and its effect on health. Study the prevention and treatment of high cholesterol.	HE - 3
05H12	Learn to test for cholesterol, glucose, and harmful substances in your body.	HE - 1 each test
05H13	Analyze the nutritional value of the meals your family eats over the course of a few days. Look for ways to add nutrition and cut down on fats, sugar, and other negatives.	HE - 2 HM - 3
05H14	Study vitamin and food supplements and decide which are best to meet specific nutritional needs of your family.	HE - 2
05H15	Investigate any prescription drugs taken by members of your family for digestive or food disorders. Learn what the medications contain and what risks, if any, they pose.	HE - 2 SC - 2

	Points
05H16　Study vegetarian sources of protein and amino acids.	HM - 2
05H17　Study **Homemade Health** or another good book on whole foods nutrition.	HE - 5
05H18　Study food safety and the prevention of food poisoning.	HE - 2
05H19　Instead of # 05H01, 05H09 - 05H011, and 05H014 you may take an introductory nursing course.	HE - 1 credit per course
05H20　Color and study *Taste Testing* (54-55) and *Food into Energy* (76-77) in **Gray's Anatomy Coloring Book**.	HA - 2 each section completed
05H21　Read and outline sections about nutrition (pages 248-249, 253) in **ABC's of the Human Body** by Reader's Digest.	HA - 5 EC - 2

		Points
05P01	Complete *The Creative Cooking Course*.	HM - 30
05P02	Read *Once a Month Cooking* or *Dinners in the Freezer*. Shop, prepare, and freeze meals for a month.	HM - 50
05P03	Plan and prepare all of your family's meals every day for at least one full week, balancing all meals nutritionally and staying within a given budget.	HM - 35
05P04	Prepare casseroles, one-dish dinners, and other good meals to share with sick or bereaved friends and their families.	HM - 3 each meal
05P05	Keep a scrapbook or card file of healthy, inexpensive recipes which you can make and which your family especially enjoys. Add to it periodically throughout this entire course.	HM - 2
05P06	Learn several methods of presenting a wide variety of food in an appealing, eye-catching manner.	HM - 3
05P07	Learn to cook a variety of new dishes low in sugar, cholesterol, fats, salt, etc.	HM - 2 each dish
05P08	Alter some of your favorite recipes to make them healthier by eliminating or minimizing fat, cholesterol, sugar, etc.	HM - 2 each HE - 2 each
05P09	Learn to cook as many different types of food as possible, concentrating on things your family particularly enjoys.	HM - 3 each dish : 30 max.
05P10	Plan and arrange appealing table settings and decorations for several different types of meals and occasions.	HM - 2 each meal: 10 max.
05P11	Make a tablecloth or placemat set and use it in one of your table arrangements.	HM - 5
05P12	Make napkins and napkin rings to go with the tablecloth or placemats you made.	HM - 5
05P13	Prepare an attractive meal tray with decorations for a sickbed patient or an invalid.	HM - 3
05P14	Tour the kitchen of a hospital, prison, or other institution. Talk with the dietitian in charge and observe the facility in operation.	HM - 3
05P15	Attend a Southern Living Cooking School.	HM - 10

		Points
05P16	Help prepare and/or serve meals in a soup kitchen, rescue mission, or homeless shelter. Plan special things to make the meals appealing and enjoyable.	HM - 3 each time; 12 max.
05P17	Help cook and/or clean in a commercial or institutional kitchen.	HM - 3
05P18	Learn to decorate cakes, candies, etc.	HM - 5
05P19	Volunteer as a nurse's assistant or in the food service department of a hospital or nursing home.	HE - 1 per hour up to 1/2 credit

Creative and Performing Arts

		Points
05A01	Draw onto transparencies and color with highlighters each of the organs studied in this unit—digestive and excretory systems. Prepare transparencies to overlay each other. Use to demonstrate what you have learned.	HA - 1 VA - 1 each organ
05A02	Draw a life-size outline shape of a human being and fill in the organs studied either by drawing them on directly or by making cut-outs to be fastened on where they belong.	HA - 10 VA - 5
05A03	Draw and color each of the organs studied in this unit—digestive and excretory systems. Use to demonstrate what you have learned.	HA - 1 VA - 1 each organ
05A04	Use calligraphy, drawing, or other graphic arts to make tray cards to go with meals for hospital or nursing home patients.	VA - 1 per card
05A05	Design and make banners, posters, or other decorations to brighten the walls of a soup kitchen or the dining hall of a shelter or mission.	VA - 5 each
05A06	Learn to create floral and other types of centerpieces for a variety of table settings.	VA - 10
05A07	Draw pictures of all field trips in this unit.	VA - 1 each
05A08	Make a collage or mosaic picture using whole or cut-up food labels.	VA - 5
05A09	Make a picture or design using beans, pasta, rice, or other dried food items.	VA - 5
05A10	Paint or draw a still-life featuring fruits, vegetables, or other foods.	VA - 5
05A11	Illustrate all timeline entries.	VA - 1 each
05A12	Listen to and analyze several spirituals and other songs popularized by slaves in the American South.	MA - 1 each song
05A13	Learn to sing some of the above songs.	MA - 5 each
05A14	Learn to play some of the above songs.	MA - 5 each
05A15	Complete one or more of the Dover coloring books related to the Civil War.	H - 3

Unit 6 🍂

> *She considereth a field, and buyeth it:*
> *with the fruit of her hands she planteth a vineyard.*
>
> Proverbs 31:16

Introduction to Unit 6

In this unit we see the ideal wife as an industrious gardener and real estate owner. We will look at Biblical principles for buying, selling, and owning property. We will study God's demands concerning land purchases, boundaries, and property ownership in both the Old and New Testament. We will examine parables and teachings of the Lord concerning vines and vineyards as well as taking a look at the Lord's Supper and its importance for the believer.

We will study gardening, vineyards, and fruit growing. We will learn how and where various crops grow best and how to improve growing conditions on our land for plants of choice. We will study farming and gardening in various parts of the world and take a look at the world's major vine crops and the nations which produce them. We will examine the economic impact of various crops on specific locations.

We will become familiar with laws regarding real estate and the processes involved in buying or selling. This includes a study of such concepts as appraisal, mortgage insurance, title search, abstract of property, and equity. The opportunity is afforded for further study in real estate law.

We will study the various processes which occur in growing plants, and what materials are needed to further that growth. We also will look at types of soil, soil erosion, its prevention and ways to enrich poor soils. We will compare organic and chemically-enhanced gardening to see the pros and cons of each. We will also look at other environmental issues as well as health concerns associated with wine and other alcoholic beverages.

You will try your hand at growing a wide variety of products, both edible and ornamental. You will learn a variety of uses for the products you grow and how to make the most of each crop. We will take every opportunity to use plants for beauty as well as utility and to develop an attractive landscape. There will be suggestions on ways to make money from your crops.

You will learn geometry and measurement as they relate to land and home building. This will also offer an introduction to basic trigonometry if you are interested.

Bible

		Points
06B01	Read your Bible daily as started in #01B01. You can read the Bible through each year by reading three chapters each day or by following the Daily Bible Reading Schedule in *The Narrated Bible.* ☺	B - 1 per 7 chapters
06B02	Read the following verses on spiritual growth: Rom 12:1-2, II Cor 3:18, and Eph 4:11-15.	B - 3
06B03	Write a paper entitled *Spiritual Growth*, using scriptural references and quotes whenever possible. Include the following verses in your research: Deut 6:6, 8:3, Ps 199:9, 175, John 15:3, Eph 5:25, Col 3:16, I Thess 2:13, II Tim 3:16, and I Pet 1:22-23, 2:2.	B - 5 EC - 10
06B04	Study and analyze current application of the parable of the vineyard in Matthew 20.	B - 3
06B05	Study the parable of the sower in Matthew 13, Mark 4, and Luke 8.	B - 5
06B06	Study the parable of the wicked vine-growers in Matthew 21:33-41. Compare to the account of the same parable in Mark 12 and Luke 20.	B - 5
06B07	Study the teaching of the true vine in John 15:1-8 and apply its teaching to your life.	B - 3
06B08	Read all four gospel accounts of the institution of the Lord's Supper from Matthew 26, Mark 14, Luke 22, and John 13. Compare the various accounts for a complete description of the event.	B - 2
06B09	Look up and read all Biblical references to wine, grapes, or other vineyard products. List each and whether it is used in a literal or symbolic sense (or maybe both).	B - 5
06B10	Use the concordance to locate and read passages which refer to vineyards or fields. Examine the significance of each.	B - 3
06B11	Study all passages in the Old and New Testament regarding the use of wine and "strong drink." Analyze these to reach your own conviction on this issue with advice from parents or pastor.	B - 8
06B12	Read the parable of the mustard seed in Luke 13:19.	B - 3

Far Above Rubies © 1995

06B13	Read Galatians 5:22. Make a list of the spiritual fruits. Look up the original Greek words for each fruit in the dictionary and write the definition.	B - 8
06B14	Memorize Galatians 5:22-25.	B - 2
06B15	Study Biblical teaching with regards to land boundaries and honest measure.	B - 3
06B16	Study the Biblical commands about stewardship and dominion of the Earth.	B - 2
06B17	Study the apostle Paul's teaching on the Lord's Supper as he wrote in I Corinthians.	B - 1
06B18	Give a definition of the "tree of life" from Gen 2:9, 3:22 and Rev 22:2.	B - 1
06B19	Find out our responsibility to the land. Read the following verses: Gen 2:15; Exod 23:11; Psa 8:6.	B - ½
06B20	Find out how God feels about land distribution and boundaries. Read the following verses: Num 34:1-28, Deut 2:5-3:2; Josh 1:2-5; Jer 27:6-8; and Act 17:26.	B - 1
06B21	Write a paper about property rights in the Bible by reading the following verses: Exo 20:15-17; 21:33-36; 22:1-15; Lev 24:18,21; Deut 22:1-3; Josh 13-19; 1 King 21:17-19; Prov 22:28; and Eze 46:18; 47:22,23. Refer to *Writing Summaries* (180-182) in **Writer's INC**.	B - 3 EC - 2
06B22	Find out if women have property right in the Bible. Read verses Num 27:1-9; and Acts 5:7-10.	B - ¼

Cultural Studies

		Points
06C01	Continue adding to the timeline started in #01C01. Prepare an entry for each person or event studied in this unit. ☺	H - 1 VA - 1 each
06C02	Continue adding reports to the geography notebook started in #01C04. Write a 1-3 page report on any vine-growing or other countries studied in this unit. ☺	G - 2 EC - 1 each
06C03	Obtain a topographical map of your state from your nearest United States Geological Survey Office, and study it learning the various uses for such maps and how to read them.	G - 1
06C04	Study the topography and geological make-up of the various parts of your state.	SE - 2 G - 2
06C05	Make a relief map of your state to show its land elevations, major bodies of water, and any natural boundaries.	G - 5
06C06	Use encyclopedias, or information from your state's agriculture department to study the economic impact of agriculture on your state, including major products, areas in which they grow, and other agribusiness industries.	G - 2 CE - 2
06C07	Place symbols on your relief map or draw them on a flat map to show major crops and industries within your state.	CE - 1
06C08	Talk with real estate, tax, and insurance appraisers about the purpose and methods used for each type of appraisal. List factors each has to consider.	CE - 3
06C09	Study the real estate laws of your state and any additional ordinances your local area may have on that topic.	CE - 5
06C10	Examine a real estate contract, title abstract, surveyor's report, and/or a real estate appraisal.	CL - 2 each
06C11	Interview a mortgage loan officer and/or a real estate lawyer to find out how appraisals, surveys, and title searches are used in the real estate business.	CE - 3
06C12	Talk with a real estate agent to learn about his job and how he helps clients purchase homes and other property.	CE - 2
06C13	Mark on a map all major producers of grapes, olives, or other vine crops.	G - 2

		Points
06C14	Study the economics of nations which rely heavily on agricultural exports for their trade.	CE - 5
06C15	Study chapters 3-8 in volume 2 of *God and Government*.	CG - 8 each chapter
06C16	Talk with your local officials to learn about pollution laws in effect in your area and how they are enforced.	SE - 1 CG - 2
06C17	Study all governmental agencies which are connected with agriculture, conservation, or the environment. Prepare a chart or display showing the jobs of these agencies and the relationships between them.	CG - 4
06C18	Interview employees in one or more of the above agencies to learn about their particular jobs and what they see as the best way to accomplish the goals of their agencies.	CG - 2 each interview
06C19	Tour an environmental laboratory of the EPA or any state or local agency.	CG - 1 SE - 1
06C20	Investigate your city's policies on recycling. Learn about any recycling programs currently in operation, and find ways to help in the recycling effort in your community.	CG - 2
06C21	Study the history of agriculture in your area.	H - 2
06C22	Trace the various significant developments in agriculture by making timeline cards for each.	VA - 1 H - 1 each
06C23	Study the lives of inventors and scientists whose work improved agriculture in this country.	H - 2 each
06C24	Study the history of land grant colleges and learn about the one in your state.	H - 3
06C25	Tour your state's land grant college and learn what type of educational opportunities it offers.	H - 2
06C26	Learn the procedures in applying for a mortgage or similar loan and the factors considered in granting it.	CE - 3
06C27	Use *Kingfisher's Illustrated History of the World* to read about people and events studied during this unit. Look up farming in each time period starting with the first farmers in the Fertile Crescent to the 19th century. See pages: 18-19, 53, 63, 108-109, 188-189, 268-269, 323, 348-349, 428-429, 508-509, 488-489, 594-595 and 600-601.	H - 1 each time period

Reading and Literature

06R01 Study the relationship of spiritual fruits to physical fruit by reading, studying, and outlining *A Gardener Looks at the Fruits.* It includes a compelling and comprehensive look at what the fruits of the Spirit really mean on a day to day practical basis in the life of the believer.

L - 5
B - 5

06R02 Read the book or watch the video *The Grapes of Wrath.*

L - 5

06R03 Read about the seasons in *Spring and Summer in North Carolina Forest* or *Fall and Winter in North Carolina Forest.*

L - 3 each

06R04 Read about the discovery and uses of the peanut, soybean, and sweet potato by reading the biography *George Washington Carver.*

H - 5

06R05 Read a biography of Luther Burbank and/or others who made important contributions to the world of agriculture.

L - 2
H - 3

06R06 Read a book or several articles from your local library about regional gardening.

PA - 1 each

06R07 Read several how-to guides on gardening, landscaping, etc.

PA - 3 each
book

06R08 Memorize the poem "Trees" by Joyce Kilmer. Refer to *How to Read a Poem* (211) in *Writers INC.*

L - 1

06R09 Study the life of Joyce Kilmer.

L - 1

06R10 Study the life and pastoral poetry of John Donne.

L - 2

06R11 Memorize one or more English pastoral poem totaling at least 50 lines.

L - 5

06R12 Read the classic, *The Secret Garden.*

L - 5

06R13 Read all sections of *The Hidden Art of Homemaking* which relate to gardening, landscaping, flowers, etc.

PA - 2

06R14 Read biographies of Mendel, Carver, and other scientists whose work produced better crops and/or crop yields or otherwise improved agriculture in our country.

H - 4 each

06R15 Read biographies of Cyrus McCormick and other inventors of farm machinery.

H - 4 each'

06R16 Read *Farmer Through History.*

H - 4

Composition

	Points

06W01 Continue handwriting practice in your notebook started in #01W01. Include every Bible verse studied or memorized from this unit. ☺ — EG - 1 / B - 1 **each page**

06W02 Continue placing vocabulary words in the spiral notebook you started in #01W02. Add at least 10 new words per week. Include new financial terms. ☺ — EG - 1 **per 10 words**

06W03 Continue adding to your school journal started in #01W03. Review *Journal Writing* (470-471) in **Writers INC**. ☺ — EC - 1 **per week**

06W04 Have someone dictate several paragraphs to you, using passages from books used in this unit. Proofread and correct the paragraphs. — EC - 1 **per 3 paragraphs**

06W05 Have someone dictate several Bible verses to you, using verses you have studied this unit. Proofread and correct the verses. — EC - 1 **per 3 verses**

06W06 Write a letter to your local soil conservation agency asking for information on erosion and its prevention, soil types, and soil replenishment methods. Refer to *Writing a Business Letter* (412) in **Writers INC**. — SE - 1

06W07 Write thank you notes to all field trip hosts and others who helped you with this unit. — EC - 1 **each**

06W08 Write a symbolic poem using horticultural terms to describe an unrelated person or object. Refer to *Writing the Poem* (205-216) in **Writers INC**. — EC - 1

06W09 Write a report on one or more of the people in this unit. Refer to *Writing About a Person* (119) in **Writers INC**. — EC - 2 **each**

06W10 Take a spelling test using words from your spelling notebook. Look up the spelling rule for each word spelled incorrectly. — EG - 1 **per 10**

06W11 Write one book report per week on a book related to this unit or another approved by parents. Refer to *Writing About Literature* (250-256) in **Writers INC**. — EC - 2 **each**

06W12 Write a sample legal brief explaining some specific aspect of your state's real estate laws. — CL - 2

06W13 Keep written reports, journals, and other records of your gardening projects in this unit. — PA - 3

06W14 Write an analysis of the term "The Grapes of Wrath." Refer to *Writing Metaphorically* (052) in **Writers INC**. — EC - 2

	Points

06W15 Write a poem about plants or some other aspect of creation. Refer to *Writing the Poem* (205-216) in **Writers INC**. — EC - 1

06W16 Write several paragraphs explaining what you believe the Bible teaches about the use of alcoholic beverages. Back up your conclusions with Scripture. Refer to *Writing Paragraphs* (090-103) in **Writers INC**. — EC - 1 / B - 1

06W17 Proofread and correct all grammar and punctuation errors in all written work. Refer to *Proofreader's Guide* (600-714) in **Writers INC**. — EG - 1 each page

06W18 Proofread and correct spelling errors in all written work. Add any misspelled words to your spelling notebook. — EG - 1 each page

06W19 Prepare written reports for all of the science experiments and/or investigations which you do as a part of this unit. — EC - 2 each

06W20 Write an analysis of the meaning of the quote, "It is the little foxes that spoil the vine." Refer to *Writing Metaphorically* (052) in **Writers INC**. — EC - 1

06W21 The parables Jesus told about plants are a form of writing metaphorically. Write metaphorically about your spiritual condition. Refer to *Writing Metaphorically* (052) and *Parables* (334) in **Writers INC**. — EC - 1

06W22 Look up any prefixes, suffixes, and roots of new vocabulary words. Refer to section 446-448 in **Writers INC**. — EG - 1 per 10 words

Math and Personal Economics

06M01 Study an amortization chart for a real mortgage. Use it to find what percentage of each of several selected payments will go toward interest and principle. M - 5

06M02 Use the above chart to set up different pre-payment plans to complete the loan payoff in fewer years than the original contract. M - 5

06M03 Learn formulas to figure interest, APR, total payment, and principal on loans given the other information on each. M - 3

06M04 Study basic geometric shapes and measurements used in real estate and learn to use formulas to find area and perimeter of each. M - 5

06M05 Use your geometry formulas to find the perimeter and area of your family's home, land, and other real estate, including the rooms in the home. M - 10

06M06 The above activities can be expanded to include a standard geometry course if you wish. (See also unit 1) 1 credit for complete course

06M07 Keep records of your garden showing how much you planted, how much it yielded, cost of supplies, and market value of produce. M - 5

06M08 Draw appropriate graphs to show the above information. M - 3 each graph

06M09 Examine and/or fill out a capital gains tax form for the sale of real estate. M - 3

06M10 Use gardening records referred to above as a source of problems for practice with fractions, decimals, percents, ratios, etc. M - 3

06M11 Determine the equity your family has in your home based on actual principal payments, repairs, and improvements. Compare those figures with the total arrived at by deducting payoff value from market value. M - 2

06M12 Memorize and learn to use all formulas for finding area, perimeter, and/or circumference of circles, triangles, rectangles, squares, and other regular polygons. M - 10

06M13 Memorize and learn to use all formulas for finding the measurements of complementary and adjacent angles. M - 4

06M14 Learn all necessary axioms and formulas for dealing with parallel and perpendicular lines. M - 5

Science

		Points
06S01	Use material from your county extension service or soil conservation office to study types of soil and soil testing.	SE - 2 PA - 1
06S02	Study various forms of fertilizer and learn the appropriate uses of each.	SE - 2 PA - 1
06S03	Learn how organic refuse turns into compost and how compost improves soil.	SE - 2
06S04	Study and prepare an exhibit on the different methods of plant propagation.	SB - 10
06S05	Through interviews or books and magazines, learn about organic gardening and why many people prefer it.	PA - 1 SE - 2
06S06	Tour an organic garden and observe the procedures used to enrich the soil, eliminate weeds, and control pests.	SE - 1 PA - 1
06S07	Investigate the pros and cons of chemical fertilizers, herbicides, and insecticides to make an informed decision about them.	SE - 2
06S08	Prepare an exhibit on seeds, showing the plant from which each comes, where each grows, and how each is propagated.	SB - 10
06S09	Prepare a chart, exhibit, or report on seed germination, showing requirements and the effects of different conditions. Include at least one experiment or demonstration.	SB - 10
06S10	Plant a green plant in a mixture of sand and peat moss in a large bottle. Add one to two pieces of charcoal, water well, and seal the container. Watch and record plant's growth. Prepare an exhibit and a report to show the results of this experiment and an explanation of the processes involved.	PA - 10
06S11	Read through a number of seed and nursery catalogs to learn as much as you can about different varieties of the fruits, vegetables, and ornamentals you plan to grow. Choose those which appear best suited for your climate and soil.	PA - 5
06S12	Study and perform experiments about photosynthesis, transpiration, and other life processes in plants.	SB - 2 each
06S13	Read Usborne's *Mysteries and Marvels of Plant Life.*	SB - 10
06S14	Study the parts of various types of plants and make charts labeling parts on some common plants.	SB - 3 per plant

                                                    Far Above Rubies © 1995

06S15 Go on a nature walk and identify as many trees and wildflowers as you can. Enter drawings, descriptions, notes and pressed leaves in a nature journal. Use the resources *Audubon Pocket Guide to Familiar Trees* and *Audubon Pocket Guide to Familiar Wildflowers*.

SB - 1 each journal entry

06S16 Tour a nursery or apple orchard.

SB - 2

06S17 Have a nursery worker or gardener demonstrate grafting a tree or plant. Read about being grafted into God's family in Romans 11.

SB - 2
B - 2

06S18 Play the computer game *SIM Farm.*

PA - 1 each hour

06S19 Study how God reveals Himself through creation by reading *Thinking Christianly*. Complete all work pages.

B - 15

06S20 Learn about different methods of pollination and cross-pollination.

SB - 3

06S21 Study plant genetics and cross-breeding.

SB - 5

06S22 Learn the value of mulching and the purposes for which it is done.

SB - 2

06S23 Learn the benefits of crop rotation and crops that should be used together.

SB - 2
PA - 2

06S24 Study the insects, fungi, and other pests which threaten fruit and vegetable crops in your area. Find out what protective measures are taken by community agencies and how you can protect your own plants.

SB - 2
SE - 2
PA - 2

06S25 Tour a recycling plant of some type.

SE - 2

06S26 Tour an agricultural experiment station.

SE - 2

06S27 Tour a nursery or gardening center to examine and choose your plants.

SE - 2

06S28 Take a course in botany, agriculture, or horticulture, using library or textbooks.

1 credit for each complete course

06S29 Use materials from the library or 4-H to do a thorough study of entomology.

1/2 credit for complete course

06S30 Study the plants from which some of your family's favorite foods come. Learn how to plant and grow them.

SB - 2
PA - 2

06S31 Make a booklet of bugs that are harmful to your garden and one for those who are helpful.

PA - 5

06S33 Find out how a greenhouse works to make plants grow faster.   PA - 2

06S34 Write a paper describing how herbs and other plants are used in home remedies for treating everything from headaches and burns to more serious illnesses.   PA - 3
HE - 5
EC - 2

06S35 Compare and contrast bulbs, seeds, tubers and runnels.   PA - 2

06S36 Learn the difference between perennials and annuals.   PA - 2

06S37 Study the pros and cons of starting seeds indoors or sowing straight into the garden outdoors.   PA - 2

06S38 Read books on how to use herbs.   PA -3 each book

06S39 Use *The Way Things Work* and/or other books to study the processes used in various farm machinery.   SP - 5

06S40 The structure and functions of plants, a survey of the plant kingdom, and associated botanical terminology are all learned through the coloring process in *The Botany Coloring Book*. Complete all 100 units.   SB - 1 credit

06S41 Complete the first 16 units in *The Botany Coloring Book*. These units contain material about plant cell structure, call division, simple growth, asexual and sexual reproduction, and the general plant life history cycles.   SB - 50

06S42 Read through *Botany for All Ages*. This ia wonderfully conceived introduction to botany around the principles of observation, experimentation, and self expression. Filled with fascinating information and suggested activities using plants. Points will depend on activities you choose to do. Includes instructions on how to create: An herb garden, thirst-quenching sumac-ade, bean sprouts, pressed flower book marks, an open terrarium, a carrot pump and more.   Parents discretion

Health and Physical Fitness

		Points
06H01	Study and chart the nutritive value and calorie count of several common vine-grown fruits and vegetables.	HE - 2
06H02	Read articles about herbs from magazines	PA HE - 1 each
06H03	Learn about plants which are natural sources of vitamins and other nutritional supplements.	HE - 2
06H04	Make a chart of areas of the body which would normally be exercised in the course of gardening activities.	HA - 3
06H05	Study first aid for blisters, backaches, sunburn, muscle cramps, insect bites, and other ailments which one might get while gardening.	HE - 15
06H06	Study the health hazards of insect bites and insect-borne diseases.	HE - 3
06H07	Study common pollen allergies and the plants most often responsible for them.	HE - 3
06H08	Study all available information about the effects on health of residual chemicals which may be found in foods.	HE - 3
06H09	Study the effects on health of various kinds of alcoholic beverages in varying amounts.	HE - 2
06H10	Read about poison ivy and poison oak (140) in ***ABC's of the Human Body*** by Reader's Digest.	HA - 1
06H11	Read about pollen (122-123) in ***ABC's of the Human Body*** by Reader's Digest.	HA - 1

Practical Arts

		Points
06P01	Test your soil and take necessary steps to enrich it for growing your own plants.	PA - 2
06P02	Learn to mix fertilizers, peat, topsoil, etc. to make whatever type of mixture a particular plant needs.	PA - 2
06P03	Prepare a compost heap and use the compost in your garden or flower bed.	PA - 4
06P04	Learn to mulch different plants with a variety of products.	PA - 3
06P05	Learn to read appraisals, survey reports, and abstracts of real estate titles.	BE - 3
06P06	Type all major written work for this unit.	BE - 2 per paper
06P07	Plan and execute one or more new landscape arrangements for your home.	PA - 5
06P08	Plant and grow several edible plants, from ground preparation to harvesting.	PA - 25
06P09	Learn to care for your lawn or other property, including mowing, edging, weeding, and pruning.	PA - 10
06P10	Start and grow plants through various forms of propagation. Keep records and exhibit your plants in some manner.	PA - 10
06P11	Grow at least one type of fruit or berry which makes a vine.	PA - 5
06P12	Plant and care for at least one dwarf or mini-dwarf fruit tree.	PA - 5
06P13	Learn several ways to keep birds and other animals from raiding your fruits and vegetables.	PA - 2
06P14	Create attractive floral arrangements from plants you have grown.	VA - 3
06P15	Use a variety of lettering styles to make the posters required for the various exhibits elsewhere in this unit.	VA - 5
06P16	Learn to use a tiller and other garden tools.	PA - 2
06P17	Learn to use protractor, compass, and T-square for drawing, measuring, and bisecting various shapes and angles.	CR - 2
06P18	Measuring and cutting your own materials, make one or more frames for one of the pictures you made in this unit.	CR - 3

Creative and Performing Arts

Points

06A01 Draw aspects of God's creation using the book ***Drawing from Nature.***
VA - 2 each

06A02 Use drawing, painting, and graphic arts to create displays and make posters as called for in this study.
VA - 3 each

06A03 Make posters to promote soil and/or water conservation, wise use of pesticides, and other environmental concerns.
VA - 3 each poster

06A04 Make a pottery or ceramic flowerpot or vase to use with the ornamental plants you will be growing.
VA - 10

06A05 Draw landscapes featuring a variety of plant life, natural and/or cultivated.
VA - 10 each

06A06 Sketch a detailed plan for your vegetable or flower garden.
VA - 3

06A07 Press some of your cut flowers and make a picture or collage from them.
VA - 3

06A08 Dry flowers and other plant products and use in floral arrangements.
VA - 3

06A09 Illustrate one or more of the poems studied or memorized for this unit.
VA - 3 each drawing

06A10 Set one or more of this unit's poems to music.
MA - 3 each poem

06A11 Listen to a "pastoral" symphony and discuss why it is called that.
MA - 3

06A12 Tour an exhibition of landscape art. Look especially for works featuring cultivated areas.
AA - 2

06A13 Use your protractor and compass to create a picture or design suitable for framing.
VA - 5

06A14 Draw a picture or design using only one or more specific geometric shape.
VA - 5

06A15 Research different types of gardening such as French intensive, companion planting, raised beds, terracing, rock and water gardens.
VA - 2 each

06A16 Create a book with one of the following titles: *Plants, Real Estate, Agriculture,* or *Gardening.* This can be a simple notebook that includes all the reports and art work during this unit or a bound story book written as a nonfiction book. You may include text and illustrations as you desire. Points will depend on the amount of time spent on this project. Share the book with someone.
Parents discretion

Unit 7 ❦

She girdeth her loins with strength,
and strengtheneth her arms.

Proverbs 31:17

Introduction to Unit 7

In this unit, we will investigate health, fitness, and strength, physical and spiritual. We will begin by studying God's commands to his people concerning the care of the body. We will also look at all Scripture passages which liken the Christian life to some type of physical contest or challenge. We will do a thorough examination of the "whole armor of God" and what it means to each individual Christian.

We will look into sports and athletic traditions of other countries and other periods of history. We will study the history and political significance of Ancient Greece and the Olympic Games. We will look at the lives of some notable Olympic medalists. We will also study the impact that team sports, professional athletes, and the like, have on society as a whole. Our reading will include biographies and stories of and by well-known professional, champion amateur athletes and stories occuring in Ancient Greece.

We will do a complete study of human anatomy and physiology, including the value of a good fitness program. In this unit you are encouraged to start on a personal fitness program to meet your individual health needs. In this unit you will also learn and practice basic skills needed for a variety of team and individual sports. The emphasis is on getting yourself in better physical condition.

Practical arts include various health and first aid related skills, including a complete CPR class. Art activities explore the full realm of active recreational and fitness programs.

Bible

		Points
07B01	Read your Bible daily as started in #01B01. You can read the Bible through each year by reading three chapters each day or by following the Daily Bible Reading Schedule in *The Narrated Bible*. ☺	B - 1 per 7 chapters
07B02	Read what the Bible says about the body in the following verses: Matt 6:22-24, Luke 11:33-36, Rom 6:6, 6:13, 18-10, 8:10-13, 12:1, I Cor 9:24-27, Phil 3:21, Heb 10:22, and James 3:2-6.	B - 8
07B03	Write a paragraph on what the Bible says about each of the following parts of the body: *Bones*: Ps 31:10, 32:3, 38:3, 102:3-5, Prov 14:30, 15:30, 16:24, 17:22, 25:15, Jer 20:9, Ezek 37:11, *Stomach*: Job 20:15, 20-23, Prov 18:8 and Phil 3:19. *Human blood*: Gen 9:4 -6, and Lev 17:10. Heart: (there are many, many verses about the heart, most represent inmost thoughts, mind and understanding) Jer 4:19, Lam 1:20, Deut 28:67, I Chron 28:9, I Sam 2:1, Ps 25:17, 27:3, 28:7, 102:4, Isa 66:14, II Cor 2:4, 7:3, Phil 1:7 and James 4:8	B - 3 EC - 3 each body part
07B04	Study and/or memorize Ephesians 6:13.	B - 2
07B05	Use a concordance or Bible dictionary to learn the various uses of the word translated in this verse as "girds".	B - 2
07B06	For an in-depth look at the above passage, read *The Christian in Complete Armor*.	B - 15
07B07	Study and/or memorize I Corinthians 9:24-27 as it relates to the issue of girding one's strength.	B - 5
07B08	Study and/or memorize Ecclesiastes 9:11 and/or Hebrews 12:1-2.	B - 3 each
07B09	Study II Timothy 2:3-16 as it relates to readiness, alertness, and perseverance.	B - 3
07B10	Use a concordance and other reference materials to study other Scripture passages which teach the need for perseverance in the Christian life.	B - 5
07B11	Study I Corinthians 6:15-19 and discuss the inferences which may be made from this passage concerning the importance of caring for our bodies.	B - 2

Cultural Studies

		Points
07C01	Continue adding to the timeline started in Unit 1. Prepare an entry for each person or event from Ancient Greece. ☺	H - 1 each VA - 1 each
07C02	Continue adding reports to the geography notebook started in #01C04. Write a 1-3 page report on Greece or other countries who hosted the Olympic games. ☺	G - 2 EC - 1 each
07C03	Study the history of the Olympic games, tracing them back to ancient Greece.	H - 5
07C04	Study the history of Greece chronologically using *Greenleaf's Famous Men of Greece.*	H - 10
07C05	Use *Greenleaf's Guide to Famous Men of Greece* to study Bible, geography, and vocabulary, for the book above.	H - 30
07C06	Study Greek culture and history in Usbone's *The Greeks.*	H - 5
07C07	Read the chapter 6 on the Classical Greece and Hellenization in *Streams of Civilization.* Answer the questions on page 115.	H - 5
07C08	Identify and mark on a world map all countries which have hosted the Olympic Games.	G - 3
07C09	Study in depth each of the countries which hosted the Olympics.	G - 3 each
07C10	Look at the political issues which have affected various Olympic contests and decide if you feel these things were handled in the best way to achieve the goals of the Olympics —- international unity and goodwill.	H - 2 CG - 2
07C11	Examine terrorist acts related to organized sports.	H - 2 CG - 2
07C12	Study international terrorism; identify the primary countries and groups involved; determine the most effective methods of dealing with terrorists.	H - 2 CG - 2
07C13	Study the lives of professional or Olympic athletes who distinguished themselves in other fields of endeavor.	H - 2
07C14	Investigate recreational and physical fitness programs available in your area. Determine who sponsors and pays for each.	CG - 2

07C15 Study each agency in your city, county, and or state government which deals with recreation, sports, or athletics. Compare the jobs of each and see if there is any overlap. CG - 2

07C16 Find out from your local school district and community or state colleges what percent of their budgets are spent on athletics. CE - 2

07C17 Study all countries which became gold medal winners in the most recent Olympics. G - 2 per country

07C18 Use *Kingfisher's Illustrated History of the World* to read about sports through history: Ancient Greece (89), Middle Ages (276), and 19th Century (603). H - 1

07C19 Use *World History Dates* or *Kingfisher's Illustrated History of the World* (82-95) to read about people and events in Ancient Greece. H - 1

Reading and Literature

		Points
07R01	Read the *Iliad* and/or *The Odyssey*.	L - 5 each
07R02	Read *The Children's Homer* (a retelling of the *Iliad* and *The Oddsey* at an easier reading level).	L - 7
07R03	Read *The Last Days of Socrates*.	L - 5
07R04	Study the human body and compare to the body of Christ by reading *Fearfully and Wonderfully Made* or *In His Image*.	HA - 5 / B - 2 each
07R05	Read *Chariots of Fire* or another biography of missionary athlete Eric Liddel.	H - 4
07R06	Read a biography of Jesse Owens.	H - 4
07R07	Read biographies of other Olympic record holders or athletic champions.	H - 4 each
07R08	Read biographies of well-known Christians in professional sports.	L - 4 each
07R09	Read novels or stories about sporting events or athletics.	L - 4 each book
07R10	Memorize a minimum of 50 lines of poetry related to the subject of sports, games, or athletics.	L - 3
07R11	Read one or more books written by famous athletes or athletic coaches.	L - 4 each
07R12	Read a biography of Joni Eareckson Tada, *Joni*.	L - 3
07R13	Read one or more manuals on how to play the sports which particularly interest you.	PE - 2 each
07R14	Read and study *Sportworks*.	PE - 4
07R15	Read the autobiography of the Christian baseball player who lost his arm, *Dave Dravecky*.	L - 4
07R16	Add book reviews to your Reading Log created in Unit 1. Refer to the *Reading Log* (257-261) in *Writers INC*.	EC - ½ each

Composition

	Points
07W01 Continue making entries in your handwriting notebook started in #01W01. Include every Bible verse studied or memorized from this unit. ☺	EG - 1 B - 1 each page
07W02 Continue placing vocabulary words in the spiral notebook you started in #01W02. Add at least 10 new words per week. ☺	EG - 1 per 10 words
07W03 Continue adding to your school journal started in #01W03. Review *Journal Writing* (470-471) in **Writers INC.** ☺	EC - 1 per week
07W04 Have someone dictate several paragraphs to you, using passages from books used in this unit. Proofread and correct the paragraphs.	EC - 1 per 3 paragraphs
07W05 Have someone dictate several Bible verses, to you, using verses you have studied this unit. Proofread and correct the verses.	EC - 1 per 3 verses
07W06 Write a story as if you lived during the Ancient Greece time period. Write the story again using the same events but as if you lived in Greece today. Refer to *The Writing Process* (002-024) in **Writers INC.**	EC - 5 each
07W07 Write a report on Greece. Include farming, marketing, methods of travel, etc. used today and in ancient times. Review *Showing Versus Telling* (051) in **Writers INC.**	EC - 2
07W08 Learn Latin and Greek roots by playing the card game **Rummy Roots**.	EG - 1 FL - 1 each game
07W09 Write one book report per week on a book related to this unit or another approved by parents. Refer to *Writing About Literature* (250-256) in **Writers INC.**	EC - 2 each
07W10 Write a report for your Geography notebook on each country which has ever hosted the Olympics.	G - 2 each country
07W11 Write a brief description of each sport in the Olympics, including how to play it, its objective, and where it is most popular.	PE - 1 each
07W12 Take a spelling test using words from your spelling notebook. Look up the spelling rule for each word spelled incorrectly.	EG - 1 per 10
07W13 Proofread all written work and correct any errors in grammar, punctuation, etc. Refer to rules (600-714) in **Writers INC.**	EG - 1 each page

	Points

07W14 Write a paragraph on the Bible's teaching about each of the body parts in #07B03. — EC - 10

07W15 Write thank you notes to anyone who helped you during this unit. — EC - 1 each

07W16 Write an analysis comparing aerobics, jazzercise, calisthenics, and other types of organized exercise. — EC - 2

07W17 Proofread and correct spelling errors in all written work. Add misspelled words to your spelling notebook. — EG - 2 per paper

07W18 Look up any prefixes, suffixes, and roots of new vocabulary words. Refer to section 446-448 in *Writers INC*. — EG - 1 per 10 words

Math and Personal Economics

		Points
07M01	Using a standard weight chart available from a doctor or weight control program or the American Heart Association, find out how much your own weight and that of family members fluctuates from the norm.	M - 2
07M02	Use the above figures to calculate the percentage points by which members of your family are overweight or underweight.	M - 2
07M03	Obtain from your doctor a chart showing the percentiles for a range of weights in relation to age, height, etc. Graph your own weight trends and those of your family onto such a graph.	M - 4
07M04	Prepare a bar graph comparing the calories burned per hour for a wide range of exercises.	M - 4
07M05	Prepare a line graph to track the number of calories you consume and burn each day for one or more weeks.	M - 4
07M06	Using information from the **World Almanac**, calculate the percentage of gold, silver, and bronze medals won by each country involved in the most recent Olympics.	M - 5
07M07	Make a pie graph to show the above information.	M - 4
07M08	Calculate the percentage of each county's total medals that were gold, silver, and bronze.	M - 5
07M09	Perform ratios and proportions with the facts in any or all of the above graphs.	M - 5
07M10	Do research about Thales, Pythagoras, Euclid or other Greek mathematicians.	SP - 2 each

Far Above Rubies © 1995

Science

		Points
07S01	Read **Blood and Guts**.	HA - 10
07S02	Study and color the sections about muscles and bones (8-9, 24-25, 58-65, 90-101, 106-111) in **Gray's Anatomy Coloring Book**.	HA - 5 each system
07S03	Listen to the set of tapes **Walking in Divine Health**.	HE - ½ credit
07S04	Study muscles, tendons, and ligaments, learning where they are, what they do, and the names of major ones.	HA - 5
07S05	Read and outline *The Bones and Muscles* (158-187) in **ABC's of the Human Body** by Reader's Digest.	HA - 5
07S06	Animals with backbones are called vertebrates. They include the most highly developed animals--fishes, amphibians, reptiles, birds, and mammals. Write a research paper about vertebrates.	SB - 5
07S07	A broken bone should be suspected whenever a person complains of pain with the loss of the normal use of a limb. Do research to find out the proper first aid for a broken bone.	HA - 5
07S08	Physical activity keeps bones strong and healthy. Do research to find out what happens to the bones when a person is inactive for long periods of time.	HA - 5
07S09	Study any of all of the above systems in one or more animals.	SB - 5
07S10	Put together a plastic model of the human skeleton.	HA - 3
07S11	Put together a complete model of the human body such as The **Visible Man** or **Visible Woman** series.	HA - 10
07S12	Study the Usborne book **How Your Body Works**.	HA - 5
07S13	Read and study **The Human Body Pop up Book**.	HA - 5

Health and Physical Fitness

		Points
07H01	Read the Christian view about the years of transition from childhood to womanhood that are filled with wonderful interest and promise in *Beautiful Girlhood*.	H - 5
07H02	Learn the effects of proper and improper exercise on each of the systems and organs studied above.	HA - 10
07H03	Study common health problems which affect one or more of the systems or organs under study.	HE - 3 per system
07H04	Investigate different types of exercise and fitness machines and try your hand at several of them. Learn what each one does for your body.	PE - 2 per machine
07H05	Try a variety of different types of exercise programs, including aerobics, calisthenics, sports, and weight training.	PE - 15 per month per activity
07H06	Attend an aerobics class or exercise with an aerobics video for at least 30 minutes twice a week.	PE - 5 each week
07H07	Walk or jog for 30 minutes or more at least 3 times a week, alternating days with the aerobics class.	PE - 5 each week
07H08	Participate in some sort of organized team or individual sport at least twice a week.	PE - 15 each month
07H09	Consult with a doctor or fitness coach to set fitness goals and plan an exercise program customized for your needs.	PE - 5
07H10	Join a health club, YMCA, or other fitness group instead of trying to plan your own program.	PE - 15 per month of involvement
07H11	Diligently follow your prescribed exercise program throughout the rest of this study, and on into the future.	PE - 5 each week
07H12	Choose and follow a nutritious diet designed to meet your caloric needs and help control any weight problems.	HE - 5 each week
07H13	Join a class to learn a particular sport or sports skills and attend faithfully for 6 weeks or longer.	PE - 30

Practical Arts

		Points
07P01	Use **Basic Greek in 30 Minutes a Day** or a similar self-study course to learn the original language of the New Testament.	FL - 1 credit
07P02	Build your word power by incorporating Latin prefixes and English words playing the board game **Ludi at the Circus Maximus**.	EG - 1 FL - 1 each game
07P03	Learn and practice first aid for all types of common sports injuries.	HE - 10
07P04	Take a water safety and/or lifeguard course.	HE - 30 full course
07P05	Learn to read x-rays.	HE - 2
07P06	Examine and learn to use different types of braces, casts, and bandages for various injuries.	HE - 3
07P07	Type any or all written work.	BE - 2 each
07P08	You may wish to go ahead and complete a full first aid course at this time.	HE - 1/2 credit full course
07P09	Take a CPR training course.	HE - 10
07P10	Assist in coaching a children's sports team or teaching sports skills to younger children.	HF - 5 PE - 5

Creative and Performing Arts

		Points
07A01	Use markers and highlighter pens to draw transparencies of all organs and systems studied in this unit.	VA - 5 each system
07A02	Draw or paint pictures of sports and/or sports equipment.	VA - 3
07A03	Design a logo for a real or imaginary sports team.	VA - 3
07A04	Paint or otherwise decorate a sweatsuit to use in your exercise program.	VA - 5
07A05	Listen to and compare the fight songs of a variety of well-known college or pro sports teams.	MA - 3
07A06	Learn to play some of the above tunes.	MA - 1 each
07A07	Study movement exploration exercises as used in dance or drama. (A good course manual in either should have some.)	DR - 5
07A08	Complete a Dover coloring book about the Olympics.	VA - 3
07A09	Create a book with one of the following titles: *Exercise, Ancient Greece, The Skeletal and Muscular System* or *Sports*. This can be a simple notebook that includes all the reports and art work during this unit or a bound story book written as a nonfiction book. You may include text and illustrations as you desire. Points will depend on the subject you choose and amount of time spent on this project. Share the book with someone.	Parents Discretion

Unit 8 ❧

She perceiveth that her merchandise is good:
her candle goeth not out by night.

Proverbs 31:18

Introduction to Unit 8

This unit relates to the Christian character traits of preparedness, readiness, and attentiveness to duty. We will study the parable of the 10 virgins and other Scriptural teachings on the need for vigilance and readiness. We will also look at Biblical references to lamps and light, both realistic and figurative. We will learn the value of self-examination and evaluation and to count our blessings and see that our "merchandise is good."

This unit leads to the study of light, both natural and artificial, and its various sources. In this context, we will study animal and vegetable oils, petroleum products, and natural gas as well as the industries which developed around them. We will learn about some of the important people in these various fields. We will study the discovery and progress of electricity and the various ways it is used and produced. We will look at the solar system and the universe.

We will study vision and the organs which make it possible. This will include an examination of various diseases or disorders of the eye and their treatment and prevention. We will learn about the causes of blindness and investigate the lives of famous blind people.

We will study household inventories, asset management, and other methods which may relate to measuring one's "gain" from a financial as well as spiritual standpoint. This will include learning about interest and the formulas for computing it. We will look into investments as a means to assure that your gain is good, and learn how to choose wise investments. This will involve us in a study of the banking system, the stock market, and other types of investments.

Bible

		Points
08B01	Read your Bible daily as started in #01B01. You can read the Bible through each year by reading three chapters each day or by following the Daily Bible Reading Schedule in *The Narrated Bible*. ☺	B - 1 per 7 chapters
08B02	Read Job 12:7, Ps 8:1, 19:1-6, 104:10-25, 148:7 and Acts 14:15-17. Write a paper explaining examples of how God's existence is supported by nature.	B - 5 EC - 5
08B03	Study II Corinthians 15 and apply its teaching in your life by taking a good, hard look at your own relationship with the Lord.	B - 4
08B04	Study the parable of the ten virgins in Matthew 25.	B - 2
08B05	Study the account of the poor widow and her oil in II Kings 4:1-7.	B - 3
08B06	Explain in discussion or a paper the importance of not letting one's light go out, as if you were speaking to someone from Bible times.	B - 2 EC - 1
08B07	Study and memorize Christ's teaching in Matthew 5:14-16.	B - 3
08B08	Memorize Psalm 119:105.	B - 2
08B09	Study and explain the prophecy about Christ in Isaiah 9:2.	B - 2
08B10	Study and memorize John 1:1-9.	B - 4
08B11	Use the concordance to look up other Bible verses about light or lamps. Read each to determine its meaning.	B - 5
08B12	Use a concordance or topical Bible to find and study a variety of verses teaching attentiveness and readiness.	B - 5
08B13	Study Scripture references on borrowing, lending, usury, and debt.	B - 5
08B14	This unit studies astronomy, not to be confused with the cult, astrology. Look up the difference between astrology and astronomy.	B - 3
08B15	Read Psalm 19:1-6 in several versions and try to determine the actual meaning of this passage, bearing in mind the growing tendency among well-educated Christians to return to a belief in geocentricity. Look for other passages to substantiate your view.	B - 5
08B16	Insofar as you are able, do a word study on the above verses in the original Hebrew.	FL - 2

Cultural Studies

		Points
08C01	Continue adding to the timeline started in Unit 1. Prepare entries for all inventors, scientist, other persons and any historical events studied in this unit. ☺	H - 1 each VA - 1 each
08C02	Continue adding reports to the geography notebook started in #01C04. Write a 1-3 page report on the major oil producing countries. ☺	G - 2 EC - 1 each
08C03	Study the history of lamps and other forms of artificial light, making a chart of the ones used at various times.	H - 3
08C04	Instead of a poster, you may put together a collection of lamps and lights from different periods. Many early ones are very easy to duplicate as they were made of clay and other common material.	H - 3
08C05	Study and prepare a chart or display of the various oils and other fuels which have been commonly used in lamps.	H - 3
08C06	Study the whaling industry and its ships.	H - 2
08C07	Study and chart the history of the use of kerosene and other petroleum products for the production of light.	H - 3
08C08	Study the life of Benjamin Franklin and his contributions to electricity.	H - 2
08C09	Study the life of Thomas Edison, including how and when he created his incandescent bulb.	H - 2
08C10	Study the lives of other inventors and scientists who made major contributions to the development of modern lighting.	H - 2 each
08C11	Identify and trace on a map all major petroleum exporting nations.	H - 2
08C12	Study the history of the oil and gas industry in the United States.	H - 3
08C13	Study the lives of men who were involved in the enterprise of whaling.	H - 2 each
08C14	Study the lives of important figures in the history of the oil and gas industry.	H - 2 each
08C15	Study the history of the Federal Reserve system and how it operates today.	H - 2 CE - 2
08C16	Tour a large bank and learn how its various departments operate.	CE - 2

		Points

08C17   Study about the minting of coins and the printing of paper money. Learn where and how it is done and the laws regarding it.   CE - 2

08C18   Study the history of the stock exchange in America and worldwide.   CE - 1   H - 1

08C19   Study the laws which govern the sale and purchase of stocks, bonds, etc.   CL - 2

08C20   Study the lives of people who overcame blindness to accomplish important things.   H - 2

08C21   Interview a stock broker to find out about his job and the stock market.   CE - 2

08C22   Study bankruptcy laws and analyze them in light of the Old Testament customs with regard to release from debt.   B - 2   CL - 2

08C23   If possible, visit a stock exchange and observe the trading process.   CE - 2

08C24   Use Usborne's **World History Dates** or Kingfisher's **Illustrated History of the World** to read about people and events studied in this unit.   H - 1

Reading and Literature

		Points
08R01	Read the short biographical sketches of scientists who believed in God in **Men of Science, Men of God.**	SE - 5
08R02	Read Usborne's **Scientists from Archimedes to Einstein**.	SE - 5
08R03	Read the biography from the Sower Series, **Johannes Kepler.**	SE - 5
08R04	Read **The Miracle Worker**.	L - 3
08R05	Read a biography of Benjamin Franklin.	H - 4
08R06	Read biographies of several men who made a name for themselves in the banking or finance business.	H - 4 each person
08R07	Read biographies of Alexander Hamilton and others who played a prominent role in the history of the Federal Reserve.	H - 4 each person
08R08	Read biographies of Tycho Brahe, Galileo, and other well-known early astronomers.	H - 3
08R09	Read biographies of one or more of the scientists and inventors in this unit.	H - 4 each person
08R10	Read **Moby Dick**, a classic whaling tale.	L - 5
08R11	Read biographies of Helen Keller, Louis Braille, Fanny Crosby, and/or other well-known blind people.	H - 4 each person
08R12	Add book reviews to your Reading Log created in Unit 1. Refer to the *Reading Log* (257-261) in **Writers INC**.	EC - ½ each

Composition

		Points
08W01	Continue making entries in your handwriting notebook started in #01W01. Include every Bible verse studied or memorized from this unit. ☺	EG - 1 B - 1 each page
08W02	Continue placing vocabulary words in the spiral notebook you started in #01W02. Learn at least 10 new words per week. ☺	EG - 1 per 10 words
08W03	Continue adding to your school journal started in #01W03. Review *Journal Writing* (470-471) in ***Writers INC***. ☺	EC - 1 per week
08W04	Have someone dictate several paragraphs to you using passages from books used in this unit. Proofread and correct the paragraphs.	EC - 1 per 3 paragraphs
08W05	Have someone dictate several Bible verses, to you, using verses you have studied this unit. Proofread and correct the verses.	EC - 1 per 3 verses
08W06	Read about God's providence at work in the universe and write a paragraph about each topic. *Eclipses*: Job 9:7, Isa 13:10, Ez 32:7, Joel 2:10, 3:15, and Amos 8:9. *The moon*: Ps 104:2, 19 & 20, Isa 30:26, and Jer 31:35. *The stars*: Job 38:31, and Isa 40:26. *The sun*: Ps 104:2, 19 & 20, Isa 30:26, Jer 31:35, and Mat 5:35.	B - 3 EC - 3 SP - 2 each topic
08W07	Write a research paper describing the processes involved in coal mining. Refer to *Writing the Research Paper* (135-173) in ***Writers INC***.	SE - 2
08W08	Write several paragraphs explaining the importance of not letting one's light go out.	H - 2
08W09	Write a paper on the importance of the electric light bulb to our modern way of life.	SP - 2
08W10	Write brief reports on any or all of the inventors and scientists studied in this unit. Refer to *Writing About a Person* (119) in ***Writers INC***.	H - 2 each
08W11	Write reports on Helen Keller, Louis Braille, and/or other well-known blind people. Refer to *Writing About a Person* (119) in ***Writers INC***.	EC - 2 each
08W12	Write a paper to help a new investor understand the differences between stocks, bonds, and other investment options.	CE - 2
08W13	Write thank you notes to all field trip hosts and/or tour guides and anyone else who helped you with this unit.	EC - 1

		Points
08W14	Write a first-person story or diary about life on a whaling ship.	H - 3 each
08W15	Write a poem about light, used in a natural or symbolic sense. Refer to *Writing the Poem* (205-216) in **Writers INC**.	EC - 2
08W16	Define geocentricity and heliocentricity from Webster's 1828 dictionary and compare with a modern one.	EG - 2
08W17	Write a paper defending Biblically and scientifically what you believe with regards to the geo-heliocentricity debate. For organization and clarifying ideas refer to *Writing to Persuade* (125) in **Writers INC**.	B - 3 EC - 5 SE - 3
08W18	Write a report or news article on the Federal Reserve and how it affects all banks in this country.	CE - 3
08W19	See the chart on the solar system and the table labeled *Planet Profusion* (953) in **Writers INC.** Write a paragraph to follow the paragraph listed. Include any interesting data from the chart.	EC - 2 each week
08W20	Write a report or news article describing each field trip.	EC - 2
08W21	Proofread and correct all grammar and punctuation errors in all written work. Refer to *Proofreader's Guide* (600-714) in **Writers INC**.	EG - 1 each page
08W22	Proofread and correct spelling errors in all written work. Add misspelled words to your spelling notebook.	EG - 2 per paper
08W23	Use a dictionary to mark pronunciation and syllables of all new vocabulary words.	EG - 1 per 10 words
08W24	Take a spelling test using words from your spelling notebook. Look up the spelling rule for each word spelled incorrectly.	EG - 1 per 10
08W25	Review some of your writings with your parents. Find occurrences that lack detail or examples. Read *Showing Verses Telling* (051) in **Writers INC**. Rewrite these sentences into paragraphs adding substance and depth.	EC - ½ per paragraph
08W26	Look up any prefixes, suffixes, and roots of new vocabulary words. Refer to section 446-448 in **Writers INC**.	EG - 1 per 10 words

Math and Personal Economics

		Points
08M01	Prepare a graph to show the amounts of electricity used by various appliances during a certain time period.	M - 3
08M02	Prepare a graph to compare the wattage output per dollar and/or per hour of the various types of power plants.	M - 3
08M03	Create a pie graph to show the number and percentage of each type of electrical power plant in your state or region and the percent of the area's power produced by each type.	M - 3
08M04	Obtain from your power company figures on the total number of miles of electric lines in your area. Perform the necessary calculations to convert these figures to other units of linear measure.	M - 2
08M05	Compute your own (or another) electric bill given the cost per kilowatt hour and the total usage.	M - 1
08M06	Study interest rates and learn to compute both compound and simple interest.	M - 3
08M07	Memorize the formula for computing interest (I=prt) and use it to find any or all of the variables when given the other two.	M - 3
08M08	Learn to figure APR when given the total interest paid.	M - 2
08M09	Compute your family's total net worth by combining the appraised or estimated value of all your belongings (assets) and subtracting everything you owe.	M - 3

Science

		Points
08S01	Study and outline each section of **Astronomy and the Bible**: the earth and moon; the solar system the stars; galaxies and universe; general science; and technical terms and ideas.	SE - 2 each section
08S02	Play the board game, **Constellation Station**.	SE - 1 each game
08S03	Visit a planetarium and learn how the equipment works.	SP - 2
08S04	Study astronomy, learning all basic facts about our solar system and general information about objects and formations in the universe.	SE - 15
08S05	Study the constellations common in your part of the world and learn to identify them in the night sky.	SE - 5
08S06	Investigate the history of astronomy, including various theories about the universe and the men who developed them.	SE - 5
08S07	Study the constellations using **The Glow in the Dark Night Sky Book**.	SE - 5
08S08	Study the astronomical theories of Tycho Brahe, Johannes Kepler, Galileo, and Aristotle.	SE - 3 each man
08S09	Study the anatomy and physiology of various types of whales.	SB - 3
08S10	List all sources of light which you can bring to mind. Study any that are unfamiliar.	SP - 2
08S11	Tour a solar energy facility.	SP - 2
08S12	Study sun, moon, and stars and the ways in which they affect our Earth, particularly as regards to length of days and nights and the provision of light.	SE - 3
08S13	Study the production of electricity and various sources of fuel used.	SP - 5
08S14	Tour a hydroelectric power plant.	SP - 2
08S15	Tour an electric power plant fired by coal or a similar fossil fuel.	SP - 2
08S16	Study about light, fuels and electricity from **The Way Things Work**.	SE - 3
08S17	Read Troll's **Energy and Fuels**.	SE - 3
08S18	Read Usborne's **Energy and Power**.	SE - 5
08S19	Read Usborne's **Magnetism and Electricity**.	SE - 5
08S20	Tour a nuclear power plant.	SP - 2

		Points
08S21	Visit a coal mine.	SP - 2
08S22	Visit an oil drilling rig.	SP - 2
08S23	Study patterns for wiring different types of circuits and the differences between them.	SP - 3
08S24	Study environmental dangers posed by oil and gas drilling and find ways to solve the problem without limiting our fuel supplies.	SE - 3
08S25	Study the chemical makeup of various types of "wax" used for candle making now and in earlier times.	SC - 3
08S26	Study fossil fuels and how they are produced and obtained.	SE - 3
08S27	Study the drilling and refining processes used in the petroleum industry.	SE - 3
08S28	Study the drilling, refining, and shipping processes used in the production of energy from natural gas.	SE - 3
08S29	Study the human eye and the sense of sight.	HA - 3
08S30	Investigate the environmental problems caused by each common method of electricity production and ways to minimize each.	SE - 5
08S31	Learn the various units of measurement connected with electricity and what each one means.	SP - 3
08S32	Study the fuel (energy source) used for each of the lights studied in the cultural studies section of this unit.	SP - 3
08S33	The recent probes sent by NASA to the sun and other planets were launched by calculations based on the model of a geocentric universe. These calculations worked when those based on the popular belief in heliocentricity did not. Explain why you think that is true.	SE - 3
08S34	Listen to and form an opinion on the tapes of the geo-heliocentricity debates available from Calcedon Audio-Visual Productions.	B - 2 SE - 4
08S35	Study and complete the ***Sources of Energy*** workbook.	SP - 10
08S36	Study the Morley-Michaelson experiment and its results in relation to the geo-heleocentricity issue.	SE - 3

Health and Physical Fitness

		Points
08H01	Study common causes of blindness, their cures and/or treatments, and methods of prevention.	HE - 3
08H02	Study cataracts, their common causes, and how they can be treated.	HE - 2
08H03	Study glaucoma, its causes and how it can be treated.	HE - 2
08H04	Study near sightedness and farsightedness and learn how the eyeball is shaped in each instance.	HE - 3
08H05	Study all other vision disorders and how each can be prevented and/or treated.	HE - 3
08H06	Learn how a doctor administers a complete eye exam and what each part of the test is for.	HE - 2
08H07	Tour an ophthalmologist's office and learn about the various pieces of equipment he uses and what each one does.	HE - 2
08H08	Tour an optical laboratory and learn how eyeglasses and contact lenses are made.	HE - 2
08H09	Learn about eye safety and how to prevent eye injury and loss of vision.	HE - 2
08H10	Tour a school or similar facility for the training of blind people.	HE - 2
08H11	Tour a facility which makes artificial eyes to see how they are made and installed.	HE - 2
08H12	Learn the difference between optometry and ophthalmology.	HE - 1
08H13	Read and outline *The Eye* (188-205) in ***ABC's of the Human Body*** by Reader's Digest. Refer to *The Outline* (110-112) in ***Writers INC.***	HA - 5
08H14	Color and study *The Blink of an Eye* (22-23) and *Do You See What I See* (48-49) in ***Gray's Anatomy Coloring Book***.	HA - 2 each section completed
08H15	Do research and write a paper on the eye from the encyclopedia or other source. Refer to *Writing to Learn* (473-474) in ***Writers INC.***	H - 4 EC - 2

Practical Arts

		Points
08P01	Conduct a household asset inventory by recording all valuable belongings along with their current appraisal or estimated market value. Keep these records in a safe place in case of fire or theft. Include receipts, pictures, bills of sale, or other proofs of ownership.	CE - 2
08P02	Make a battery from zinc and copper plates, using directions found in *World Book* or another encyclopedia.	SP - 3
08P03	Make a small electric generator using directions from *World Book* or another encyclopedia.	SP - 3
08P04	Wire an electric light bulb to run off your homemade battery and/or generator.	SP - 3
08P05	Learn to clean, fill, and trim wicks of various types of oil and gas lamps.	HM - 2
08P06	Learn to change all types of light bulbs used in your home.	HM - 1
08P07	Make several types of molded and dipped candles, using modern and folk methods.	VA - 2 HM - 2
08P08	Make one or more attractive candle holder from common household materials.	VA - 2 each one
08P09	Learn to fix broken electric cords and to replace plugs on them.	CR - 2
08P10	Learn to replace broken electric sockets in your home.	CR - 2
08P11	Learn to replace broken light switches in your home.	CR - 2
08P12	Learn to check and replace the fuses used in your home or to check and reset your home's circuit breakers.	CR - 1
08P13	Learn to wire or replace wiring in a lamp.	CR - 3
08P14	Create a working electric lamp from a glass jar or bottle.	SP - 2 CR - 2
08P15	Turn an attractive piece of driftwood into a working electric lamp.	SP - 2 CR - 2
08P16	Learn to read and use an ohm meter.	CR - 2 CR - 2
08P17	Learn to read and use a voltmeter.	SP - 4

		Points
08P18	Make a simple telescope. (Instructions are available in books about science projects.)	SP - 4
08P19	Learn to locate stars, planets, etc. through a telescope.	SE - 2
08P20	Learn to read and write in Braille.	FL - 1 Credit for a full course

Creative and Performing Arts

		Points
08A01	Draw a mural or make a model of the solar system as it is commonly believed to be.	VA - 2 SP - 2
08A02	Repeat activity # 08A01 using each popular past theory about the solar system.	VA - 2 each SP - 2 each
08A03	Make a collage or drawing of a wide variety of light sources.	VA - 3
08A04	Copy Psalm 119:105 in good calligraphy or stenciled lettering to make a poster or caption for the picture in # 08A03.	B - 1 VA - 2
08A05	Find and listen to a number of hymns and gospel songs written by Fanny Crosby.	MA - 3
08A06	Learn to sing one or more of Fanny Crosby's hymns.	MA - 5 each song
08A07	Learn to play one or more of Fanny Crosby's hymns.	MA - 5 each song
08A08	Use a kit from a craft store to make one or more suncatchers of real or simulated stained glass.	VA - 3 each, up to 3
08A09	Draw a still life featuring some type of lamp or candles.	VA - 5
08A10	Create attractive centerpieces and/or arrangements using lamps or candles you made.	VA - 3
08A11	Create a book with one of the following titles: *The Eyes Have it, Scientists, Light, Banking,* or *Astronomy.* This can be a simple notebook that includes all the reports and art work during this unit or a bound story book written as a nonfiction book. You may include text and illustrations as you desire. Points will depend on the subject you choose and the amount of time spent on this project. Share the book with someone	Parents Discretion

Unit 9 ❧

*"She layeth her hands to the spindle
and her hand holdeth the distaff."*

Proverbs 31:19

Introduction to Unit 9

This unit deals with the diligence of the godly woman and her commitment to hard work. We will also see examples in Scripture of women who put their time and skills to good use in sewing for their families and others. In addition, we will emphasize the importance of learning a skill well and doing a good job in whatever we do.

We will investigate the textile industry in various countries, including its history and famous people involved in it. We will expand this study to learn about the Industrial Revolution and the history of the labor union movement.

We will look at the spindle, the distaff, and other tools of sewing used by women in Bible times. We will trace these items through history and see the development of their modern counterparts. We will examine other simple machines used in a typical household.

Math covered in this unit includes units of linear measurement in both English and metric systems. We will have many opportunities to measure lengths and areas of pieces of cloth, etc. and to express those measurements in a variety of ways. We will also practice conversions of measurements between units of the two systems.

We will study health problems related to co-ordination and/or perception. We will investigate ways to deal with each of these problems. We will learn exercises to improve hand-eye coordination. In human anatomy you will study cells, genes, tissues, and a general overview of the body's systems.

This unit abounds in homemaking skills as we will learn many forms of sewing and other fabric crafts. The student will have opportunity to learn spinning, weaving, tatting and other crafts which we tend to relate to an earlier time. The unit even offers instructions for making your own weaving looms and similar equipment.

Bible

09B01   Read your Bible daily as started in #01B01. You can read the Bible through each year by reading three chapters each day or by following the *Daily Bible Reading Schedule* in **The Narrated Bible.** ☺   B - 1 _{per 7} chapters

09B02   Use the concordance to find and list all examples of sewing and needlework skills found in the Bible.   B - 3

09B03   Study II Timothy 2:15, Titus 2:1-5, and other verses which contain commands about how we should do our work.   B - 5

09B04   Study the life of Hannah from the book of I Kings and pay special attention to her use of sewing skills for God's glory in the life of her son.   B - 2

09B05   Study the story of Dorcas from the book of Acts and see how she brought joy to the lives of others through her sewing ability.   B - 2

09B06   Using the book **Beggar to King: All the Occupations of the Bible**, list all occupations of Biblical times which involved sewing or other fabric arts. Look up in the Bible one person who held each occupation and study all references to him or her.   B - 5

09B07   Begin now to pray that the Lord will give you opportunities to use your skills for His glory.   B - 2

09B08   Read what the Bible says about God's providence in life work from: Esther 4:14, Eccles 2:24, 5:19, Isa 45:1-5, Luke 1:15-17, and Gal 1:15.   B - 3

09B09   Read what the Bible says about eagerness to do good work from: Matt 7:16-18, 13:23, Titus 2:13-14, and James 1:25.   B - 3

09B10   Study **Christian Character: A Course for Training Young People**. This workbook that provides an examination of the character that should be found in the lives of young people. List twenty-eight character traits, student exercises, personal evaluations, and goal settings.   B - 30

09B11   All energy was created by God and comes through Him. Read the following verses to understand this: Gen 1:3,4,16,1; 2:7; Isia 45:5-7.   B -1

09B12   Changes in form of matter and energy are continuously occurring: Psa 102:25,26; Isah 51:6; I Pet 1:24; James 1:11, and 2Pet 3:10-12.   B - 1

Cultural Studies

09C01 Continue adding to the timeline started in Unit 1. Prepare entries for all the inventions, discoveries, scientists, inventors and important events during the time of the Industrial Revolution. ☺

H - 1
VA - 1 each

09C02 Continue adding reports to the geography notebook started in #01C04. Write a 1-3 page report on any country studied this unit. ☺

G - 2
EC - 1 each

09C03 Study the various ways in which women have created and used fabrics during each period of history from Biblical times through today. Compare the skills and tools of each period.

HM - 2
H - 3

09C04 Read Usborne's *The Age of Revolutions*.

H - 5

09C05 Study the living and working conditions of textile workers at various times during and since the Industrial Revolution, including reforms made at various times and the reasons for them.

H - 3

09C06 Study the Industrial Revolution, with emphasis on how it affected the textile industry.

H - 5

09C07 Study the lives of some of the reformers of the Industrial Revolution.

H - 2 each

09C08 Study the history of labor unions and the abuses which the unions sought to correct.

H - 3

09C09 Study the lives of some of the leaders of the labor union movement here and abroad.

H - 2 each

09C10 Study current labor laws in your country and find out what the history is of each. When were they passed and what abuse or problem were they addressing?

H - 4

09C11 Tour a living history museum or pioneer demonstration and observe spinning, weaving, and other steps involved in making clothing.

H - 2

09C12 Use Usborne's *Invention and Discovery* to find the dates and inventors of various machines and equipment related to spinning, weaving, or the production of textiles.

H - 1

09C13 Study the history of the United States textile industry.

H - 2

09C14 Use Usborne's *World History Dates* or Kingfisher's *Illustrated History of the World* to read about people and events studied in this unit.

H - 1

09C15 Read Book 8: *The Age of Extremes* in A History of US series.

H - 30

Reading and Literature

09R01 Read all chapters of *The Hidden Art of Homemaking* that apply to hand sewing, needlework, or other handicrafts.

HM - 1 each chapter

09R02 Read historical novels about the textile industry during the Industrial Revolution.

H - 2
L - 2

09R03 Read one or more Charles Dickens novels or other classics written and/or set during the Industrial Revolution.

L - 5 each

09R04 Read about the Depression years and how they effected a migrant family in the novel *Blue Willow.*

L - 4

09R05 Read biographies of some of the leaders in the movements for social reform during the Industrial Revolution.

H - 4 each person

09R06 Read and memorize *Portrait of a Southern Lady*, from **John Brown's Body** by Stephen Vincent Benet.

L - 3

09R07 Read sections of **The Foxfire Book** or **Back to Basics** which deal with spinning, weaving, and similar skills.

HM - 2

09R08 Read through Usborne's **Invention and Discovery** to pinpoint those items which strongly affected the development of the textile industry.

H - 2 each person

09R09 Read biographies of inventors whose products were responsible for the mass production and industrialization which characterized the Industrial Revolution.

H - 4 each book

09R10 Read at least one book per week from this unit or resource list.

L - 4 if not in unit

09R11 Find out how changes in society are not always advantageous by reading **Seven Men Who Rule the World from the Grave.** It includes short biographical sketches with a Christian perspective of Darwin, Dewy, Freud, Kienkegard, Wellhausen, Keynes and Marx.

L - 4
H - 5

09R12 Read biographies of prominent people connected with the textile industry.

H - 4 each person

Composition

	Points

09W01 Continue handwriting practice in your notebook started in #01W01. Include every Bible verse studied or memorized from this unit. ☻ — EG - 1 / B - 1 each page

09W02 Continue placing vocabulary words in the vocabulary notebook you started in #01W02. Add at least 10 new words per week. ☻ — EG - 1 per 10 words

09W03 Continue adding to your school journal started in #01W03. Review *Journal Writing* (470-471) in **Writers INC**. ☻ — EC - 1 per week

09W04 Have someone dictate several paragraphs to you, using passages from books used in this unit. Proofread and correct the paragraphs. — EC - 1 per 3 paragraphs

09W05 Have someone dictate several Bible verses to you, using verses you have studied this unit. Proofread and correct the verses. — EC - 2 per 3 verses

09W06 Write one book report per week on a book related to this unit or another approved by parents. Refer to *Writing About Literature* (250-256) in **Writers INC**. — EC - 2 each book

09W07 Write a first-person story or play about some event of the Industrial Revolution. Refer to *Writing About an Event* (123) in **Writers INC**. — H - 3 / EC - 2

09W08 Write reports on one or more of the reformers of the Industrial Revolution. Refer to *Writing About a Person* (119) in **Writers INC**. — H - 3 each / EC - 2 each

09W09 Write reports on leaders and important figures in the labor union movement. Refer to *Writing About a Person* (119) in **Writers INC**. — H - 3 each / EC - 2 each

09W10 Write thank you notes to all field trip hosts and others who helped you with this unit. — EC - 1 each note

09W11 Write reports on all field trips or other special activities during this unit. Concentrate on your writing style. Refer to *Writing with Style* (050-082) in **Writers INC**. — EC - 2 each trip

09W12 Take a spelling test using words from your spelling notebook. Look up the spelling rule for each word spelled incorrectly. — EG - 1 per 10

09W13 Write a news report of any event of the Industrial Revolution as it might have been covered by the media of the day. Refer to *Writing the News Story* (230-247) in **Writers INC**. — H - 3 / EC - 2

09W14 Proofread and correct all grammar and punctuation errors in all written work. Refer to *Proofreader's Guide* (600-714) in **Writers INC**. — EG - 1 each page

09W15 Proofread and correct spelling errors in all written work. Add misspelled words to your spelling notebook. — EG - 2 per paper

	Points

09W16 Write a research paper on the history of the textile industry, and inventions which changed it. Refer to *Writing the Research Paper* (135-173) in ***Writers INC.***

H - 4
EC - 2

09W17 Write several entries in a diary for a textile worker during the Industrial Revolution.

H - 5
EC - 2

09W18 Write a paper on the history and purposes of labor unions. Refer to *Establishing a Timetable* (140-141) in ***Writers INC.***

H - 3
EC - 2

09W19 Write a persuasive speech which might have been given to sway votes one way or the other in a decision of whether to unionize the employees of a company. Refer to *Speech Skills* (490-495) in ***Writers INC.***

CE - 3 EC - 2

09W20 Read a story from any book in this unit. Rewrite the section as a poem telling the story in a different way. Refer to *Where Short Story and Poem Overlap* (206) in ***Writers INC.***

EC - 2

09W21 Do research to find out how inherited characteristics are passed on form parents to children. Write a detailed description of your self and of each of your parents.

EC - 1
HA - 2

09W22 Look up any prefixes, suffixes, and roots of new vocabulary words. Refer to section 446-448 in ***Writers INC.***

EG - 1 per 10 words

09W23 Review some of your writings with your parents. Find occurrences that lack detail or examples. Read *Showing Verses Telling* (051) in ***Writers INC.*** Rewrite these sentences into paragraphs adding substance and depth.

EC - ½ per paragraph

09W24 Look up any prefixes, suffixes, and roots of new vocabulary words. Refer to section 446-448 in ***Writers INC.***

EG - 1 per 10 words

Math and Personal Economics

09M01 Study and memorize the relationships between all English units of linear measure. M - 5

09M02 Memorize the names and sizes of all metric units of linear measure in relation to each other and to English measurements. M - 3

09M03 Practice converting each English unit of linear measure to every other unit. M - 3

09M04 Learn and practice using the formulas to convert metric units of linear measure to their English equivalents and English units to metric. M - 3

09M05 Practice finding the area of various size pieces of fabric. M - 2

09M06 Learn to read and use size and measurement charts on the back of pattern packages. M - 2

09M07 Learn the correct way to take all of your body measurements. M - 2

09M08 Use your math skills to alter any patterns which are not the exact size of the person for whom they are being used. M - 3 per pattern

09M09 To expand on the geometry used in measuring and cutting patterns, take a basic geometry course use *Keys to Geometry*, or another curriculum. M - 1 Credit for a full course

09M10 Memorize and learn to use all formula for finding area, perimeter, and/or circumference of all common shapes. M - 10

09M11 Memorize and learn to use all formula for finding the measurements of complementary and adjacent angles. M - 4

Science

		Points
09S01	Tour a textile manufacturing facility.	SP - 2
09S02	Study the machines used in the mill you toured to learn how they are made and how they work.	SP - 10
09S03	Use the book *Invention and Discovery* to find out when each of the above machines was first invented as well as all other inventions and /or improvements that led to the form in which we use it today.	SP - 10 H - 5
09S04	Examine common household tools and appliances to determine which simple machine —screw, pulley, lever and fulcrum, inclined plane, or wheel and axle — is the basis for each.	SP - 2 each tool; 10 max.
09S05	Study each of the above simple machines and common variations of them.	SP - 12
09S06	Include in your examination of machines the spindle, distaff, carding comb, weaving loom, and other spinning and weaving equipment of an earlier day.	SP - 2 each
09S07	Study simple machines using *The Way Things Work.*	SP - 2 each machine
09S08	Read Usborne's *Machines.*	SP - 3
09S09	Read and outline *The Human Body* (20-45) in *ABC's of the Human Body* by Reader's Digest. Refer to *The Outline* (110-112) in *Writers INC.*	HA - 5
09S10	Color and study all systems and organs in *Gray's Anatomy Coloring Book* you have studied in this unit.	HA - 2 each section completed
09S11	Do research and write a paper on the cell from the encyclopedia or other source.	SB - 4 EC - 2
09S12	Draw a diagram of an animal cell. Label and explain each of the following: lysome, endoplasmic reticulum, centrosome, cytoplasm, golgi body, nucleolus, nucleus, mitochondria and cell membrane.	SB - 5
09S13	Draw and label each of following human cells: leaf, nerve, muscle and skin.	HA - 2
09S14	Do research and write a paper on the cell theory from the encyclopedia or other source.	H - 4 EC - 2
09S15	Read and outline the section about the cell (15-57) in *Fearfully and Wonderfully Made.*	H - 4 EC - 2

Health and Physical Fitness

		Points
09H01	Take tests to measure hand strength, hand-eye co-ordination, and grip.	HE - 2
09H02	Learn to administer the above tests.	HE - 3
09H03	Learn and faithfully follow exercises and activities to improve any deficiencies shown by the tests above.	PE - 5
09H04	Study perception and visual acuity as they relate to hand-eye co-ordination.	HE - 3
09H05	Take a common test series for identifying perceptual problems.	HE - 2
09H06	Learn to administer the above perception tests.	HE - 3
09H07	Learn to teach exercises to improve perception difficulties.	PE - 4
09H08	For at least 1 hour per week, play tennis, golf, softball, or some other sport which requires good hand-eye co-ordination.	PE - 3 per sport per week
09H09	Practice exercises learned above for any perception or co-ordination problems you have.	PE - 3 per hour

Practical Arts

		Points
09P01	Learn and complete one project in hand sewing, embroidery, needlepoint, crochet, or other handicraft.	HM - 10
09P02	Try your hand at spinning thread from wool, flax, or cotton. Use different types of equipment if possible.	HM - 2
09P03	Make a weaving loom, using directions from **The Foxfire Book** or **Back to Basics**.	CR - 10
09P04	Make a quilt using strip quilting methods from **A Quilt in a Day** series.	HM - 20
09P05	Make a garment or other item from the cloth you wove.	HM - 10
09P06	Learn to smock at least one item.	HM - 10
09P07	Learn to tat and use for one item.	HM - 10
09P08	Knit at least one complete item.	HM - 10
09P09	Crochet at least one complete item.	HM - 10
09P10	Decorate garment made in # 09P05 above using your skills in tatting, embroidery, smocking, or appliqué.	HM - 5
09P11	Weave or braid one rug.	HM - 10
09P12	Use your loom to weave one piece of cloth large enough to make a garment for yourself.	HM - 5
09P13	Learn to use a protractor, compass, and T-square to draw, measure, and bisect a variety of shapes and angles.	IA - 2
09P14	Measuring and cutting your own materials, make one or more frames for one of the pictures in the Creative and Performing Arts section of this unit.	IA - 3

Creative and Performing Arts

		Points
09A01	Design an original pattern to use for embroidery or painting on clothing or linens.	VA - 5
09A02	Draw pictures of the things you saw and did on each field trip.	VA - 2 each picture
09A03	Draw or paint pictures of all completed hand craft projects from the practical arts section in this unit.	VA - 2 each project
09A04	Draw a picture of each of the machines you have studied in this unit.	VA - 2 each machine
09A05	Prepare a photo montage or display featuring the garments and other items you have made in this unit.	VA - 5
09A06	Make a collage or mosaic of pictures (including advertisements) relating to the textile and garment industry.	VA - 3
09A07	Study the various uses of textiles items as decorative artwork.	AA - 2
09A08	Tour an exhibit of tapestry, crewel, or other fabric art.	AA - 2
09A09	Use your protractor and compass to create a picture or design suitable for framing.	VA - 5
09A10	Draw a picture or design using only one specific geometric shape.	VA - 5
09A11	Create a book with one of the following titles: *Machines, Work, Industrial Revolution, Sewing* or *Interior Design.* This can be a simple notebook that includes all the reports and art work during this unit or a bound story book written as a nonfiction book. You may include text and illustrations as you desire. Points will depend on the subject you choose and the amount of time spent on this project. Share the book with someone.	Parents Discretion

Unit 10 ❧

> *She stretcheth out her hand to the poor;*
> *yea, she reacheth forth her hands to the needy.*
>
> Proverbs 31:20

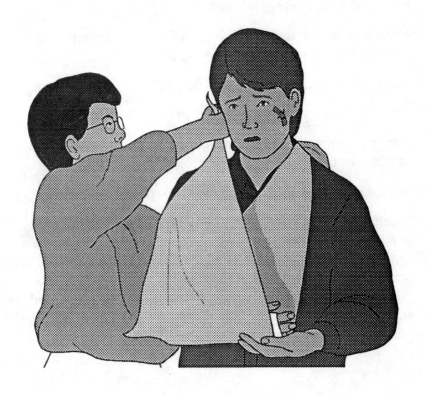

Introduction to Unit 10

In this unit, you will learn about charity and sharing with others. We will look at what the Bible says about giving of both our substance and ourselves to the Lord and His people. We will look at practical ways to give to those in need around us. We will discuss the dual Biblical concepts of stewardship and tithing and allow you to make your own commitment in this area.

We will investigate social programs, public and private, which are designed to help people with special needs, those this passage would refer to as the needy. We will try to determine from Scripture which programs are run according to God's standards and which are not. We will try to differentiate between the correct realms of government, church, and family in administering help as God outlines it in His Word. We will also look at the Bible's guidelines with regard to who is entitled to such help and what they should be required to do to get it. You will then be asked to analyze programs available in your community by the above guidelines.

This unit studies the history of domestic and foreign aid and social services programs. We also look at the lives of many of the world's foremost philanthropists and social reformers. We will study the lives of Christians who have made an impact among the poor and needy. In analyzing the causes of poverty, we look at unemployment, inflation, national debt, and other economic problems of families and nations. We will also try to examine the lifestyles of people in countries where poverty is rampant, in an effort to find ways to help those people help themselves.

The true object of this unit is to encourage you to get involved in helping others and showing compassion. In addition to learning the Biblical why's of kindness to those in need, and the actual make-up of structures which offer help, we will provide hands-on experience. This unit suggests numerous opportunities for you to serve others, alone or with your family or home school group. All students are strongly encouraged to do this part of the curriculum by choosing and participating in one or more of these volunteer opportunities listed.

Bible

		Points
10B01	Read your Bible daily as started in #01B01. You can read the Bible through each year by reading three chapters each day or by following the *Daily Bible Reading Schedule* in **The Narrated Bible.** ☉	B - 1 per 7 chapters
10B02	Read what the Bible says about how believers are to treat the poor and needy: *Afflicted and downtrodden*: Luke 4:18-19. *Samaritans*: Luke 17:11-19, John 4:1-42. *Lepers*: Mat 8:2-4, Luke 17:11-19. *Widows*: Luke 7:11-15, 20:45. Write a summary about each topic.	B - 15 EG - 5
10B03	Study the harsh words of judgment for those who ignored the poor: Mark 17-25, Luke 6:24-25, 12:16-20, 16:13-15, and 19-31.	B - 10
10B04	Memorize I Corinthians 13.	B - 5
10B05	Study the institution and function of deacons in Acts.	B - 3
10B06	Study the story of Dorcas in Acts.	B - 2
10B07	Study the Old Testament laws that relate to the poor.	B - 5
10B08	Study all New Testament commands relating to treatment of the poor.	B - 5
10B09	Compare your church's benevolence policies to the verses above.	B - 2
10B10	Participate in a project with your church or other group to help a needy family for Christmas or some other special occasion and share Christ with them as a result.	B - 2
10B11	Study and memorize Malachi 3:10-13.	B - 3
10B12	Study all Scripture relating to the institution and use of the tithe.	B - 3
10B13	Some Christians believe the entire tithe should go to the local church; others say that any church-related activity can be the recipient of tithes. Some people feel that any worthy cause is an acceptable use of tithe. Still others say tithing is no longer required at all. Discuss this with your parents and/or pastor and study it on your own to develop a definitive position on this issue.	B - 4
10B14	Look at the people with whom you come in contact with daily and single out any with special needs. Ask God to show you how you can serve each of them.	B - 1

Cultural Studies

		Points
10C01	Continue adding to the timeline started in Unit 1. Prepare an entry for each person or historical event studied in this unit. Include the Great Depression. ☺	H - 1 each VA - 1 each
10C02	Continue adding reports to the geography notebook started in #01C04. Write a 1-3 page report on underdeveloped and poor countries studied this unit. ☺	G - 2 EC - 1 each
10C03	Study chapters 9 and 10 of **God and Government** volume 2, and complete all questions and activities.	CG - 8 each chapter
10C04	Study the Great Depression and New Deal programs implemented to fight poverty caused by the Depression. Make a chart showing laws passed, agencies formed, stated purposes, and dates of each.	CG - 3 H - 3
10C05	Carefully study Clarence Carson's *The Welfare State* from **A Basic History of the United States** volume 5.	CG - 15 H - 5
10C06	Study the plight of the poor at various times in different countries.	CE - 5
10C07	Study our nation's social security system and compare it with Scriptural principles for the care of the poor.	CE - 3 B - 1
10C08	Interview an agent of some public or private social services group to learn about his/her job, clients, services offered, and guidelines for eligibility.	CG - 2
10C09	Compile a list of agencies in your city which help the poor and otherwise needy and the kind of help each gives to whom.	CE -3
10C10	Interview one lawmaker on each side of the issue of governmental help for the poor. Summarize the views of each on: kind of help to be offered, eligibility criteria, length of eligibility, private and/or church involvement, and funding. Compare the views of each with the Bible's teaching in this area.	CE -5
10C11	Study the IRS "Earned Income Credit" as a form of welfare alternative.	CE - 3
10C12	Study the "workfare" programs which have been started in some states as an alternative to traditional welfare.	CE - 2
10C13	Study the United Nations relief programs.	CE - 3
10C14	Take a class at the Red Cross or similar agency on disaster assessment and relief.	CE - 2 HE - 5

10C15	Study the child-sponsorship programs of World Vision, Compassion International, and other Christian groups.	CE - 3
10C16	Study United States foreign policy as it relates to aid to underdeveloped and poor countries.	CE - 3
10C17	Study inflation, recession, and other economic conditions which limit the financial health of our nation and its citizens.	CE - 3
10C18	Learn what our nation's "leading economic indicators" are and how they are measured.	CE - 1
10C19	Study the United States policy of deficit spending to find out what it is and why it is a problem.	CE - 2
10C20	Use a world almanac or other source to find and study the ten countries with the highest and lowest per capita income and standards of living.	CE - 2 per country
10C21	Study the historical period of each event or person in this unit and add to the timeline all major events from each era.	H - 1 each VA - 1 each
10C22	Study CARE, the Peace Corps, and other agencies involved in overseas relief.	CE - 3
10C23	Use Usborne's **World History Dates** or Kingfisher's **Illustrated History of the World** (to read about people and events studied in this unit.	H - 1
10C24	Examine the poverty level in various countries and try to learn why it is more wide-spread in some places than others.	CE - 2 G - 1
10C25	Read Book 8 in A History of US series **The Age of Extremes.** It consist of the years from 1800 up to the First World War. It includes the symbols of prosperity Andrew Carnigie, J.P. Rockefeller and Henry Ford as well as the other end of the spectrum—the immigrant workers, the rise of the Ku Klux Clan, and the appearance of John Muir, Lee Vick, and Jane Addams.	H - 30

Reading and Literature

		Points
10R01	Read biographies of Jane Adams, William Booth, Mother Teresa, and/or others who devoted their lives to helping the needy.	H - 3 each person
10R02	Read the *Autobiography of George Mueller*.	H - 5
10R03	Read *A Chance to Die; The Life and Legacy of Amy Carmichael*.	H - 5
10R04	Read *In the Shadow of Plenty*, *The Dispossessed*, and/or other Christian books on the subjects of poverty and homelessness.	CE - 3 each book
10R05	Read each of the short biographical sketches of George Muller, Isobel Kuhn, Billy Bray, David Brainerd, and Robert Annan in *God Made Them Great*.	H - 5
10R06	For a happier look at the life of a poor couple, read O'Henry's short story *The Gift of the Magi*.	L - 1
10R07	Read or see a performance of the play, *Guys and Dolls*, which is about the Salvation Army.	L - 3
10R08	Read relevant sections in *The Hidden Art of Homemaking*.	HM - 2
10R09	Read biographies of Cyrus McCormick, R. J. LeTourneau, and others who invented machines which helped improve the standard of living nations or large groups of people.	H - 4
10R10	Read *Oliver Twist* or any similar classic novel about those caught in the cycle of poverty.	L - 5
10R11	Read a biography of Franklin Roosevelt and/or other New Deal politicians.	H - 4
10R12	Read biographies of Abraham Lincoln, Booker T. Washington, Colin Powell, or other famous people who grew up in poverty but overcame it with hard work and determination.	L - 5 each
10R13	Read *Bringing in the Sheaves* and study its approach to Christian charity.	CE - 3 B - 2
10R14	Add book reviews to your Reading Log created in Unit 1. Refer to the *Reading Log* (257-261) in *Writers INC*.	EC - ½ each

Composition

		Points

10W01 Continue making entries in your handwriting notebook started in #01W01. Include every Bible verse studied or memorized from this unit. ☺ — EG - 1 / B - 1 each page

10W02 Continue placing vocabulary words in the notebook you started in #01W02. Add at least 10 new words per week. ☺ — EG - 1 per 10 words

10W03 Continue your school journal started in #01W03. Review *Guidelines to Journal Writing* in **Writers INC**. ☺ — EC - 1 per week

10W04 Have someone dictate several paragraphs to you, using passages from books used in this unit. Proofread and correct the paragraphs. — EC - 3 per 3 paragraphs

10W05 Have someone dictate several Bible verses, to you, using verses you have studied this unit. Proofread and correct the verses. — EC - 2 per 3 verses

10W06 Write a summary about the various ways God shows His concern for the poor and needy use the following verses: Ps 10:14, 12:5, 14:6, 34:6, 35:10, 40:17, 68:10, 113:7, 132:15, Is 25:4, I Sam 2:8, and Luke 1:52-53. — B - 10 / EG - 5

10W07 Write a news article about Dorcas as if covering her death in her day. Refer to *Writing the News Story* (230-247) in **Writers INC**. — B - 3

10W08 Write a paper analyzing from a Biblical perspective the social programs created by the New Deal. Refer to *Writing a Definition* (122) in **Writers INC**. — B - 2 / H - 2

10W09 Write an essay expressing your opinion on the validity of the social security system for Christians. Support your arguments from Scripture. Refer to *Writing an Explanation* (124) and *Writing to Persuade* (125) in **Writers INC**. — CE - 2 / B - 2

10W10 After you have studied these issues, write a bill you would like to see presented in your state's legislature or Congress to deal with problems in the handling of poverty, charity, or welfare. Refer to *How a Bill Becomes a Law* (964) in **Writers INC**. — CG - 3

10W11 Write reports on all field trips. — EC - 2 each

10W12 Write thank you letters to field trip hosts and others who helped you during your study of this chapter. — EC - 1 each

10W13 Take a spelling test using words from your spelling notebook. Look up the spelling rule for each word spelled incorrectly. — EG - 1 per 10

Far Above Rubies © 1995

		Points

10W14 Prepare for either side of a debate on "Who's Responsible for the Care of the Needy - the State or the Church?" **B - 3**

10W15 Write one book report per week on a book related to this unit or another approved by parents. Refer to *Writing About Literature* (250-256) in **Writers INC.** **EC - 2** each

10W16 Proofread and correct all grammar and punctuation errors in all written work. Refer to *Proofreader's Guide* (600-714) in **Writers INC.** **EG - 1** each page

10W17 Proofread and correct spelling errors in all written work. Add any misspelled words to your spelling notebook. **EG - 2** per paper

10W18 Look up any prefixes, suffixes, and roots of new vocabulary words. Refer to section 446-448 in **Writers INC.** **EG - 1** per 10 words

10W19 Review some of your writings with your parents. Find occurrences that lack detail or examples. Read *Showing Verses Telling* (051) in **Writers INC.** Rewrite these sentences into paragraphs adding substance and depth. **EC - ½** per paragraph

10W20 Read the research paper *Helping the Homeless* (169) in **Writers INC.** Write a research paper on any topic of your choosing. Use the same format as in section 169. If you need help selecting a subject refer to *Guidelines for Selecting a Subject* (031). **EC - 5**

Math and Personal Economics

		Points
10M01	Determine the official poverty level in your state and those surrounding it and make a graph comparing them.	M - 5
10M02	Obtain social security earning figures for your family and determine what your benefits would be in case one or both parents were disabled or deceased.	M - 3
10M03	Fill out an earned income credit for any given family at or near the income level determined in # 10M01.	M - 2
10M04	Determine the percentage of your church's budget which goes to benevolence and the ratios between that and other categories of spending.	M - 2
10M05	Make and save your own money to buy gifts for worthy needy persons or families.	M - 2
10M06	Determine what your tithe would be at 10% of all your personal income.	M - 2
10M07	Find out how economic indicators are figured on a national basis.	CE - 3
10M08	Keep up with figures on unemployment, consumer prices, rate of inflation, and other economic indicators for a period of six months and chart them on a line graph.	M - 8
10M09	Read *Biblical Economics in Comics.*	CE - 5
10M10	Read *What Ever Happened to Penny Candy?*	CE - 5
10M11	Study and complete *Get a Grip on Your Money.*	CE - 1 Credit
10M12	Learn to read statistics on per capita income and the cost of living in various countries.	M - 2
10M13	Using the *World Almanac* or other reference material, make a graph comparing the per capita income and/or cost of living between the ten highest and lowest nations.	M - 7
10M14	From your studies related to poverty and social services, prepare a statistical analysis of the "typical" welfare family in your state. Include information like family size, educational level, and marital status of parents and total family income.	CE - 5

Science

		Points
10S01	Study the basic needs of man and the effects of a deficiency of each.	HE - 3
10S02	Study the environmental problems which often go along with poverty, such as poor sewage, unsafe drinking water, insects.	SE - 4
10S03	Study various methods of water treatment and sewage disposal from the primitive to the modern.	SE - 3
10S04	Tour one of the laboratory farms of SIFAT or some other agricultural agency which is working on ways to improve crop yields and living standards in underdeveloped nations.	SE - 3
10S05	Research solutions for the problems identified in # 10S02.	SE - 4
10S06	Study hybrids and other improved forms of grains and food crops and learn about how each improves yield from a particular plot of ground.	PA - 3
10S07	Study various types of farm equipment used to increase yields or ease production of food crops.	PA - 3
10S08	List and study hurricanes, volcanoes, earthquakes and other forces of nature' which sometimes cause major disasters and the ways they affect people's standard of living.	SE - 10 if complete
10S09	Study fire hazards and fire safety as a way of preventing one form of poverty.	SE - 2 SP - 2
10S10	Use Usborne's ***Discovery and Invention*** to find information about dates and inventors of machines which help fight poverty and related conditions by improving farming, sanitation, or general health problems.	SP - 10
10S11	Use Usborne's ***Machines***, ***The Way Things Work,*** and other books to study the processes involved in the operation of the above machines.	SP - 10
10S12	Study the various chemical and natural methods of insect and rodent pest control and the possible environmental effects of each.	SE - 4
10S13	Study the life cycle of the mosquito, the roach, and the fly. Show how poor living conditions and/or sanitation can effect the population of each.	SE - 4

Health and Physical Fitness

		Points
10H01	Study the health hazards most common in truly poor neighborhoods and/or countries and examine measures that could be taken to prevent or correct them.	HE - 2 CE - 2
10H02	Look at the public health system in our country and visit a health clinic to see what services they offer.	HE - 2 CE - 2
10H03	Study the symptoms and long-term effects of malnutrition.	HE - 2
10H04	Prepare a chart showing low-cost sources of all required nutrients.	HM - 2
10H05	Plan and supervise a fitness/recreation day for needy children.	PE - 3
10H06	Study malaria, dysentery, and other diseases caused by poor sanitation.	HE - 2 each
10H07	Study the vaccines and other treatments or preventive measures available to combat each of the above diseases.	HE - 2 each
10H08	Study the various health problems caused by parasites and how to prevent them.	HE - 3
10H09	Study the health hazards presented by flies, mosquitoes, and other insects and the importance of pest control.	HE - 3
10H10	Study the negative health effects of continued use of DDT and other insecticides.	HE - 3

Practical Arts

		Points
10P01	Visit and serve meals in a soup kitchen, rescue mission, and/or homeless shelter.	HM - 2 each time
10P02	"Adopt a Grandparent" by ministering to a lonely elderly person.	B - 5 per month
10P03	Participate with a group to entertain at a nursing home, mission, or shelter.	3 in area of performance
10P04	Make clothing for a needy child or adult.	HM - 4
10P05	Organize a group to provide practical help for victims of a house fire, tornado, hurricane, or other disaster.	BE - 2 B - 2
10P06	Help in a thrift shop or yard sale which benefits some type of charity.	BE - 2
10P07	Provide free baby-sitting for a needy mother to look for work or to take care of necessary business.	HM - 2
10P08	Help a relief organization sort or man its food pantry or clothing closet.	BE - 2
10P09	Bake cookies, cupcakes or other snack for a nursing home, shelter, or orphanage.	HM - 2
10P10	Take part in a project for the needy, using your talents in whatever way seems appropriate.	B - 2
10P11	Help some organization collect and/or distribute food or gifts, including wrapping, sacking, and organizing.	BE - 2
10P12	Plan a special meal in your home for your family to share with someone in need.	HM - 3
10P13	Help in an international relief effort to victims of war or oppression by wrapping, shipping, collecting, dispatching, etc.	BE - 2
10P14	Take a needy child shopping to buy gifts to give loved ones.	CE - 2
10P15	Work with your family to provide a needy family with dinner and gifts.	CE - 3
10P16	Volunteer to work on a disaster relief team with the Red Cross or other agency.	BE - 3 CR - 5

Creative and Performing Arts

		Points
10A01	Make a birthday card for your adopted "grandparent", or another needy person whom you see on a regular basis.	VA - 1 each card
10A02	Make and mail valentines to all widows and others who live alone in your church family.	VA - 1 per card
10A03	Sing with a group at a shelter, mission church, or other facility for the poor.	MA - 3
10A04	Play a musical instrument alone or as an accompanist for a poor church or ministry to the needy.	MA - 3
10A05	Sing or lead singing in a service with a poor congregation or at a nursing home or similar facility.	MA - 3
10A06	Direct and/or perform in a Christian play or skit for shelter residents or other needy people.	DR - 3
10A07	Use your artistic talents to decorate a shelter or the home of a needy family.	VA - 3
10A08	Make and distribute valentines or other greeting cards for shelter or nursing home residents.	VA - 1 per card

Unit 11 &

> *"She is not afraid of the snow for her household, for all her household are clothed with scarlet."*
>
> Proverbs 31:21

Introduction to Unit 11

We will examine the need for God's people to be prepared for anything that may happen to them or those around them. We will study and memorize a variety of Scriptural commands on this topic. We will also look at the weather as part of God's creation and call attention to the times when God exercised control over weather conditions in order to provide a sign or perform a miracle for His people.

We will study weather, weather forecasting and the ways in which movements of the sun, Earth, and other heavenly bodies affect our weather. We will study latitude, longitude, and the various climatic zones into which the Earth is divided. We will try to find average climate conditions for various countries and parts of the world. We will examine climate variations along each of several specific latitudes and try to determine why the conditions are different. We will study the respiratory system and health problems related to cold weather and/or other bad weather conditions and how to treat them.

We will look at the various health hazards which could result from any of the common methods of home heating and precautions to take to prevent them. In terms of physical fitness, we will look at various cold weather sports. Practical arts will feature the skills that are needed to prepare our homes, cars, and other property for severe weather. We will learn to maintain our home heating and air conditioning systems, choose and install insulation, weather-stripping, and remove snow and ice from walks and steps. We will also deal with those skills needed to properly prepare an automobile for winter.

Bible

11B01   Read your Bible daily as started in #01B01. You can read the Bible through each year by reading three chapters each day or by following the Daily Bible Reading Schedule in **The Narrated Bible.** ☉

B - 1 per 7 chapters

11B02   Read about these topics in the earth's atmosphere. Write a summary paragraph about each topic. *Clouds*: Job 37:11-16, Job 38:34, Ps 97:2, 135:7, 147:8, Jer 10:13, and Ezek 30:18. *Dew*: Gen 27:28 and Job 38:28. *Frost*: Job 38:29 and Ps 147:16. *Hail*: Exod 9:18-33, Job 38:22, Ps 105:32, 147:17, Isa 28:2 and Hag 2:17. *Lightning*: Exod 9:23, 19:16, 2 Sam 2:22, Job 36:30, 37:3, 38:35, Ps 18:12, 97:4, and Jer 10:13. *Rain*: Gen 7:4, Deut 28:12, I Kings 18:1, II Chron 6:26, Job 5:10, 36:27, 37:6, 38:25, Ps 147:8, Jer: 14:22, Ezek 34:26, Joel 2:23, Zech 10:1, Mat 5:45, and Acts 14:17. *Rainbow*: Gen 9:12-17. *Sky*: Job 37:18. *Snow*: Job 37:6, 38:22, Ps 147:16. *Thunder*: Exod 9:23, 20:18, Job 36:33, 37:4, and Jer 10:13. *Wind*: Job 37:17, Ps 135:7, 137:18, Jer 4:11, 49:36, Ezek 13:13 and Mark 4:41.

B - 3
SE - 2
EC - 3 each topic

11B03   Read about the following Earth's disasters. Write a summary paragraph about each topic. *Earthquakes:* Job 9:6, Ps 18:7, 104:31, Isa 13:13, Jer 4:24, and Ezek 38:19. *Famine and drought*: Lev 26:18, Deut 28:23, I Kings 17:1, Ps 107:33, Jer 8:13, 51:36 Ezek 22:24, 30:12, Hos 13:15, Amos 4:6-8, Nah 1:4, and Hag 1:9. Fire: Isa 66:16, Ezek 20:45-48, 30:8, and Amos 7:4. *Plagues and clamities*: Exod 9:1-4, 2 Chron 6:28-31, Isa 29:6, 34:9, Ezek 38:22, Hos 2:12, Amos 4:9, Nah 1:3 and Luke 21:11. *Flood:* Gen 6:17, 7:11, and Job 38:34.

B - 3
SE - 2
EC - 3 each topic

11B04   Use a concordance to look up all references in Scripture which list or discuss preparations one should make for winter, cold weather, etc.

B - 5

11B05   Study God's example of the ants given in Proverbs 6:6-8.

B - 3

11B06   Use a concordance to find other verses addressed to sluggards.

B - 2

11B07   Using a concordance, find and study all passages in which God uses a weather phenomena to achieve a specific spiritual purpose or create a miracle.

B - 3

11B08   Study the gospel account of Jesus calming the storm.

B - 3

		Points
11B09	Study the parable of the wise and foolish builders in Mat 7:24-27.	B - 3
11B10	Use a Bible dictionary to determine the meaning of the word "scarlet."	B- 2
11B11	Study Genesis to explain the weather during the time from the first rains until Noah and his family leave the ark.	B - 4
11B12	Read Psalm 29 and discuss how this Psalm describes a storm.	B - 2
11B13	Discuss the Biblical reasons for rain from Job 37:13 and other sources.	B - 2
11B14	Read Isaiah 55:10 and explain this metaphor about snow.	B - 2
11B15	Read and discuss these verses about snow: Job 37:6, 38:22 and Psalm 147:16.	B - 2
11B16	Read *Wonder O' the Wind* by Phillip Keller.	B - 2

Cultural Studies

		Points
11C01	Continue adding to the timeline started in Unit 1. Prepare entries for important natural disasters throughout history, Arctic and Antarctic explorations or other events studied in this unit. ☉	H - 1 each VA - 1 each
11C02	Continue adding reports to the geography notebook started in #01C04. Write a 1-3 page report on any countries studied this unit. Include the winter clothing of people in each country and countries #11C04 or 11C05. Use as many pictures as you can. ☉	G - 2 EC - 1 each
11C03	Look at each of Earth's five climate zones: north polar, north temperate, tropical, south temperate, south polar. Find the latitudes of each and which countries are in which ones.	G - 3
11C04	Follow your latitude around a globe and list all countries, states, and/or other areas on approximately the same latitude and having about the same climate.	G - 5
11C05	Repeat #11C04 with the same latitude South as yours is North, or vice versa.	G - 5 each
11C06	Study other variables which may account for climatic deviations at the same latitude.	SE - 3
11C07	If you have not previously studied latitude and longitude, do so now.	G - 3
11C08	Play *Global Pursuit* with the physical earth questions to learn about Earth's climate, weather, and physical features.	G - 2 each time; 10 max.
11C09	Write reports on all countries which lie mostly or entirely within polar regions.	G - 2 each
11C10	Do research and write an essay about Arctic and Antarctic exploration. Refer to *Writing Essays* (105-118) in **Writers INC**.	H - 4 EC - 2
11C11	Tour a museum or exhibit to see clothing of different periods and/or areas.	CE - 2
11C12	Use ***Beggar to King: All the Occupations of the Bible*** to identify all workers who dealt with the manufacturing of clothing. Use a concordance to find and study a person in Scripture who held each job.	B - 8
11C13	Use ***Kingfisher's Illustrated History of the World*** to read about the Antarctic (635, 672, 719 and 742) and Arctic (12).	H -1

Reading and Literature

		Points
11R01	Read *Noah's Ark and the Lost World*.	L - 4
11R02	Read *Discovered! Noah's Ark*.	H - 5
11R03	Read at least one book of your choice per week from this unit or resource list.	L - 4 each book
11R04	Read all chapters of *The Hidden Art of Homemaking* that apply to sewing, clothing manufacturing, and/or fashion.	HM - 2
11R05	Read short stories set in any or all of the countries studied in this unit.	G - 2 each country
11R06	Read short stories written by people from each of the countries studied in this chapter.	L - 2 each author
11R07	Read one or more novels set in an Arctic or Antarctic area.	L - 4 each
11R08	Read one or more novels in which snow plays a major role.	L - 4 each
11R09	Read and memorize 40 - 50 lines of poetry about weather.	L - 3
11R10	Read biographies of Arctic or Antarctic explorers.	H - 4 each person
11R11	Read sections of *The Foxfire Book* which explain ways of keeping a house warm without gas or electric heat.	IA - 3
11R12	Read *The Genesis Flood*, take notes on it, and discuss it with your parents.	SE - 5 B - 4
11R13	Read Usborne's *Weather and Climate*.	SE - 3

Composition

		Points
11W01	Continue making entries in your handwriting notebook started in #01W01. Include all Bible verses studied or memorized from this unit. ☺	EG - 1 B - 1 each page
11W02	Continue placing vocabulary words in the notebook you started in #01W02. Add at least 10 new words per week. ☺	EG - 1 per 10 words
11W03	Continue adding to your school journal started in #01W03. Review *Journal Writing* (470-471) in ***Writers INC***. ☺	EC - 1 per week
11W04	Have someone dictate several paragraphs to you, using passages from books used in this unit. Proofread and correct the paragraphs.	EC - 1 per 3 paragraphs
11W05	Have someone dictate several Bible verses, to you, using verses you have studied this unit. Proofread and correct the verses.	EC - 1 per 3 verses
11W06	Take a spelling test using words from your spelling notebook. Look up the spelling rule for each word spelled incorrectly.	EG - 1 per 10
11W07	Write one book report per week on a book related to this unit or another approved by parents. Refer to *Writing About Literature* (250-256) in ***Writers INC***.	EC - 2 each
11W08	Write a fictional story in which bad weather plays a major role.	EC - 2
11W09	The words "weather" and "whether" are frequently confused. Scan the section *Using the Right Word* (715-837) in ***Writers INC***. Choose 10 words. Write a paragraph using each of the words.	EG - 1
11W10	Write your own weather report after studying a given set of weather charts.	SE - 3
11W11	Write reports on one or more of the people studied in this chapter. Refer to *Writing About a Person* (119) in ***Writers INC***.	H - 3 each
11W12	Write a news report on one or more of the following types of storms when it occurs in your area: hurricane, tornado, blizzard, or hail storm. Refer to *Writing About an Event* (123) in ***Writers INC***.	SE - 3
11W13	Look up "weather" and "climate" in a good dictionary and write a paper comparing them.	EG - 1 each page
11W14	Proofread and correct all grammar and punctuation errors in all written work. Refer to *Proofreader's Guide* (600-714) in ***Writers INC***.	EG - 1 each page
11W15	Proofread and correct spelling errors in all written work. Add any misspelled words to your spelling notebook.	EG - 2 per paper

Math and Personal Economics

		Points
11M01	Compare and graph the low and high temperature for several selected cities as given on daily weather reports for one week.	M - 5
11M02	Prepare a graph showing the percentage of difference in #11H01.	M - 3
11M03	Follow the forecasted and actual high and low temperatures in your area each day for a month and show that information on a graph.	M - 8
11M04	Use figures on the above graph to find the percentage of error in your local weather forecasts.	M - 3
11M05	Research figures on the weather in different areas for one full month, and use them to find each area's mean and median temperatures for the month.	M - 3 each area
11M06	Use information from any or all of the above graphs to practice making and solving problems with percent, ratio, and proportion, if review of this topic is still needed.	M - 3
11M07	Compare and graph the amounts of rainfall in your area each day for a month.	M - 5
11M08	Use math skills for needed calculations in your damage assessment activities.	varied

Science

		Points

11S01 Study and outline each of the 5 sections of *Weather and the Bible:* weather basics; water, wind and clouds; stormy weather; past weather; and future weather.
— SE - 20

11S02 Read *The Weather Sourcebook* and outline each aspect of weather: history, weather lore, violent weather, atmospheric pressure, wind, temperature, moisture, clouds, marine weather, weather for pilots, becoming a weather forecaster, major equipment, books, and learning more about weather. Do activities that interest you.
— SE - 2 per outline Activities - Parents discretion

11S03 Study and outline each chapter of *It Couldn't Just Happen*.
— SE - 10

11S04 Study wind, precipitation, surface and air temperature, cloud cover, and other conditions which determine our weather.
— SE - 3

11S05 Obtain a weather map from your local TV station or weather service office and learn to read the various symbols on it.
— SE - 1

11S06 Identify and study all items on the above weather chart.
— SE - 2

11S07 Learn to identify various types of clouds and the weather conditions each produces.
— SE - 2

11S08 Use available equipment to observe your local weather and try to make accurate predictions based on your observations.
— SE - 5

11S09 Study hurricanes and learn what weather conditions cause them.
— SE - 3

11S10 Study tornadoes and learn what weather conditions cause them and what warning signs to look for in predicting one.
— SE - 3

11S11 Study blizzards and the weather conditions that cause them.
— SE - 3

11S12 Learn the difference in the meaning of various levels of bad weather alerts as issued by the National Weather Service.
— SE - 3

11S13 Visit the nearest office of the National Weather Service and get employees to show you their equipment and how it works.
— SE - 2

11S14 Study sleet, snow, hale, and freezing rain and the differences between them.
— SE - 3

11S15 Study common methods of home heating and learn how each works.
— SP - 5

11S16 Study the various fuels commonly used for home heating and their sources.
— SE - 5

11S17 Use Usborne's *Spotter's Guide on The Weather* to analyze and predict weather in your area.
— SE - 5

Health and Physical Fitness

		Points
11H01	Study colds, influenza, and other illnesses which tend to spread during cold weather. Learn about the various treatments for each. See pages 118-121 in *ABC's of the Human Body*	HE - 5
11H02	Study the affects of severe cold on the human body and the importance of keeping warm.	HE - 3
11H03	Find out how weather and air pollution effect breathing.	HE - 5
11H04	Learn the proper procedures to follow during tornado or hurricane warnings in various situations.	HE - 4
11H05	Investigate the safety hazards connected with each of the different methods of home heating studied in the last section.	SP - 2 each
11H06	Learn first aid and other treatment for frostbite, hypothermia, and other effects of exposure to extreme cold.	HE - 2 each
11H07	Learn the safety precautions necessary to prevent accidents from the hazards of home heating studied in #11H05.	HE - 3
11H08	Learn first aid treatment for burns and other injuries or health problems which may be connected with home heating equipment.	HE - 2 each injury
11H09	Spend one or more hours per week in ice skating or other winter sports.	PE - 1 per hour
11H10	Take a course through the Red Cross or similar agency to learn first aid and emergency medical treatment for diseases and injuries common in various natural disasters.	HE - 10
11H11	Read and outline *The Respiratory System* (112-129) in *ABC's of the Human Body* by Reader's Digest. Refer to *The Outline* (110-112) in *Writers INC.*	HA - 5 EC - 2
11H12	Color and study *Taking a Deep Breath* (70-71) in *Gray's Anatomy Coloring Book.*	HA - 2 each section completed
11H13	Do research and write a paper on the respiratory system from the encyclopedia or other source. Refer to *Writing the Research Paper* (142-149) in *Writers INC.*	HA - 4 EC - 2
11H14	Do research and write a paper on the skin from the encyclopedia or other source. Refer to *Writing to Learn* (473-474) in *Writers INC.*	HA - 4 EC - 2

Practical Arts

		Points
11P01	Visit local fabric stores to compare a variety of fabrics for weight, type weave, texture, etc. to decide which fabrics are appropriate for which seasons.	HM - 2
11P02	Using a map from the weather service or making your own, track the next hurricane or major storm which threatens your county or area.	G - 2
11P03	Build a weather station, using ideas from Boy Scout, Girl Scout, Royal Ranger, or Christian Service Brigade manuals or science project books from the library.	SP - 5
11P04	Learn to light pilot lights and/or do whatever else is necessary to start your home's heating system.	IA - 1
11P05	Learn to change filters, clean, and maintain your home's heating system.	IA - 3
11P06	Visit a clothing store to see the variety of fabrics used for different types of clothing. Compare the texture and weight of natural and synthetic fibers.	IA - 2
11P07	Learn how to check and add antifreeze in your family's automobiles.	IA - 2
11P08	If you live where they are used, learn to put snow chains on your family's cars.	IA - 5
11P09	Type all major papers written during the study of this unit.	BE - 1 each page
11P10	Learn various methods of removing ice from car windows, sidewalks and steps.	IA - 2 each
11P11	Learn to weather-strip windows and doors, applying the technique to any spots in your own home which may need it.	IA - 3
11P12	Learn which insulation is best for your home and how to install it.	IA - 2
11P13	Learn how to install and remove storm windows and doors.	IA - 2
11P14	Learn how to insulate household water pipes to prevent freezing.	IA - 2
11P15	Take the Red Cross training course in damage assessment as related to natural disasters.	HE - 10
11P16	Take the Red Cross' training course in disaster relief and volunteer in that area as needed.	HE - 10

Creative and Performing Arts

		Points
11A01	Draw a picture of each field trip.	VA - 3 each
11A02	Use swatches, scraps, and samples of various types of cloth to make a picture or collage.	VA - 5
11A03	Make a poster or plaque of one of the Scripture passages studied in this chapter using calligraphy and original illustrations.	VA - 3 B - 2
11A04	Draw or paint a picture of a winter scene with snow, ice, etc.	VA - 5
11A05	Draw or paint pictures of your choice on velvet or similar fabric.	VA - 5
11A06	Frame and hang one or more of the above pictures.	MA- 5
11A07	Find and listen to a variety of songs about snow, rain, sleet, and other adverse weather conditions. Compare styles and messages.	MA - 1 each up to 10
11A08	Write an original song about a certain season or type of weather.	MA- 5
11A09	Learn to sing one or more Christian songs about storms, etc.	MA - 3 each song
11A10	Learn to play one or more of the above songs on a musical instrument.	MA - 3 each song
11A11	Tour an exhibit of fabric arts. Notice the varied types and styles of work.	AA - 2
11A12	Tour an art exhibit with paintings of wintry or rainy landscapes.	AA - 2
11A13	Study each work above and its artist. Compare time periods and styles.	VA - 3
11A14	Create a book with one of the following titles: *Weather, Winter*, or *Disasters*. This can be a simple notebook that includes all the reports and art work during this unit or a bound story book written as a nonfiction book. You may include text and illustrations as you desire. Points will depend on the amount of time spent on this project. Share the book with someone.	Parent's Discretion

Unit 12 🍎

> "She maketh herself coverings of tapestry;
> her clothing is silk and purple."
>
> Proverbs 31:22

Introduction to Unit 12

This unit begins with a study of the word "tapestry", which is usually translated as "covering." We will also try to trace the significance of "purple" as used during Bible times. The broadest possible use of these words allow us to study all uses of fabrics in the home, as well as fashion and dress. In human anatomy you will study your body covering—the skin. The skin forms a protective barrier against the action of physical, chemical, and bacterial agents on the deeper tissues and contains the special end organs for the various sensations commonly grouped as the sense of touch.

In history we will study the Tabernacle's construction, furnishings and areas, and how they point to Christ. We will also look at painting, sculpture, architecture, and allied arts were produced in Europe in the historical period called Renaissance. The Renaissance people draped themselves in beautiful imported linens as well as a variety of fine textiles produced locally.

You will examine current fashions and those of various periods of history. You will look at fabrics, clothing styles, modesty, and appropriateness of specific articles of clothing for male and female genders.

You will also learn to make a wide variety of clothing and household "coverings." These will include rugs, window treatments, bed coverings, and decorative items. There are also many suggestions for decorating and/or improving items of that type which you already have. You will learn to use them in interior decorating.

This unit deals with two issues which have caused much controversy among Christians. You will deal with the matter of head coverings for women in church services and what is meant by the Bible's prohibition against women dressing like men. This unit does not take a position on either topic. Instead, it will give you the chance to study the relevant documents and form your own conclusions.

Bible

		Points

12B01 Read your Bible daily as started in #01B01. You can read the Bible through each year by reading three chapters each day or by following the Daily Bible Reading Schedule in *The Narrated Bible.* ☺

B - 1 per 7 chapters

12B02 Read the verses and study the symbolism of each piece of furniture in the Tabernacle. *Bronze basin*: Exod 30:18, Zech 13:1, and Eph 5:26. *Golden Alter:* Exod 40:5, 26, Heb 13:15, and Rev 8:3. *Golden candlestick*: Exod 25:31 and John 8:12. *Mercy seat*: Exod 25:17-22, Rom 3:25 and Heb 4:16. *Table and bread of presence*: Exod 25:23-30, John 1:16, and 6:48. *Incense*: Lev 16:12, Ps 141:2, and John 17:9.

B - 15

12B03 Study and outline *Teaching From the Tabernacle*.

B - 10
EC - 2

12B04 Conduct a Scripture word study, using concordance, lexicon, Bible dictionary, or other references, to find all possible meanings of the words translated as "tapestry" or "coverings."

B - 3

12B05 Study and analyze all passages from the New Testament which refer to head coverings for women during worship.

B - 5

12B06 Draw your own conclusion from the above passages and determine what you believe about head coverings. Be prepared to defend your answer with Scripture.

B - 5

12B07 Use a concordance to find and list all Biblical references to the symbolism of certain colors in clothing and other uses. Compile a list or make chart of them.

B - 5

12B08 Study the life of Paul and his companions who were also tentmakers.

B - 3

12B09 Look up and study all Scripture verses which offer commands or teachings about appropriate modes of dress for men or women.

B - 5

12B10 Use *Beggar to King: All the Occupations of the Bible* to identify all jobs related to the clothing or fashion industry. Look for a person in Scripture who held each job. Study each one you can find.

B - 8

12B11 Examine your own preferred style of clothing in light of the Scriptures you have studied. Find any alterations you may need to make in your own style or manner of dress.

B - 5

Cultural Studies

		Points
12C01	Continue adding to the timeline started in Unit 1. Include entries for people and events during the Renaissance period and all major fashion and architecture developments throughout history. ☿	H - 1 each VA - 1 each
12C02	Continue adding reports to the geography notebook started in #01C04. Write a 1-3 page report on Bible lands or any other countries studied in this unit. ☿	G - 2 EC - 1 each
12C03	Use **Manners and Customs of Bible Lands**, **Everyday Life in Old Testament Times** or a similar book to study the architecture and decor of Bible time homes.	H - 5
12C04	Study the various artistic and creative developments in the field of architecture during the Renaissance period.	AA - 2 H - 3
12C05	Study the history of architecture and the major styles used during each period.	AA - 2 H - 3
12C06	Study the lives of famous architects and building painters of the Renaissance and other periods.	H - 1 each VA - 1 each
12C07	Study the various artistic and creative developments of the Renaissance, with special emphasis on the decorative arts as used in homes.	AA - 2 H - 3
12C08	Research and compare quilts, rugs, and other coverings used in different countries during different periods of history.	H - 3
12C09	Read and outline *Nationalism and the Renaissance* (346-369) and *The Reformation and the New World* (370-392) in **Streams of Civilization**.	H - 5
12C10	Study clothing styles and trends in various countries at different periods of history, including the time of the Bible.	H - 3 G - 3
12C11	Read and outline **Greenleaf's Famous Men of the Renaissance and Reformation**.	H - 10
12C12	Use **World History Dates** to read about people and events in Renaissance and Reformation period—1300-1600.	H - 1
12C13	Read *The Renaissance* (317-319, 330-333) and *The Reformation* (354-355) in **Kingfisher's Illustrated History of the World**.	H - 5
12C14	Read pages 48-138 in **Sketches of Church History**.	H - 5

	Points

12C15   Investigate the economic impact of the fashion industry in this country, paying special attention to any fashion centers which may be located in your area.   CE - 2

12C16   Tour a museum or similar exhibit to see clothing of different periods and/or areas.   H - 2

12C17   On your museum tour, look for examples of sewing machines and other tools of the various periods which women made clothing.   H - 2

12C18   Find out who built Stonehedge and what scientist know about it.   H - 1

12C19   Compare how different civilizations approached developing technologies by reading **Builder Through History.** Compare and discuss the difference in the buildings shown in the illustrations from one time period to another.   H - 2

12C20   Study architecture by reading the books or watching any of the videos by David Macaulay: **Castle, Cathedral, or City.**   AA - 2 / H - 2

12C21   Do research to find out how a girl your age lived during the Renaissance. Include: education, chores, entertainment, age for marriage, etc. Write a story about it.   H - 2 / EC - 2

12C22   Do research about Renaissance painters. Make a chart with columns showing when they were born, where they lived, famous pieces of work, etc.

12C23   Find out how the Renaissance is different from the Middle Ages. Find out why it is considered a distinctive time rather than just a continuation of medieval times.   H - 1

12C24   Read about everyday life during the Renaissance in **The Renaissance: History of Everyday Things**.   H - 5

12C25   Find out about the Renaissance Merchant's guilds. Write a paper comparing them to modern day labor unions.   H - 2 / EC - 1

12C26   Write journals entries as if written by Isabella d'Este or another famous Renaissance woman.

12C27   Create Renaissance paper dolls and clothing. Include clothes for both sexes for: at home, at court, at work, and at a tournament.   H - 2 / VA - 2

12C28   Put each of the following names on an index cards. Place descriptions of each on another set of index cards: Michelangelo, Leonardo de Vinci, Martin Luther, Marco Polo, Donatello, Vasco de Gama, Savonarola, Castiglione, Chaucer, Cervantes, John Calvin, Ulrich Zwingli, and Shakespere. Make and play a card game.   H - 2

Reading and Literature

		Points
12R01	Read at least one book of your choice per week from this unit or resource list.	L - 2 each
12R02	Read all chapters of *The Hidden Art of Homemaking* that apply to sewing, clothing manufacturing, and/or fashion.	HM - 2
12R03	Read all chapters of *The Hidden Art of Homemaking* that apply to floors, wall coverings, or interior design.	HM - 2
12R04	Read biographies of artist during the Renaissance.	H - 3 each
12R05	Read about young Robert Upton in *A Heart Strangely Warmed* by Louise Vernon.	H - 3
12R06	Read sections of *The Foxfire Book* which relate to clothing or fashion.	HM - 2
12R07	Read the story of "Penelope and the Suitors" from *The Oddysey*.	L - 1
12R08	Read biographies of craftsmen and/or architects of the Renaissance.	H - 3 each person
12R09	Read all sections of *The Foxfire Book* on floor, wall or bed coverings, and/or skills used to make them.	H - 2
12R10	Read how-to books on quilting, knitting, weaving, or similar skills that might be used to make "coverings."	HM - 3
12R11	Read *Foxes Book of Martyrs*.	H - 4
12R12	Read any of the works by Shakespeare's that your parents approve.	L - 5
12R13	Read the story of Gutenberg and the invention of movable type in the story *Ink on His Fingers*.	H - 3
12R14	Read about Martin Luther from the perspective of his son in *Thunderstorm in Church* by Louise Vernon.	H - 3
12R15	Read about Tyndale and Luther in *The Man Who Laid the Egg* by Louise Vernon.	L - 4 H - 1
12R16	Read the story of William Tyndale in *The Bible Smuggler* by Louise Vernon.	H - 3

Composition

	Points

12W01 Continue making entries in your handwriting notebook started in #01W01. Include every Bible verse studied or memorized from this unit. ☺
EG - 1
B - 1 each page

12W02 Continue placing vocabulary words in the spiral notebook you started in #01W02. Learn at least 10 new words per week. ☺
EG - 1 per 10 words

12W03 Continue adding to your school journal started in #01W03. Review *Journal Writing* (470-471) in **Writers INC**. ☺ ·
EC - 1 per week

12W04 Have someone dictate several paragraphs to you, using passages from books used in this unit. Proofread and correct the paragraphs.
EC - 1 per 3 paragraphs

12W05 Have someone dictate several Bible verses to you, using verses you have studied in this unit. Proofread and correct the verses.
EC - 1 per 3 verses

12W06 Write one book report per week on a book related to this unit or another approved by parents. Refer to *Writing About Literature* (250-256) in **Writers INC.**
EC - 2 each

12W07 Write a first-person short story about a Renaissance painter. Refer to *Writing a Short Story* (218-227) in **Writers INC**.
EC - 4

12W08 Read a sonnet by Shakespeare and one by Petrarch. Write a summary explaining how they are alike or different.
EC - 2

12W09 Write a newspaper article about the events in 1494 that made the turning point in Renaissance history.
EC - 1
H - 1

12W10 Create a Renaissance newspaper. Write articles, news events, sports, funnies and advertisements.
EC - 1 each page

12W11 Write a paper on the effect the bubonic plague had on art and culture.
H - 1

12W12 With your parents help, write a paper defending your beliefs about the wearing of head coverings by women for worship. Use Scripture references to support conclusions.
B - 3
EC - 2

12W13 Write an exegesis of the passages which decry the wearing of clothing of the opposite gender. Explain both in light of clothing styles in Bible times and how it applies today.
EC - 2
B - 3

12W14 Write a report about anyone living during the Renaissance or Reformation periods.
EC - 2 each

12W15 Proofread and correct all grammar and punctuation errors in all written work. Refer to *Proofreader's Guide* (600-714) in **Writers INC.**
EG - 1 each paper

Math and Personal Economics

		Points
12M01	Measure all walls in your home. Use formulas to find perimeters and areas of each.	M - 5
12M02	Use the above figures to determine the amounts of various kinds of wall paper needed for each room.	M - 8
12M03	Calculate the costs of various wallpaper in quantities needed for each room.	M - 3
12M04	Calculate the amount of paint needed to adequately cover the walls in each room and the cost.	M - 3 each
12M05	Measure the dimensions of each room in your home and find areas and perimeters.	M - 5
12M06	Calculate the amount of carpet needed for each of the rooms in your home.	M - 3
12M07	Calculate the cost of carpeting each room in your home and the savings you can achieve by doing it all together.	M - 2
12M08	Measure all dimensions of all rooms in your doll house and find the areas and perimeters of each.	M - 5
12M09	Measure the exact dimensions of your bed and determine the amount of different fabrics you will need to make a bedspread or other covering. Be sure to allow for hems and seam allowances.	M - 2
12M10	Measure all windows in your home to find correct sizes for blind.	M - 6
12M11	Use your window measurements and add required allowances to determine the amount of fabric needed to make curtains for each room.	M - 3
12M12	Build your doll house as an exact scale model of your own home.	M - 5
12M13	If you are using a kit to build your doll house, measure the finished rooms and see how close you can come to setting up a scale in relation to the size of the rooms in your own home.	M - 5
12M14	Graph the population of Europe from 600 A.D. to 1600 A.D.	M - 1 H - 1

Science

		Points
12S01	Study sound waves and the sound absorption qualities of carpets and drapes. Compare different materials for these qualities.	SP - 8
12S02	Study the chemical processes involved in the removal of stains.	SC - 5
12S03	Learn formulas for homemade stain removers and what products remove what kinds of stains.	SC - 3
12S04	Find out how the invention of gunpowder transformed warfare.	H - 1
12S05	Galileo applied mathematical models to the subject matter of physics. Find out what impact this made on the science.	SP - 2
12S06	Write a report about Johannes Gutenbergs inventions and how it changed life.	SP - 1 H - 1
12S07	Read about Leonardo Da Vinci's inventions. Make a list of them.	SP - 1
12S08	Do research and compare Aristole achievements with Leonardo Da Vinci's. Write a paper explaining who was the most outstanding.	SP - 2 EC -1
12S09	Learn about the construction and operation of each of the machines used in any of the factories studied or toured in this unit.	SP - 1 (each machine)
12S10	Study the various natural and chemical sources of pigment for coloring cloth items.	SC - 5
12S11	Read and outline *The Skin* (115-151) in **Fearfully and Wonderfully Made.**	SC - 3
12S12	Read and outline *The Skin* (130-157) in **ABC's of the Human Body** by Reader's Digest. Refer to *The Outline* (110-112) in **Writers INC.**	HA - 5 EC - 2
12S13	Color and study *It's Only Skin Deep* (58) in **Gray's Anatomy Coloring Book.**	HA - 2 each section completed
12S14	Do research and write a paper on hair and nails from the encyclopedia or other sources. Refer to *Writing to Learn* (473-474) in **Writers INC.**	HA - 4 EC - 2
12S15	Do research and write a paper on the skin from the encyclopedia or other sources. Refer to *Writing to Learn* (473-474) in **Writers INC.**	HA - 4 EC - 2
12S16	Do research to find out why some people have freckles, birthmarks or moles.	HA - 1
12S17	Do research to find out cures for sunburn and frostbite.	HA - 1
12S18	Do research to find out why people are different colors.	HA - 1

Health and Physical Fitness

		Points
12H01	Study the kind of support a mattress should provide for a person's back and how to test for the proper support.	HE - 3
12H02	Study the anatomy of the vertebrae and spinal column.	HE - 5
12H03	Study the health factors relating to the need for sleep and its effects on the body.	HE - 3
12H04	Study encephalitis and the mosquitoes that cause it.	HE - 3
12H05	Study insomnia and other sleep-related disorders and their causes and cures.	HE - 3
12H06	Study common allergens which may be used in bedding, carpets, or other household coverings. Learn how to check for each.	HE - 5
12H07	Study the safety hazards of electric blankets and rules for their safe use.	SE - 1
12H08	Study scoliosis and the kind of sleep support needed by people who have it.	HE - 3
12H09	Study the effects of good and/or poor posture on general back health.	HE - 5
12H10	Study the medical field of chiropractic and compare their basic philosophy with that of more traditional doctors.	HE - 6
12H11	Compare the back support given by various kinds of traditional and waterbed mattresses.	HE - 2

Practical Arts

		Points
12P01	Build a doll house to use for the decorating ideas you can't do in your home. (alternatives are given for each option.)	CR - 50 VA - 50
12P02	Make a bedspread or comforter for one of the beds in your home.	HM - 20
12P03	Piece and complete one patchwork quilt to fit a bed in your home.	HM - 20
12P04	Use embroidery, appliqué, or other needle crafts to decorate a complete set of sheets and pillowcases for a double or larger bed.	HM - 20
12P05	Weave a rug or wall hanging using a homemade or bought weaving loom.	HM - 10
12P06	Braid a rag rug using strips from old garments or sewing scraps.	HM - 10
12P07	Choose and hang wallpaper for one or more rooms of your home or doll house.	VA - 5 or 50
12P08	Choose and lay appropriate carpet in one or more rooms in your home or doll house.	HM - 5 or 50
12P09	Lay vinyl or other tile flooring in one or more rooms in your home or doll house.	CR - 5 or 30
12P10	Use pictures, plaques, needlework or other items you have made to decorate one or more of the walls in your home.	VA - 5
12P11	Take a class to learn braiding, weaving, latchhook, macramé, or other processes often used to make wall and floor coverings.	HM - 30
12P12	Plan and hang one or more attractive wall groupings in your home.	VA - 5
12P13	Learn to mount all types of curtain and drapery rods and to hang the curtains on them.	CR - 5 each
12P14	Learn to hang, clean, and maintain each of the various kinds of blinds and shades.	HM - 5 each
12P15	Learn proper methods to clean, mothproof, store, and care for blankets, quilts, and other bed coverings.	HM - 3
12P16	Learn how to correctly and safely clean and store electric blankets.	HM - 2
12P17	Crochet a bedspread, tablecloth, or other covering.	HM - 10
12P18	Knit an afghan, blanket, or similar covering.	HM - 10

		Points
12P19	Make one or more pairs of drapes or curtains.	HM - 10 each
12P20	Latchhook a rug, pillow top, or wall hanging.	HM - 10
12P21	Learn proper cleaning techniques to use with various kinds of rugs and carpets.	HM - 3 each
12P22	Prepare a booklet showing current fashion styles, trends, and colors.	HM - 3
12P23	Recover one or more pieces of upholstered furniture or make a slipcover for it.	HM - 10 each
12P24	Replace cloth bottoms in one or more straight dining chairs.	HM - 5 each
12P25	Monogram a set of sheets or pillowcases for yourself or for a gift.	HM - 3 each
12P26	Use embroidery, fabric paint, or other needle arts to decorate a plain tablecloth.	HM - 6
12P27	Make a set of place mats and cloth napkins for a special occasion.	HM - 10
12P28	Decorate and set an attractive table for each regular meal and for some special occasions.	HM - 3 each up to 15
12P29	Decorate and arrange tables for a formal banquet, reception, or tea.	HM - 5
12P30	One fourth of all trips to the doctor have to do with a problem with th eskin, usually cuts or burns. Put together a first aid kit.	HA - 3

Creative and Performing Arts

		Points
12A01	Create an original painting or drawing to be used on a wall or in a wall grouping in one of the rooms in your home.	VA - 8
12A02	Tour an art exhibit featuring decorative weaving, needlework, or other fabric arts.	AA - 2
12A03	Draw an original design to be embroidered, appliquéd, or painted onto a tablecloth or bed covering.	VA - 3
12A04	Draw a detailed sketch of your room as you would like it to be decorated.	VA - 5
12A05	Study and compare artistic elements of various types of architecture.	AA - 5
12A06	Create an original mosaic artwork using tiles, beads, bark, stones, or any other appropriate material.	VA - 5
12A07	Design and make a string art to be used in your wall grouping.	VA - 5
12A08	Use calligraphy to create a poster, picture, or other wall hanging.	VA - 5
12A09	Design an original pattern for a patchwork quilt.	VA - 3
12A10	Paint pictures or decorations onto sheets tablecloths, and other coverings.	VA - 3 each
12A11	Study the Renaissance paintings such as Michelangelo, Botticelli, Pisanello, Mantegna, Masacco, and de Vinci, decide which is your favorite. Write a summary explaining why.	VA - 2 EC - ½
12A12	In Renaissance art, the decisive break with medieval tradition occurred in Florence about 1420 with the invention of linear perspective, which made it possible to represent three-dimensional space on a flat surface. Draw or paint an example of three-dimensional art.	VA - 2
12A13	Create a book with one of the following titles: *The Tabernacle, Architecture Through History, The Renaissance Period, The Reformation Period, Interior Design*, or *Fashion Through History*. This can be a simple notebook that includes all the reports and art work during this unit or a bound story book written as a nonfiction book. You may include text and illustrations as you desire. Points will depend on the subject you choose and the amount of time spent on this project. Share the book with someone.	Parents Discretion

Unit 13

"Her husband is known in the gates when he sitteth
among the elders of the people."

Proverbs 31:23

Introduction to Unit 13

This unit deals with the godly woman's support of her husband in his business, church, and community involvement. We look at the truth of the old adage about the woman behind a successful man and examine Scripture relating to that aspect of the woman's being a "helpmate" to her husband.

You will examine at length the various terms used in Scripture to name or designate church leaders. We will seek to fully understand the requirements set by Scripture for those who would hold those positions and the Biblical pattern of choosing them. We will look at various forms of church government and try to find the Biblical teachings on the subject. You also use this unit as an opportunity to study civil government positions and the procedures used for filling them. This expands into a study of local, state, and national politics and will include a study of our nation's political process and the individual's place of responsibility in it. Ideally, this unit can best be covered during a national or state election year. You will read biographies of famous church and civil government leaders and their wives. You will study present day leaders and the relationships they have with their wives.

Geographically, we learn about a wide variety of cities which were built with walls and gates. You will compare those cities and the cultures of which each was a part. You will also learn about different types of fences and gates and how they are built.

You will also explore special ways in which a wife can and should care for the health and physical well-being of her husband. We deal with stress reduction, business related entertaining, organizing for the husband's benefit, and other areas in which a wife can support her husband's rise to the top in his chosen profession, whatever that might be.

Bible

		Points
13B01	Read your Bible daily as started in #01B01. You can read the Bible through each year by reading three chapters each day or by following the Daily Bible Reading Schedule in *The Narrated Bible.* ☺	B - 1 per 7 chapters
13B02	Make a list of a wife's responsibilities to her husband. I Cor 7:3, Titus 2:4, Prov 12:4, I Cor 7:2, 10, 33-34, 39, Exod 20:14, Rom 7:2-3, Eph 5:22, 33, Col 3:18, I Pet 3:1-6.	B - 10
13B03	Use a concordance and other research aids to do a thorough study of the Old Testament term "elders of the land" to determine who they were and what they did.	B - 5
13B04	Use a concordance to list and study all New Testament references to elders (also look up presbyter, bishop, and overseer).	B - 5
13B05	Do a word study of the Greek word(s) normally translated "elder," "overseer," or "bishop."	B - 3
13B06	Compare Old Testament elders of the tribes of Israel to elders of the New Testament church as ordained by Paul and others in Acts.	B - 5
13B07	Study the requirements for deacons and elders (or overseers and bishops) as outlined in I Timothy 3 and Titus 1.	B - 2 (if not done as # 13B03 instead)
13B08	Study all references to women or wives of the aforementioned church officers in the passages under study.	B - 2
13B09	Study I Timothy 5:17-18 and examine its teaching on payment to elders or preachers.	B - 1
13B10	Listen to the tape *Christian Leadership in the Home* from Pilgrim Tape Ministry.	B - 2
13B11	Read *Political Sermons of the American Founding Era* to see the impact of godly Christian leaders on our nation in its early days.	B - 3 L - 2
13B12	Read the following verses to see that human government was established by God as a means of controlling sinful man: Gen 9:5, 6; and Rom 13:3, 4.	B - ½
13B13	Read the following verses to see that civil authorities are a deterrent to evil, not to good: Rom 13:3, 4; ITim 2:1, 2; and IPet 2:13, 14.	B - ½

Cultural Studies

	Points
13C01 Continue adding to the timeline started in Unit 1. Prepare entries for each person or major event studied in this unit. Include United States founding fathers, presidents, church leaders, wars, signing of major documents etc. ☉	H - 1 each VA - 1 each
13C02 Add an extensive report on the United States to the geography notebook started in #01C04. Include all relevant information from this unit. ☉	G - 3 EC - 2
13C03 Listen to the series of lectures teaching on our Godly heritage with *America 350 years*. Complete the worksheets.	H - 50
13C04 Read about the persecution and flight from England, voyage to America, and landing at Plymouth in Mantle Ministries republished book, *The Plymouth Settlement*.	H - 30
13C05 Read about the little known miracles in Washington's life in *Bulletproof George Washington*.	H - 5
13C06 Read "Little Bear" Wheeler's republished 1899 extraordinary collection of biographical accounts *Great American's and Their Noble Deeds*.	H - 10
13C07 Read about founding of America and events in other countries during that time in *Kingfisher's Illustrated World History*. Compare with a book written form a Christian view. List any differences.	H - 5
13C08 Watch the video *What the Founding Fathers Really Meant by Separation of Church and State* and discuss it.	H - 5
13C09 Examine the civil government set up for Israel by God as described in Exodus - Numbers and chart the system.	B - 5
13C10 Examine your church's governmental structure and look for scriptural reasons for its particular set up.	B - 2
13C11 Study the history of democracy and the republican form of government from any good Christian world history book.	H - 5
13C12 Study the founding of our nation using any applicable chapters of *God and Government*, volume 1 or other appropriate material.	H - 5
13C13 Study the *Declaration of Independence* and memorize it.	CG - 5
13C14 Study the lives of the individuals who signed the *Declaration of Independence*.	CG - 2 each man

		Points
13C15	Study and complete all chapters in *God and Government*, volume 1 on church government.	CG - 8
13C16	Study chapter 4 in *God and Government*, volume 3 and applicable chapters in volume 1 to learn how our governmental system works and how Christians can make it better.	CG - 8 per chapter
13C17	Read the fascinating story of how each colony was formed and what social, economical, and religious factors caused the English colonist to set out for North America in a quest for freedom. The founding of Jamestown, the beginning of slavery in North America, the Salem witch trails, and a cast that includes Pocahontas, Roger Williams, Daniel Boone, and Oliver Cromwell are all part of this dramatic adventure in *A History of US: Making the Thirteen Colonies* (book 2 of this series).	H - 30
13C18	Study all United States presidents and their wives. Write a few paragraphs about each.	H - 1 each
13C19	Tour the Capitol, Supreme Court, city hall, your county courthouse, and/or any other governmental buildings at the state and/or national level.	CG - 2 each tour
13C20	Interview a political official of your choice. Ask him about the campaign process and what part his family played in helping him get elected.	CG - 2
13C21	Study the lives of famous church leaders and their wives during and since the Protestant Reformation.	H - 2 each
13C22	Read Usborne's *Politics and Government.*	H - 2
13C23	Play *Hail to the Chief.*	CG - 1 each time played
13C24	Read Clarence Carson's *Basic History of the United States* to understand the processes which made and continue to mold our government.	H - 5 per volume
13C25	Watch the historical video *America's Godly Heritage* to see God's hand in the establishment of our country.	H - 4
13C26	Study the kings of England and their wives.	H - 2
13C27	Study other forms of government and compare them to ours.	H - 4
13C28	Contact your Congressman, the local chapter of the league of women voters, or a campaign headquarters for information on the election process and specific upcoming elections in your area.	CG - 2

Reading and Literature

		Points
13R01	Read *Light and the Glory* by Daniel Manuel and Peter Marshall.	H - 4
13R02	Read *From Sea to Shining Sea*, a sequel to the previous book.	H - 4
13R03	Read and discuss *Rebirth of a Nation*.	H - 4
13R04	Read and analyze political essays by Thomas Paine, Benjamin Franklin, Daniel Webster, and other writers throughout our nation's history.	H - 2 each person
13R05	Read biographies of any or all of the Presidents of our country.	H - 4 each book
13R06	Read biographies of several American First Ladies and decide whether each was an asset or a hindrance to her husband.	H - 4 each book
13R07	Find and study several poems on patriotic subjects.	L - 2
13R08	Read poems about famous political figures.	L - 1 per poem
13R09	Memorize a total of 50-60 lines of poetry from poems in #13R07 and #13R08.	L - 10
13R10	Read biographies of famous kings and/or queens.	H - 4 per book
13R11	Read one or more of Shakespeare's plays about the lives of kings or emperors.	H - 3 per play
13R12	Read the Sower Series biography *Daniel Webster*.	L - 2 H - 3
13R13	Read *Kings and Queens of England* from Usborne Books.	H - 3
13R14	Read *The Open Church* to understand how the New Testament church met and worshipped.	H - 2 B - 2
13R15	Read *Thunderstorm in Church* about Martin Luther, the great reform preacher.	H - 2
13R16	Read *Morning Star of the Reformation* about John Wycliffe.	H - 2

13R17 Read *The Hawk that Dare not Hunt by Day,* the story of how William Tyndale translated the Bible to English.

H - 2

13R18 Read the Sower Series biography *George Washington*.

L - 3
H - 3

13R19 Read the Sower Series biography *Noah Webster*.

L - 3
H - 3

13R20 Read "Little Bear" Wheeler's republished book *One Nation Under God*. It was used for three decades in the one room school house when God's providence was still taught to students.

H - 10

13R21 Read biographies of Martin Luther, John Calvin, and/or other leaders of the Reformation. Pay special attention to ways in which their wives aided or influenced them.

H - 2
L - 3 each

13R22 Read biographies of a wide variety of well-known current and historical preachers and Christian leaders. Look for ways in which their wives aided or influenced them.

L - 4 each

Composition

		Points
13W01	Continue making entries in your handwriting notebook started in #01W01. Include every Bible verse studied or memorized from this unit. ☺	EG - 1 B - 1 each page
13W02	Continue placing vocabulary words in the vocabulary notebook you started in #01W02. Learn at least 10 new words per week. ☺	EG - 1 per 10 words
13W03	Continue adding to your school journal started in #01W03. Review *Journal Writing* (470-471) in ***Writers INC***. ☺	EC - 1 per week
13W04	Have someone dictate several paragraphs to you, using passages from books used in this unit. Proofread and correct the paragraphs.	EC - 1 per 3 paragraphs
13W05	Have someone dictate several Bible verses to you, using verses you have studied in this unit. Proofread and correct the verses.	EC - 1 per 3 verses
13W06	Write an essay giving your opinion of some aspect of our governmental system. Back up all statements and suppositions with evidence; such as quotes, examples, and passages from material read.	EC - 3
13W07	Rewrite in summary form each section of the *United States Constitution*. Refer to the *U.S. Constitution* (962) in ***Writers INC***.	EC - 4 CG - 4
13W08	Write a paraphrase of each amendment to the *United States Constitution*, summarizing where it is advantageous to do so. Refer to the *Constitutional Amendments* (963) in ***Writers INC***.	EC - 4 CG - 4
13W09	Write letters to public officials to support or protest specific issues or legislation. Refer to *Writing a Business Letter* (418) in ***Writers INC***.	EC - 2 each
13W10	Write thank you notes to all who helped you in this unit, including guides, etc. for field trips.	EC - 2 each
13W11	Write a poem to express your feelings for your country. Refer to *Writing a Poem* (212) in ***Writers INC***.	EC - 2
13W12	Write a news article about the public official you interviewed. Refer to *Writing the News Story* (230-247) in ***Writers INC***.	EC - 3
13W13	Write one book report per week on a book related to this unit or another approved by parents. Refer to *Writing About Literature* (250-256) in ***Writers INC***.	EC - 2 per book
13W14	Critique various political speeches of history from a Biblical perspective. Refer to *Speech Skills* (490-495) in ***Writers INC***.	EC - 1 each H - 1 each

	Points
13W15 Choose one president and first lady and write an extensive term paper on their life together as husband and wife. Choose from *U.S. Presidents* (966) in **Writers INC**.	EC - 10
13W16 Write an essay comparing and contrasting the "elders of the twelve tribes" in the Old Testament with the elders of the churches in New Testament times.	EC - 3
13W17 Proofread and correct all grammar and punctuation errors in all written work. Refer to *Proofreader's Guide* (600-714) in **Writers INC**.	EG - 1 each page
13W18 Proofread and correct spelling errors in all written work. Add any misspelled words to your spelling notebook.	EG - 2 per paper
13W19 Write a paper describing and comparing each of the major forms of government: monarchy, oligarchy, dictatorship, democracy, confederation, and republic. Refer to *The Traditional Essay* (116) in **Writers INC.**	EC - 7
13W20 Take a spelling test using words from your spelling notebook. Look up the spelling rule for each word spelled incorrectly.	EG - 1 per 10
13W21 Research and write short reports on any or all members of the Constitutional Convention.	EC - 2
13W22 Outline each book in the **Carson History Series**.	EC - 5 each book
13W23 The noun "capitol" refers to a city or to money. The adjective "capital" means major or important. The noun "Capitol" refers to a building. Scan the section *Using the Right Word* (715-837) in **Writers INC**. Choose 10 words. Write a paragraph using each of the words.	EG - 2
13W24 Read the traditional essay *America—Land of the Plenty* (116) in **Writers INC**. Rewrite each transitional sentence. Refer to section 99 and 103 for ideas.	EG - 2
13W25 Look up any prefixes, suffixes, and roots of new vocabulary words. Refer to section 446-448 in **Writers INC**.	EG - 1 per 10 words

Math and Personal Economics

		Points
13M01	Use a history book or Bible atlas to learn the dimensions of the walled portion of the city of Jerusalem. Use these to find area and perimeter.	M - 1
13M02	Draw a scale model of the wall and/or other features of the city of Jerusalem as it was in Bible times.	M - 3 VA - 5
13M03	Use math skills and formulas to determine the dimensions of the four sides of a fence. Use several fences of different sizes.	M - 2
13M04	Determine the number of bricks needed to build a fence or wall of each of the above sizes.	M - 2
13M05	Determine the number of feet and yards of wire that would be needed to fence a given area.	M - 1
13M06	Use the formulas in reverse to find the perimeter and area of the space which could be enclosed by a certain number of fence posts spaced a certain distance apart.	M - 2
13M07	Watch election returns and prepare your own graphs of votes earned by various candidates in various states, counties, or districts.	M - 5
13M08	Use the above election returns to find the percentage of the vote that each candidate got and what percent each candidate's vote was of each of the others.	M - 2

Science

		Points

13S01 Examine the tools and materials commonly used in the building of walls, fences, and gates.

SP - 2

13S02 Study the inventions of Benjamin Franklin, and other important members of the American political community who also dabbled in science.

SP - 2
H - 2

13S03 Study the scientific discoveries of Sir Isaac Newton, especially those made during his years as a member of the House of Lords in Parliament.

SP - 5
H - 2

13S04 Learn all you can about the sealed thermometer which was invented by Grand Duke Ferdinand of Tuscany in 1654.

SP - 2

13S05 If you did not do so in a previous chapter, study and learn to make and use a rain gauge and a hygrometer, both of which were invented by clergymen.

SP - 2
SE - 2

13S06 Research in an encyclopedia or other reference to find out about the different types of voting machines that are used and the history of their development.

SP - 2
H - 2

13S07 Contact your local election commission, voter registrar's office, or political precinct chairman to find out as much as you can about the type of voting machine used in your area and how it operates.

CG - 1
SP - 3

Health and Physical Fitness

		Points
13H01	From a good medical encyclopedia or health book, study stress and the adverse effects it can have on the body.	HE - 4
13H02	Study the causes and health effects of high blood pressure and its treatment.	HE - 2
13H03	Study the causes, symptoms, and effects of ulcers and their treatment.	HE - 2
13H04	Study other ailments often related to stress or a sedentary lifestyle.	HE - 2
13H05	Study the vitamin B-complex as it relates to problems with stress.	HE - 2
13H06	Study medical findings on the anti-stress properties of chamomile, pasta, and other foods and herbs.	HE - 2
13H07	Using materials available from doctors, pharmacists, or the extension service, learn stress-avoidance and stress management techniques and begin putting them into practice in your home.	HE - 5
13H08	Learn and regularly do exercises designed to reduce stress.	PE - 3 per week
13H09	Learn how to give a back and neck massage to help someone relax and reduce tension.	PE - 5

Practical Arts

		Points
13P01	Listen to the tape by Jonathan Lindvall, ***Preparing for Romance.***	HF - 5
13P02	Listen to the tape by Jonathan Lindvall, ***A Talk to Godly Teens About Sex and Romance.***	HF - 5
13P03	Learn to mix and apply mortar and lay bricks for a simple patio, barbecue pit, or garden wall.	VA - 10
13P04	Learn to use caulk, mortar, and other substances to repair cracks in walls and other brick structures.	VA - 10
13P05	Learn to hang a gate or door on hinges.	VA - 5
13P06	Go with a parent or other adult to vote, going into the booth if possible.	CG - 2
13P07	If your family's beliefs allow it, help in a political campaign, doing office work or handing out literature.	CG - 5 BE - 3
13P08	If you don't wish to campaign or can't choose a candidate to support, you may call local election officials and offer to be a volunteer worker at the polls.	CG - 5 BE - 3
13P09	Learn to test your own or someone else's blood pressure using the home kits available for that purpose.	HE - 3
13P10	Buy and learn to use a Badge-a-Minit or other button maker.	BE - 2

Creative and Performing Arts

		Points
13A01	Draw pictures and designs for political flyers or posters for the campaign in which you are working.	VA - 5
13A02	Design one or more campaign buttons for your favorite candidate. Make them yourself or have them made by someone else.	VA - 3 each
13A03	Draw pictures of all field trips.	VA - 3 each
13A04	Use your calligraphy or other lettering skills to make a poster of the Preamble to the Constitution.	VA - 10
13A05	Copy one or more of the verses to be memorized in your best calligraphy.	VA - 2 each
13A06	Draw one or more political cartoons about an issue of importance to you.	VA - 5 CG - 2
13A07	Use your artistic talents to illustrate one or more of the papers written for this unit.	VA - 3
13A08	Write a campaign song for your favorite candidate.	MA - 5
13A09	Learn to play and sing the song you wrote.	MA - 3
13A10	Learn to sing your country's national anthem.	MA - 3
13A11	Learn to play your country's national anthem on your choice of instrument.	MA - 3
13A12	Learn to sing one or more patriotic songs from our country's history.	MA - 3 each
13A13	Create a book with one of the following titles: *Civil Government, Church Government, Early American History,* or *Politics.* This can be a simple notebook that includes all the reports and art work during this unit or a bound story book written as a nonfiction book. You may include text and illustrations as you desire. Points will depend on the subject you choose and the amount of time spent on this project. Share the book with someone.	Parents Discretion
13A14	Listen to the tape *History Alive Through Music: America*. Includes 16 American folk and patriotic songs from the French and Indian War chronologically through to the first transcontinental railroad.	MA - 3 each tape

Unit 14 ❧

> "She maketh fine linen and selleth it and delivereth girdles to the merchants."
>
> Proverbs 31:24

Introduction to Unit 14

This unit takes a look at the business skills which a wife and mother could use to increase her family's income without ever leaving home. We deal with Biblical teachings which apply to business transactions and to working as unto the Lord. We will look at the occupations pursued by godly women mentioned in the Bible.

You will study various trades and crafts as they were pursued and have changed throughout history. This will include a study of trade guilds, originating in Medieval Europe, and culminating in the unions and trade associations of today. We will look extensively at various economic factors related to the business community in our country.

You will study the businesses, history and geography of Ancient Rome in a Biblical context and read classic literature selections set in Ancient Rome during Jesus' times.

During this unit, you will be encouraged and led, step by step, to develop your own interests and talents into a home business or to get involved in your family's business. It is our hope that each student completing this unit will have established herself, alone or with other family members, in a business which can be operated entirely or mostly from home or in which the entire family can participate.

We will walk you through the actual filing of required business papers and tax forms. There will also be much work with accounting and bookkeeping. You will improve your math skills as you do the calculations needed to fill out the various forms presented.

Bible

		Points
14B01	Read your Bible daily as started in #01B01. You can read the Bible through each year by reading three chapters each day or by following the *Daily Bible Reading Schedule* in **The Narrated Bible.** ☺	B - 1 per 7 chapters
14B02	Use a concordance to list and study Biblical rules or commands which would apply to business transactions.	B - 5
14B03	Study godly men and their character traits from "Little Bear" Wheeler's republished classic **Gaining Favor With God and Man**.	B - 20
14B04	Research and list the business or occupation of all prophets, apostles, and missionaries in the Bible.	B - 5
14B05	List all verses which refer to merchants or trade.	B - 5
14B06	Study the story of Lydia.	B - 2
14B07	Use the book **Beggar to King: All the Occupations of the Bible** to find and list all businesses or occupations which could be pursued by a woman working from home.	B - 3
14B08	Use a Bible and concordance to find and study examples of each of the jobs from the list made in #14B07 above.	B - 8
14B09	Study Larry Burkett's course **Business by the Book**, which presents Biblical teaching on running a business.	BE - 10 B - 5
14B10	Read, study, and outline **Knowing God**. Refer to *The Outline* (110-112) in **Writers INC.**	B - 5 EC - 3
14B11	Read and outline **The Disciplined Life**. Refer to *The Outline* (110-112) in **Writers INC.**	B - 5 EC - 3
14B12	Read the following verses: Gen 1:26,28; 2:15; 3:19; Exod 20:9; Prov 14:23; 28:19; Acts 20:34,35; Ephes 4:28; 1Thes 4:11,12; and 2Thes 3:10-13. Write a summary of these verses titled *Work is Part of God's Plan for Man*. Refer to *Writing Summaries* (180-182) in **Writer's INC.**	B - 1 EC - 2
14B13	Read the following verses to find out the result of honest work: Ps 128:2; Prov 12:12; 31:21,28-31; Eccl 5:12; 4:28; and 1Thes 4:11,12.	B - 1

Cultural Studies

		Points
14C01	Continue adding to the timeline started in Unit 1. Include entries for famous persons or events that occurred in Ancient Rome. ☺	H - 1 VA - 1 each
14C02	Continue adding reports to the geography notebook started in Unit 1. Include a 1-3 page report on Ancient Rome. ☺	G - 2 EC - 1 each
14C03	Study trades and businesses in Ancient Rome using Usborne's *The Romans.*	H - 5
14C04	Study the history of Rome chronologically using *Greenleaf's Famous Men of Rome*.	H - 10
14C05	Use *Greenleaf's Guide to Famous Men of Rome* to study Bible, geography, and vocabulary with the book in #14C04.	H - 30
14C06	Read about the physical layout of a typical Roman city, military camps, construction techniques and aqueducts in *City*.	H - 5
14C07	Study shops and marketing in Ancient Rome using the Usborne Time Traveller Book, *Rome and Romans*.	H - 5
14C08	Study Roman history, and geography from a Biblical perspective using *In Jesus' Times*.	H - 5 B - 5
14C09	Watch the video, *The Last Days of Pompii*.	H - 5
14C10	Read chapter 1 about Ancient Rome in *How Should We Then Live*.	H - 3
14C11	Read chapter 7 - 9 about the Roman Empire and Christianity in *Streams of Civilization*.	H - 5
14C12	Contact tax and licensing agencies in your area to learn what registration, licenses, etc. are needed to start a business there and how to apply for each.	CG - 3
14C13	Study zoning laws and other restrictions on business use of your home.	CG - 2
14C14	Secure and study incorporation papers for some company to learn what is involved in that form of business.	BE - 2
14C15	Obtain and study all tax forms, from IRS, needed for each of the three primary types of businesses: corporations, partnerships, and sole proprietorships.	BE - 3

		Points
14C16	Study trade guilds in Medieval Europe and how they have developed since then.	H - 3
14C17	Study the primary economic indicators used today. Discover how they are determined and what they mean.	CE - 3
14C18	Study Larry Burkett's tape series *God's Principles for Operating a Business*.	BE - 10 B - 5
14C19	Play *Made for Trade* as often as possible.	H - 2 per time
14C20	Find out what projects in your city and state are financed through sales tax and business license fees.	CE - 2
14C21	Study contract law in your state.	CG - 5
14C22	Investigate laws of your nation, state, and/or local area which affect the type of business you may have in your home.	CG - 3
14C23	Read Adam Smith's *Wealth of Nations* to learn about the principles of the free market system.	CE - 3 L - 3
14C24	For a more complete course, in place of # 14C12-14C18, you may take a course in business or corporate law by special arrangement with a local college, law school, or through correspondence.	CG - 1 Credit for an entire course
14C25	Use *World History Dates* or *Kingfisher's Illustrated History of the World* to read about people and events in Ancient Rome.	H - 1
14C26	Learn to use a simple computer accounting program such as *Quick Books, MYOB (Managing Your Own Business), Peach Tree*, etc.	A - 10
14C27	Learn to use a word processing program.	BE - 5

Reading and Literature

		Points
14R01	Read the 1890 classic, ***Stories about Jesus: Our Lord and Saviour***.	B - 5
14R02	Read about first century believers and their courage, in witnessing, in the novel ***Quo Vadis***.	H - 5
14R03	Read about the Palestinian boy whose hatred toward Roman soldiers changes after he meets Jesus in ***The Bronze Bow***.	L - 5
14R04	Read the fictional account of the soldier who drew lots for Jesus' robe and how he became a Christian in ***The Robe***.	L - 5
14R05	Read the story of the Syrophenician woman and Jesus in ***Runaway***.	L - 5
14R06	Read the story of Stephen, the first martyr, in ***Forbidden Gates***.	L - 4
14R07	Read any or all sections not yet read of ***Beggar to King: All the Occupations of the Bible***.	H - 4
14R08	Read either or both of the Living History books: ***Living History: Ancient Greece, Living History: Classical Rome***.	H - 4 each
14R09	Read ***The Merchant of Venice***.	L - 3
14R10	Read ***All the Way Home***.	L - 4
14R11	Read biographies of businessmen who built large companies and/or became famous from very small beginnings.	H - 4 each person
14R12	Read biographies of Mary Kay and/or other people who started and are at the head of major "work from home" businesses.	H - 4 each
14R13	Read ***Teenage Entrepreneurs' Guide*** and choose businesses you would like to investigate further as possibilities for yourself.	CE - 4
14R14	Read ***Found Money, Money in my Cookie Jar***, or another good book on businesses to be run from home.	CE - 4
14R15	Read and outline ***Minding Your Own Business***.	BE - 5
14R16	Read David Schwartz's book ***If I Made a Million***.	BE - 5

Composition

	Points
14W01 Continue making entries in your handwriting notebook started in #01W01. Include every Bible verse studied or memorized from this unit. ☺	EG - 1 B - 1 each page
14W02 Continue placing vocabulary words in the vocabulary notebook you started in #01W02. Add at least 10 new words per week. ☺	EG - 1 per 10 words
14W03 Continue adding to your school journal started in #01W03. Review *Journal Writing* (470-471) in **Writers INC**. ☺	EC - 1 per week
14W04 Have someone dictate several paragraphs to you, using passages from books used in this unit. Proofread and correct the paragraphs.	EC - 1 per 3 paragraphs
14W05 Have someone dictate several Bible verses to you, using verses you have studied in this unit. Proofread and correct the verses.	EC - 1 per 3 verses
14W06 Write a story as if you lived in Ancient Rome during Jesus' times.	EC - 4
14W07 Write a story as if you were a persecuted Christian in the early church in Rome. Refer to *Writing the Short Story* (218-227) in **Writers INC**.	EC - 4
14W08 Write a résumé listing your abilities, interests, and training. Use it to choose a home business or profession for yourself. Refer to *Writing Résumés* (424) in **Writers INC**.	EC - 3 CE - 2
14W09 Listen to the tape by Inge Cannon **Writing Résumés for Teens**.	EC - 3
14W10 Outline any or all of the books read in #14R13 through 14R17.	EC - 5 each
14W11 Continue writing book reports on a regular basis, using the books in this unit or others of your choice.	EC - 2 each book
14W12 Write reports on all field trips taken in relation to this unit.	EC - 2 each
14W13 Take a spelling test using words from your spelling notebook. Look up the spelling rule for each word spelled incorrectly.	EG - 1 per 10
14W14 Write an essay on the Christian's Responsibility in Business, using information from the tapes and books in this unit.	EC - 2
14W15 Write a proposal like you would use to initiate a particular partnership or business deal. Refer to *Writing to Persuade* (125) in **Writers INC**.	EC - 3 CE - 2
14W16 Proofread and correct all grammar and punctuation errors in all written work. Refer to *Proofreader's Guide* (600-714) in **Writers INC**.	EG - 1 each page

Math and Personal Economics

		Points
14M01	Obtain profit and loss statements, operating expense information, and similar figures from various home businesses run by women you know or fictional women. Prepare a graph to compare the productivity and profitability of these businesses.	M - 10
14M02	Prepare a schedule C with all necessary attendant forms for your own or someone else's home business.	M - 5
14M03	Study and learn to complete all income tax forms for a real or imaginary corporation.	BE - 3
14M04	Study and learn to complete all income tax forms for a real or imaginary partnership.	BE - 3
14M05	Play *The Richest Christian* board game.	CE - 3
14M06	Learn to track and record expenses for a real or imaginary home business. Keep records for a minimum of two months.	M - 5
14M07	Complete a spreadsheet, computerized or otherwise, for a family or home business.	M - 5
14M08	Compile information on licenses fees, tax prepayments, materials required, and any other startup costs and determine how much capital you will need to launch the home business of your choice.	CE - 3 M - 2
14M09	Visit your local bank and discuss the services they offer to businesses which are not traditionally needed by consumers.	BE - 2

Science

		Points
14S01	Examine different types of leather, comparing them for various qualities.	SB - 2
14S02	Study the anatomy and physiology of various animals whose hides are used for common leather goods.	SB - 4
14S03	Study the manufacturing and use of various synthetic leathers and leather substitutes.	SC - 3
14S04	Study the physical and chemical processes involved in the art of taxidermy.	SC - 5
14S05	Study the various physical and chemical processes involved in the tanning of hides.	SC - 5
14S06	Study various types of traps used to capture different animals for different purposes.	SB - 2
14S07	Study the anatomy and physiology of a variety of fur-bearing mammals.	SB - 4

Far Above Rubies © 1995

Health and Physical Fitness

		Points
14H01	Examine your own physical condition and determine any restrictions which your health might place on your choice of a business or profession. Consider such things as allergies, back problems, vision or hearing impairment, and handicaps.	HE - 6
14H02	List all health-related businesses you can think of which could be ran from home.	BE - 2
14H03	Take a course in nursing, home health care, or something else related to the health care profession.	HE - 1/2 Credit per semester course
14H04	Examine your home for things which might create health or safety hazards for customers or associates of your home business. Make arrangements to correct or warn people of each hazard.	HE - 2
14H05	Investigate any home business you are considering for any dangers it may possibly present to you, your customers, or associates. Look for ways to correct the problems or warn others about them.	HE - 3
14H06	Plan a fitness program for yourself to strengthen those muscles you will need for the business you have chosen, prevent the health hazards you discovered in #14H04, and provide the kinds of exercise you will not get as a regular part of your work.	HE - 5

Practical Arts

		Points
14P01	Market and sell some of your needle work or other crafts.	BE - 5
14P02	Tour craft shops and shows which specialize in items similar to what you intend to make. Comparison shop so you can set realistic prices for your items.	BE - 2 each trip
14P03	Examine your own abilities and interests and choose a home business to match them.	BE - 2
14P04	Learn to make belts, wallets, and/or other leather items.	CR - 2 (per item)
14P05	Set up and run your own home business, handling all record keeping, advertising, and all other aspects of the business.	BE - 30 for one month of operation
14P06	Complete schedules C and SE and any other forms needed for tax purposes on a home business.	BE - 3 per type form
14P07	Design and order your own business cards.	VA - 2
14P08	Open your own bank account and keep all bank records successfully for 2 quarters.	FM - 20 per quarter
14P09	Learn to endorse and cash checks.	BE - 2
14P10	Learn the difference between personal and commercial bank accounts and the way your bank handles each.	CE - 2
14P11	Investigate various forms of advertising available to you and determine which would be the best buy for your type of business.	BE - 5
14P12	Play the computer game *Rome*. Start as a slave and work your way to Emperor.	H - 1 per game - limit 5
14P13	Attend the *Apprenticeship Plus* seminar (or listen to the tapes) by Inge Cannon.	BE - 20

Creative and Performing Arts

14A01   Make a model of a Roman Fort and/or Roman Villa using your own materials or Usborne's *Make This Roman Fort* or *Make this Roman Villa*.

VA - 10 each

14A02   Design your own logo for your business using original artwork and/or calligraphy.

VA - 10

14A03   Use your logo or other artwork to make posters or produce flyers to advertise your business.

VA - 5

14A04   Design your own business stationery, using your logo, calligraphy, or other artwork.

VA - 5

14A05   To improve your artistic skills for drawing ads and such, you may wish to take drawing lessons from an art school or private teacher.

VA - 1/2 Credit per school year of classes

14A06   Instead of the above lessons, you can teach yourself to draw better using the book *Drawing on the Right Side of the Brain*.

VA - 1/2 Credit for completing entire book.

14A07   Create a book with one of the following titles: *Ancient Rome, Business, or Home Industries*. This can be a simple notebook that includes all the reports and art work during this unit or a bound story book written as a nonfiction book. You may include text and illustrations as you desire. Points will depend on the subject you choose and the amount of time spent on this project. Share the book with someone.

Parents Discretion

Unit 15 🦜

> "Strength and honor are her clothing;
> and she shall rejoice in time to come."
>
> Proverbs 31:25

Introduction to Unit 15

This unit begins with a detailed study of dignity and related words from a Biblical perspective. You will look at what constitutes a dignified woman and how to become one. In the quest, you will examine the lives of a number of Christian women who displayed strength and dignity, often in the face of great adversity. You will study the Middle Ages and read classic literature selections set in that time period.

Though this unit stresses trust in the Lord for deliverance in the trials of life, you will also learn ways to best prepare our families to meet these trials. We will look at life and health insurance and the costs of hospitals, nursing homes, funerals, etc. Discuss these issues with your parents to find their views on them and how they would like you to approach this unit. You may then work with your family to find ways to provide for those eventualities. In human anatomy we will study hormones, glands, and the rest of endocrine system.

In looking toward the future, you will study Biblical prophecy, looking at that which is fulfilled and that which may not yet be fulfilled. We will not take a position on issues such as the Millennium or seek the identity of the Anti-Christ. Instead, the student is encouraged to study and find her own beliefs. We will look at the past to find out the impact of various national and international disasters on the lives of the women of the period.

We study provisions made by governments for widows and victims of wars and other catastrophes. We will also investigate secular predictions such as global warming, ozone depletion. Again, we will try to offer an opportunity for you to examine the evidence for yourself and make your own conclusions. We do encourage action in conservation of natural resources and those environmental issues you decide are legitimate.

Bible

		Points
15B01	Read your Bible daily as started in #01B01. You can read the Bible through each year by reading three chapters each day or by following the *Daily Bible Reading Schedule* in **The Narrated Bible.** ☺	B - 1 per 7 chapters
15B02	Read the following verses about strength: 1 Kings 19:5, Mark 5:2-4, and Acts 19:16.	B - 3
15B03	Read and memorize Matt 26:41 about strength against temptation.	B - 5
15B04	Define strength as it deals with Christian virtue based on the following verses: Ps 84:7, 1 Cor 4:10, 16:13, 2 Cor 12:10, Eph 6:10 and 1 John 2:14.	B - 10
15B05	Read the following verses and write a prayer petitioning God for strength against trouble. Neh 9:32, Ps 20:1, 22:11, 61:1, 86:7, 88:1-9, 102:2, 116:3-9, 138:3 & 7, Isa 33:2 and Lam 3:55.	B - 10
15B06	Read, study, and outline **Knowing God**. Refer to *The Outline* (110-112) in **Writers INC.**	B - 5 EC - 3
15B07	Read and study **The Disciplines of a Beautiful Woman.** List the page number for each reference to one of the specific character traits from Proverbs 31.	HF - 5 B - 3
15B08	Study the New Testament church's treatment of widows and the Bible's commands to them on the subject.	B - 3
15B09	Memorize passages in which God promises to be a husband to the widow.	B - 3
15B10	Study all books of the Old Testament considered to be the major prophets.	B - 25
15B11	Study all books of the Old Testament considered to be the minor prophets.	B - 20
15B12	Study Revelation with a good commentary to help in your understanding of it.	B - 10
15B13	Study each of the following Psalms which deal with trusting God: 11, 31, 34, 40, 46, 55, 62, 64, 73, 100, 105, 115, and 131.	B - 2 each
15B14	Memorize one or more of the above Psalms.	B - 5 each

		Points

15B15 Study a topical Bible series on prayer. B - 8

15B16 Choose or develop a personal Bible study program and pursue it diligently. B - 20 per month

15B17 Prepare a list of Scriptures which give comfort to those undergoing various types of trials. B - 5

15B18 Set up and keep a prayer journal of requests, promises, and answers. B - 5 per month

15B19 Work through Bible study and other parts of **The Christian Charm Course**. B - 10

15B20 Write a summary paragraph titled *God Rewards Diligence*. Use the following verses: Prov 10:4,5; 13:4; 20:13; 31:27; Eccel 9:10; Ezek 34:2-6, Rom 12:11. Refer to *Writing Summaries* (180-182) in **Writer's INC**. B - 2 / EC - 2

15B21 Write a prése titled *Why and How to Plan Ahead*. Answer after reading the following verses: Prov 6:6-11; 30:25-28; 31:16,21,27; Matt 25:1-13; Luk 14:28-32; and James 4:13-15. Refer to *The Prése* (182) in **Writer's INC**. B - 2 / EC - 2

Cultural Studies

		Points
15C01	Continue adding to the timeline started in Unit 1. Include entries for persons or events during the Middle Ages. ☺	H - 1 VA - 1 each
15C02	Continue adding reports to the geography notebook started in Unit 1. Include a 1-3 page report on Europe during the Middle Ages. ☺	G - 2 EC - 1 each
15C03	Study the history of the Middle Ages chronologically using *Greenleaf's Famous Men of the Middle Ages.*	H - 10
15C04	Use *Greenleaf's Guide to Famous Men of the Middle Ages* to study Bible, geography, and vocabulary with the book above.	H - 30
15C05	Read chapter 11 and 12 about the Middle Ages in *Streams of Civilization*. Answer all chapter questions on page 228 and 250.	H - 8
15C06	Read about the various stages of construction of a castle by reading *Castle* and/or watching the video *Castle*.	H - 4
15C07	Read about the various stages of construction of a cathedral by reading *Cathedral* and/or watching the video *Cathedral*.	H - 4
15C08	Read about everyday life in the Middle Ages using Usborne's *Knights and Castles.*	H - 4
15C09	Study the maps, charts, and photos of life in the Middle Ages using the *Cultural Atlas of the Middle Ages*.	H - 3 G - 3
15C10	Study lives of early Christian women such as Constantine's mother and the King of Kent's wife. Write a paper on how they influenced history.	H - 1 EC - 2 each woman
15C11	Study the Middle Ages by reading chapter 2 in *How Should We Then Live*.	H - 4
15C12	Research Stonehedge in England.	H - 2
15C13	Study Christianity in Medieval Europe. Use *Sketches of Church History* or *Streams of Civilization.*	H - 5
15C14	Mohammed was born during the Middle Ages. He started the false religion of Islam. Followers of Islam are called Muslims. Use *Streams of Civilization* or an encyclopedia to study the Islam religion. Find out what percentage of the world are Islam today.	H - 3
15C15	Study the feudal system.	CG - 2

15C16 Study the lives of women who triumphed in the face of great odds. Some to include are Helen Keller, Corrie Ten Boom, and Joni Eareckson Tada.

H - 2 each person

15C17 Use *The Christian Legal Advisor* or a similar book to study probate court, wills, and inheritance laws and taxes on the national, state, and local levels. Contact your local probate court for information on specific laws, taxes, etc. for your area.

CE - 5

15C18 From history books, study the various methods of treating and/or providing for widows in other places and time periods.

H - 5

15C19 Use library and other resources to study the major wars of United States history and how they affected women and families.

CE - 5

15C20 Use Larry Burkett's book or others on the subject to study the United States economy. Try to determine what its problems are and how you can make the best plans to avoid a personal crisis.

CG - 2

15C21 Talk with a funeral home director to learn about your state and local laws with regards to funerals. Find out what type caskets, embalming, etc. is required and what other services the director recommends and why.

CG - 2

15C22 Talk to an investment counselor and look at various investment plans and pensions, including social security, to see what provisions they make for survivors.

CE - 2

15C23 Listen to tape 3 from *History Alive Through Music* it includes the time period from Stephen's life through the Middle Ages.

H - 2

15C24 Read *The Early Middle Ages* (157-236) and *The Middle Ages* (237-316) in *Kingfisher's Illustrated History of the World*.

H - 2

15C25 Read about the Middle Ages in pages 111-155 in *Everyday Life Through the Ages*.

H - 3

15C26 Use Usborne's *World History Dates* to read about people and events during the Middle Ages.

H - 1

Reading and Literature

		Points
15R01	Read *The Door in the Wall*, a story about a ten-year-old boy left crippled by illness and how he finds purpose in life. Set in late medieval England.	L - 4
15R02	Read about the monastic life in the 11th century in *The Hawk and the Dove*.	L - 4
15R03	Read the novel about an innkeeper's daughter during the Middle Ages, *Jackaroo*.	L - 4
15R04	Read the classic about the Black Knight in 13th century England, *Ivanhoe*.	L - 5
15R05	Read *The Story of King Arthur and His Knights* or *Tristan*.	H - 5 each
15R06	Read biographies of Helen Keller, Joni Eareckson Tada, Fanny Crosby, and others who overcame handicaps with strength and dignity.	L - 4
15R07	Read *A Chance to Die: A Biography of Amy Carmichael*.	L - 5
15R08	Read *God Made Them Great*, inspiring stories of five lives: George Muller, Isobel Kuhn, Billy Bray, David Brainerd and Robert Annan.	L - 5
15R09	Read biographies of Elizabeth Elliott, Catherine Marshall, Edith Shaeffer, and other Christian women who maintained a ministry in dignity after widowhood.	H - 4
15R10	Read *John Brown's Body* and critique Mary Lou Wingate.	L - 3
15R11	Memorize *Portrait of a Southern Lady* from *John Brown's Body* by Stephen Vincent Benet.	L - 8
15R12	Read 3 other poems relating to women of strength and dignity.	L - 3
15R13	Read *The Coming Economic Earthquake* by Larry Burkett.	CE - 4
15R14	Read the biography *Florence Nightingale*.	H - 4
15R15	Read *The Trumpeter of Krakow*, set in medieval Poland in 1461.	L - 4
15R16	Read *Otto of the Silver Hand*.	L - 4

	Points

15R17 Read *The Parousia* by J. Stuart Russell, *Days of Vengeance* by David Chilton, and *The Late, Great Planet Earth* by Hal Lindsay and compare the three different views of the end times as taught in Scripture.

CD - 20 no partial credit

15R18 Read *This Present Darkness* and/or *Piercing the Darkness,* both novels by Frank Peretti.

L - 4 each

15R19 Read writings of any or all of the women of whom you are reading or have read biographies in this unit.

L - 4

15R20 Read and outline *All the Way Home*.

L - 5
EC - 4

15R21 Read *Beowulf*.

L - 5

Composition

		Points
15W01	Continue making entries in your handwriting notebook started in #01W01. Include every Bible verse studied or memorized from this unit. ☺	EG - 1 B - 1 each page
15W02	Continue placing vocabulary words in the vocabulary notebook you started in #01W02. Learn at least 10 new words per week. ☺	EG - 1 per 10 words
15W03	Continue adding to your school journal started in #01W03. Review *Journal Writing* (470-471) in **Writers INC**. ☺	EC - 1 per week
15W04	Have someone dictate several paragraphs to you, using passages from books used in this unit. Proofread and correct the paragraphs.	EC - 1 per 3 paragraphs
15W05	Have someone dictate several Bible verses to you, using verses you have studied in this unit. Proofread and correct the verses.	EC - 1 per 3 verses
15W06	Write a story about a person living in a feudal manor. Describe their customs and family life.	EC - 2
15W07	Write as if you lived in a castle during the Middle Ages. Describe customs and family life. Refer to *Writing the Short Story* (218-227) in **Writers INC**.	EC - 2
15W08	Copy the poems and verses you are trying to memorize for handwriting practice. Refer to *Writing the Poem* (205-216) in **Writers INC**.	EG - 2 each
15W09	Write a complete character sketch of Mary Lou Wingate from **John Brown's Body**.	EC - 2
15W10	Write an essay paper or extensive report on one of the women you have studied in this unit. Refer to *Writing Essays* (105-118) in **Writers INC**.	EC - 10
15W11	Write letters of encouragement and comfort to friends undergoing trials.	EC - 2
15W12	Outline **Disciplines of a Beautiful Woman** as you study it.	EC - 5 L - 3
15W13	Proofread and correct all grammar and punctuation errors in all written work. Refer to *Proofreader's Guide* (600-714) in **Writers INC**.	EG - 1 each page
15W14	Proofread and correct spelling errors in all written work. Add any misspelled words to your spelling notebook.	EG - 2 per paper

	Points
15W15 Take a spelling test using words from your spelling notebook. Look up the spelling rule for each word spelled incorrectly.	EG - 1 per 10
15W16 Write a character sketch of a personal acquaintance who is a woman of dignity.	EC - 2
15W17 List reasons a person may fear for the future. Write a paper giving the Biblical response to each reason/problem.	EC - 3 CD - 5
15W18 Write a paper giving predictions of your own concerning the future of our society based on trends you observe now.	EC - 5
15W19 Write a detailed analysis of the future world as you see it taught in the book of Revelation. If you do not believe this book is a prediction of the future, explain in writing what you do think it means.	EC - 5 B - 5
15W20 Look up any prefixes, suffixes, and roots of new vocabulary words. Refer to section 446-448 in *Writers INC*.	EG - 1 per 10 words
15W21 Scan the section *Using the Right Word* (715-837) in **Writers INC.** Choose 10 words. Write a paragraph using each of the words. Include the words their, they're and there and any words you have trouble with.	EG - 1

Math and Personal Economics

		Points
15M01	Prepare an investment plan for the future of your family.	BE - 4
15M02	For the above activity, compute your total expected expenses at various periods, your current disposable income, and the insurance and other investments. Determine how much income you need and the investment required to produce it.	A - 3 M - 3
15M03	Examine your insurance policy and determine the rate of return.	M - 3
15M04	Investigate your family's health insurance to find any deductibles, limits, and/or exclusions. Prepare a budget to allow some savings to meet those needs if they should arise.	A - 3
15M05	Investigate the Medicare and Medicaid programs as administered in your state and compare the benefits to the actual cost of the listed services to determine percentages of differences.	CE - 2
15M06	Obtain typical charges for various services at one or more local hospitals and use the figures to determine the cost of an average stay for a patient needing a certain procedure.	CE - 2 M - 2
15M07	Compute your family's payments for hospitalization insurance over the period of one year. Determine the cost of hospital care and associated expenses. Compare to the cost of insurance.	M - 2

Science

		Points
15S01	Watch the video *City of the Bees* from Bob Jones.	SB - 5
15S02	Study ants and bees as examples of insects that prepare for the future.	SB - 5
15S03	Study squirrels and other rodents, especially with regards to their hoarding trait and preparation for winter.	SB - 5
15S04	Get books from the library which deal with environmental concerns which cause many to fear for the future, such as global warming, acid rain, etc. Examine evidence in support of all predictions in those areas.	SE - 5
15S05	In any of the above areas where you see evidence of a legitimate problem, look for solutions you can help implement.	SE - 3
15S06	Research widespread fears within our society in the past and the extent to which any of them came true. (Look in the library under environment, ecology, futurology, and/or predictions.)	H - 3
15S07	Study the work of John Nesbitt or another futurologists and evaluate their predictions for validity.	SE - 3
15S08	Investigate the primary natural resources of your area to find their main uses, level of supply, and suggested methods of conservation. You can obtain this information from your Chamber of Commerce or State Conservation Department.	SE - 3
15S09	Study various natural disasters and how you can prepare for them to minimize danger and/or damage.	SE - 5
15S10	For a Christian perspective on environmental issues, read *Caring for Planet Earth*.	SE - 5
15S11	Study the methods and standards used by the Red Cross and other agencies for damage assessment in a time of natural disaster.	A - 3 SE - 3 BE - 2
15S12	Roger Bacon lived during the 1200's. Write a report on his discoveries. Refer to *Writing Summaries* (180-182) in *Writer's INC*.	SP - 2 EC - 2
15S13	Do research and write an essay about science during the Middle Ages. Include superstition, magic, alchemy and astrology. Refer to *Writing Essays* (105-118) in *Writers INC*.	SP - 2 EC - 2

Health and Physical Fitness

		Points
15H01	Research the many plagues that occurred in Europe during the Middle Ages. Find out where they came from.	HE - 4
15H02	Study cancer and other "catastrophic" illnesses. Investigate causes, fatality rates, preventive measures, and effects of these diseases on patient and family. Make charts, posters, or a notebook for easy reference.	HE - 5 complete study of one illness
15H03	Interview in person or by phone a representative of the American Cancer Society or a similar group to discover what services they offer cancer victims and their families.	HE - 2
15H04	Conduct an interview like #15H03 with a representative of the American Heart Association or another group who deals with victims of heart attacks and related problems.	HE - 2
15H05	Study medical literature to determine the major causes of death in different age groups and learn how to treat and/or prevent each.	HE - 5
15H06	Study medical literature to determine the major causes of permanent disabilities in persons of various age groups and learn how to prevent each.	HE - 5
15H07	Visit or talk with a worker from a hospice and compare their purposes, facilities, and services with those of a hospital.	HE - 2
15H08	Volunteer to work in a hospital or hospice.	HE - 2
15H09	Read and outline *The Endocrine System* (74-87) in ***ABC's of the Human Body*** by Reader's Digest. Refer to *The Outline* (110-112) in ***Writers INC.***	HA - 5
15H10	Find, color and study sections related to the endocrine system in ***Gray's Anatomy Coloring Book.*** Include these glands: pineal, thyroid, pituitary, adrenal. Include these organs: and the thymus, hypothalamus, pancreas, ovaries and testes.	HA - 2 each section completed
15H11	Do research and write a paper on the endocrine system from the encyclopedia or other source. Refer to *Writing to Learn* (473-474) in ***Writers INC.***	HA - 4 EC - 2
15H12	Do research to find out what happens to the endocrine when you are under stress and when you age.	HA - 3
15H13	Do research to find out what causes dwarfs, midgets and giants.	HA - 1

Practical Arts

		Points
15P01	Using ***Putting Food By***, a similar book, or pamphlets from your county extension office, learn to can foods for storing without electricity.	HM - 5
15P02	Using the books and/or pamphlets which are mentioned above, learn to dry foods for storing without electricity.	HM - 5
15P03	Use the books and/or pamphlets in #15P01 to learn how to smoke foods so they will keep without electricity.	HM - 5
15P04	Learn ways of cooking, heating. and cooling without dependence on utility companies or other outside entities.	HM - 3
15P05	Implement procedures to enable your family to conserve your personal resources and store up needed items for an uncertain future.	CE - 3
15P06	Build a water wheel to capture water power for household use in case of permanent disruption of electric services.	VA - 10 SP - 10
15P07	Build a windmill to use in case of permanent disruption of electric services.	SP - 10 VA - 10
15P08	Build a generator and hook it up to be used with either #15P06 or #15P07.	SP - 10 VA - 10
15P09	Learn to prepare fresh foods for freezing. (Use resources in #15P01.)	HM - 5
15P10	Learn as much as you can about various kinds of life insurance policies and choose the best one for your family.	BE - 2
15P11	Study about wills and practice making one using a common will kit available in book stores and from some lawyers.	BE - 2
15P12	Plan and implement a program for your family to get involved in recycling and other conservation activities within your community.	SE - 3

Creative and Performing Arts

		Points
15A01	Make a model castle using your own materials or Usborne's **Make this Model Castle**.	VA - 5
15A02	Make sympathy or get well cards to send to friends or relatives whenever the occasion arises.	VA - 2 per card
15A03	Freehand or with drafting tools, draw plans for any or all of the building projects in the practical arts section.	VA - 2 each
15A04	Learn to use your artistic talent to make life better for elderly friends or relatives	Parent's discretion
15A05	Listen to a number of hymns and spiritual songs which deal with trusting God in times of adversity.	AA - 2 per song
15A06	Find out as much as you can about the author of each of the above hymns with special emphasis on any particular trial that person may have faced which led to the writing of that hymn.	AA - 1 H - 2
15A07	Learn to sing one of the above songs or hymns.	MA - 3 each song
15A08	Learn to play one or more of the above songs or hymns.	MA - 3 each song
15A09	Write an original tune for one or more Psalms you studied or memorized about trusting God in times of trouble.	MA - 5 each song
15A10	Memorize and learn to sing your original song from #15A09 above.	MA - 3
15A11	Create a book with one of the following titles: *Life During the Middle Ages, The Endocrine System or Diligence*. This can be a simple notebook that includes all the reports and art work during this unit or a bound story book written as a nonfiction book. You may include text and illustrations as you desire. Points will depend on the subject you choose and the amount of time spent on this project. Share the book with someone.	Parents Discretion

Unit 16 ❦

"She openeth her mouth with wisdom
and in her tongue is the law of kindness."

Proverbs 31:26

Introduction to Unit 16

This unit deals with the meaning of wisdom from a Biblical perspective as the knowledge and obedience of the ways of God. We will study those books of the Bible which are often called the Wisdom Literature: Job, Proverbs, and Ecclesiastes, giving special consideration to those passages which specifically speak of wisdom. We will also study the New Testament Epistles and other parts of Scripture which relate to wisdom and doctrine. You will be encouraged to commit large portions of Scripture to memory. One main thrust of this unit is to teach the student how and why to set up a regular program of personal Bible study.

The remainder of this unit addresses the ability and willingness of the godly woman to share her wisdom, knowledge, and spiritual gifts with others. This includes mentoring, teaching facts and skills, training children or women in church programs, and home schooling. In this context, we will look at the existing school programs and the problems with them. We will also study the history of home education and the laws and major court cases concerning it. We will seek to obtain and compile data on student performance and other factors in public, private, and home schools.

We will investigate the various learning styles and methods of home schooling, seeking to pinpoint the strengths and weaknesses of each type. We will read biographies and case histories of home schooling families and famous people who received some or all of their education at home. You will be encouraged to hear tapes, go to workshops, and read books by well-known experts in the field of home education. You will be asked to study various learning styles and practice choosing material for each. You will write a unit study and make several different types of teaching materials. We will help you learn to write lesson plans for a student of your own.

This unit will study most complex organ in the body, the brain. We see how the brain functions, and how the amazing network of nerves get messages to other parts of your body.

Bible

		Points
16B01	Continue your daily Bible reading started in #01B01. Read three chapters each day or use a Bible study plan. ☺	B - 1 per 7 chapters
16B02	Write a paper explaining the impact of the tongue from the following verses: Psalms 141:3, Proverbs 18:7, 2 Tim 3:3, James 3:2.	B - 8 EC - 3
16B03	Read about Solomon in I Kings 3:5-28.	B - 3
16B04	Read Proverbs 2:1-22 and Proverbs 3:13-24. Make a list of the rewards of wisdom.	B - 2
16B05	Read Proverbs 1:20-33 and Proverbs 9:13. Make a list of the dangers of rejecting wisdom.	B - 2
16B06	Define human wisdom according to Galatians 6:14, Proverbs 3:19. and I Corinthians 1:26-30.	B - 5
16B07	Read the classic *The Kneeling Christian*.	B - 5
16B08	Study the wisdom of the book of Job.	B - 20
16B09	Read a chapter of Proverbs each day using the day of the month as the chapter number. Repeat each month.	B - 10 per month
16B10	Do an in depth study of all Scriptures relating to wisdom.	B - 25
16B11	Study all New Testament epistles to learn more of God's wisdom for His people.	B - 30
16B12	Memorize Deuteronomy 6:4-9.	B - 10
16B13	Complete Bible Memory Association's *Daily Words of Wisdom* youth memory course.	B - 50
16B14	Read *How the Bible Came to Us*.	B - 5
16B15	Study Paul's instructions regarding the women mentors found in Titus 2:1-5.	B - 3
16B16	Study the role of women in the New Testament church. See #01B09.	B - 10
16B17	Learn one of the common approaches to tell the Gospel to another person.	B - 5

	Points

16B18 Read the book ***How to Lead an Evangelistic Bible Study***.

B - 10

16B19 Study ***How to Lead a Child to Christ*** from Child Evangelism Fellowship.

B - 5

16B20 Read ***Lifestyle Evangelism*** and compare it to other common methods of evangelism.

B - 8

16B21 Study the ***Bible Visual Resource Book*** to gain a chronological understanding of the Bible.

B - 10

16B22 Use a concordance to develop and complete a Bible study on the parent's responsibility to train their children.

B - 3

16B23 Proverbs is the most practical book in Scripture, establishing God's universal moral code. God Himself said in Proverbs that it was written to: know wisdom and instruction; to perceive the words of understanding; To receive the instruction of wisdom, justice, and judgment, and equity; To give subtlety to the simple, to the young man knowledge and discretion. Complete the Bible study on Proverbs in the workbook ***The Principle Thing***.

B - 25

16B24 Man is distinct from animals because he was created with intelligence and vocabulary. Read Gen 1:22, 2:15.

B - 1/4

Cultural Studies

		Points
16C01	Continue adding to the timeline started in Unit 1. Prepare an entry for each person or event studied in this unit. ☺	H - 1 VA - 1 each
16C02	Include a report on education in the United States to the geography notebook started in #01C04. ☺	G - 2 EC - 1
16C03	Read and outline the chapters about the history of American education in *Why Christians are Going Home to School*. Refer to *The Outline* (110-112) in *Writers INC*.	H - 5 EC - 2
16C04	Watch the video, *Education and the Founding Fathers*.	H - 5
16C05	Listen to the lecture #29 on the history of American education from *America 350 Years* (audio tapes and workbook). Answer the questions in the workbook.	H - 20
16C06	Read *Thinking Christianly* or Francis Schaeffer's *A Christian Manifesto* to be able to explain the philosophy of a Christian World View and a secular world view.	HF - 8
16C07	Study *The Messianic Character of American Education* by R. J. Rushdoony.	CG - 5
16C08	Study *Government Nannies* by Cathy Duffy.	CG - 5
16C09	Study *The Bible, Home Schooling, and the Law* by Karl Reed.	CG - 5
16C10	Study Constitutional law and court cases relating to home schools.	CG - 8
16C11	Study the lives of famous people who were home taught.	H - 2 each
16C12	Study *Home Education and Constitutional Liberties*.	CG - 5
16C13	Find out how false religion is taught in the public school system, use *A Christian Manifesto*, *Why Christians are Going Home to School* or another reference to study the *Humanist Manifesto*.	HF - 5
16C14	Obtain a copy of your state's education code and study it, paying special attention to the compulsory attendance law and anything relating to home education.	CG - 5
16C15	Attend a meeting or public forum of your local school board on an issue of interest to you.	CG - 2
16C16	Read in *The Light and the Glory* to learn about the first so-called public schools which were opened by Christian churches in early New England. Find out how they differed from the public schools of today.	H - 4

		Points
16C17	Study *The Old Deluder Satan Act* as passed in colonial America and analyze the impact it had on the beginning of our public schools.	H - 3
16C18	Watch the video, ***What the Founding Fathers Really Meant by Separation of Church and State***.	H - 5
16C19	Study the lives of Horace Mann and John Dewey to understand the origins and purpose of the public schools.	H - 5 each man
16C20	Study the *Bill of Rights* of the *United States Constitution* and the freedoms it guarantees.	CG - 5
16C21	***Understanding the Times*** is the story of the Biblical Christian, Marxist/Lenninst and Secular Humanist Worldviews from Summit Ministries. It is a study designed especially for Christian high school and college students emphasizing the importance of understanding the Christian world view's relevance in an academic environment. Read through each chapter and write a summary on each world view in each subject: Theology, Philosophy, Ethics, Biology, Psychology, Sociology, Law, Politics, Economics, and History.	B - 1 credit H - 20 EC - 1 each summary
16C22	Use ***Kingfisher's Illustrated History of the World*** to read about education through history: Jewish (179), Renaissance (317), Harvard College (475), and the 20th Century (676).	H - 2
16C22	Use Usborne's ***World History Dates*** to read about people and events studied in this unit.	H - 1 each person or event

Reading and Literature

		Points
16R01	Watch the home schooling video *Foundation for Excellence.*	HF - 3
16R02	Read *The Right Choice: Home Schooling*.	HF - 5
16R03	Study the godly principles in child rearing by reading *Child Training in the Home School: A Legacy of Grace* by Jeff and Mary Barth.	HF - 5
16R04	Study about the New Age movement and occult practices in the public school system by reading *Thieves of Innocence* by John Ankerburg.	HF - 5
16R05	Read about the public school system from the Teacher of the Year's viewpoint by reading *Dumbing Us Down*.	HF - 5
16R06	Read *Learning Styles and Tools*. Take the learning styles test. Write a paper about the strengths and weaknesses of the type of learner you are.	HF - 10 EC - 2
16R07	Study and outline *What the Bible Says About Child Training*. Refer to *The Outline* (110-112) in *Writers INC.*	B - 3 HF - 3
16R08	Read *For the Children's Sake* by Susan Schaeffer Macauley.	HF - 5
16R09	Read and report on several (3-5) good how to books on home schooling.	HF - 5 each
16R10	Read James Dobson's *Dare to Discipline* and discuss with a parent its application to child training.	HF - 5 each
16R11	Read Jay Adam's *Competent to Counsel*.	HF - 5
16R12	Study *Home Grown Kids, Home Spun Schools*, and *Home Style Teaching* for an understanding of Dr. Raymond Moore's philosophy with regards to home education and delayed schooling.	HF - 5 each book
16R13	Read *Never Too Early* for the opposite viewpoint of #16R12.	HF - 5
16R14	Read biographies of famous people who were home taught.	H - 4 each
16R15	Read *The Fine Art of Mentoring*.	HF - 4
16R16	Read Valerie Bendt's *How to Create Your Own Unit Study*.	HF - 5

	Points

16R17 Read and critique a variety of magazine articles on parenting, education, and home schooling. Use Scripture to support your analysis.

HM - 2 each
B - 1 each

16R18 Read ***The Christian Home Educator's Curriculum Manual*** by Cathy Duffy or another guide to choosing home schooling methods and materials.

HF - 5

16R19 Read the story of a home school family, ***Our Reeds Grow Free***.

HF - 4

16R20 Read ***The Peanut Butter Family Home School*** by Bill Butterworth.

HF - 4

16R21 Use articles from *Teaching Home, Home Schooling Digest, Lifestyle of Learning, Home Schooling Today* or other home school magazines to write a report on an aspect of home schooling.

HF - 4
EC - 3

16R22 Read ***Training Children in Godliness***.

HF - 3
B - 2

16R23 Read the excellent novel ***Wisdom Hunter***.

L - 4
B - 2

16R24 Read ***Home Schooling for Excellence*** by David and Micki Colfax.

HF - 4

16R25 Read the second book about the home schooling family, the Colfaxs, ***Hard Times in Paradise***.

HF - 4

Composition

		Points
16W01	Continue making entries in your handwriting notebook started in #01W01. Include every Bible verse studied or memorized from this unit. ☺	EG - 1 B - 1 each page
16W02	Continue placing vocabulary words in the vocabulary notebook you started in #01W02. Add at least 10 new words per week. ☺	EG - 1 per 10 words
16W03	Continue your school journal started in #01W03. Review *Guidelines to Journal Writing* (470) in **Writers INC**. ☺	EC - 1 per week
16W04	Have someone dictate several paragraphs to you, using passages from books used in this unit. Proofread and correct the paragraphs.	EC - 1 per 3 paragraphs
16W05	Have someone dictate several Bible verses to you, using verses you have studied in this unit. Proofread and correct the verses.	EC - 1 per 3 verses
16W06	Write a paper comparing the advantages of a Christian curriculum and the harm from a secular curriculum. See #16C06.	EC - 3
16W07	After reading the suggested Bible verses and books, write a research paper on *The Biblical Basis for Home Schooling* or *The Biblical Responsibilities of Parents*. Refer to *Writing the Research Paper* (135-173) in **Writers INC**.	EC - 15
16W08	Write a Biblical analysis of one or more of the books read in this unit.	EC - 2 B - 2
16W09	Write a letter of advice a godly mother might write to her daughter who is now beginning to raise her own children.	EC - 2
16W10	Write a description of the kind of training you plan to give your children. Refer to *Writing* (135-173) in **Writers INC**.	EC - 3
16W11	Write a paper explaining the effect of public school on our nation.	EC - 3
16W12	Write a paper explaining the motivation of the founders of the public school movement: Robert Owen, Abram Combe, Horace Mann, and Robert Dale Owen. Use #16C03, #16C05 and other references.	EC - 5 H - 5
16W13	Write a paper comparing the philosophies of Raymond Moore and Doreen Claggett.	EC - 5
16W14	Write a poem paraphrasing Proverbs 4:1-9.	EC - 2
16W15	Write a child's fictional short story to teach a moral truth.	EC - 4

		Points
16W16	Write questions you would like to ask an older woman about the Christian life. Find someone and ask them.	EC - 2 HF - 2
16W17	Look up wisdom in Webster's 1828 dictionary, and compare the definition with the definition from a contemporary dictionary.	EC - 2
16W18	Look up education in Webster's 1828 dictionary, and compare the definition with the definition from a contemporary dictionary.	EC - 2
16W19	Take a spelling test using words from your spelling notebook. Look up the spelling rule for each word spelled incorrectly.	EG - 1 per 10
16W20	Define "disciple" and "discipleship" from Webster's 1828 dictionary.	EG - 1
16W21	Define "mentor" or "mentoring" from Webster's 1828 dictionary.	EG - 1
16W22	Proofread and correct spelling errors in all written work. Add any misspelled words to your spelling notebook.	EG - 2 per paper
16W23	Write thank you notes to anyone who helped you with this unit.	EC - 1 each
16W24	Write critiques of magazine articles read in this study.	EC - 1 each
16W25	Write reports on the lives of one or more of the famous home schoolers you studied.	EC - 2 each
16W26	Outline one or more of the books in the Reading and Literature section. Refer to *The Outline* (110-112) in **Writers INC**.	EC - 3 each
16W27	The most important part of selecting curriculum is finding out the publishers world view. Write a paper explaining on your world view. For information on world views refer to **Thinking Christianly**, **Stepping Stones to Curriculum**, or **Understanding the Times**.	EC -5
16W28	Speak to a homeschool support group about your homeschooling experience. Refer to *Speech Skills* (490) and *Preparing the Speech for Delivery* (516) in **Writers INC**.	EC - 5

Math and Personal Economics

		Points
16M01	Gather and study statistics on the academic progress of home-taught students and those in other types of school settings.	M - 3
16M02	Use those statistics to make various problems, reviewing ratios, proportions, and similar comparisons.	M - 2
16M03	Show the above statistics on one or more different types of graphs.	M - 3 per graph
16M04	Use above figures and/or test scores on various groups of students to find mean, mode, and median.	M - 2
16M05	Using directions that come with teacher testing materials or books on tests and measurements, learn to plot a bell curve using figures from above statistics or imaginary ones.	M - 5
16M06	To properly prepare for teaching others, complete your math knowledge with a good course in basic algebra and other needed courses.	M - 1 Credit per full year course
16M07	Learn and teach others to play **Muggins, Knock Out**, and other math games.	M - 3 per game

Science

		Points
16S01	Relate the book of Job to creation by studying ***Dinosaurs: Those Terrible Lizards***.	SB - 5
16S02	Watch and write reviews on a variety of creation science videos by the Institute for Creation Research, Builder Books, Moody Press, or others.	SB - 3 per video
16S03	Prepare and conduct one or more science lessons for young children, each involving at least one actual experiment.	SC, SP or SE - 5 each
16S04	Color and study the *The Tongue* (54-55) in ***Gray's Anatomy Coloring Book.***	HA - 2
16S05	Study the anatomy and physiology of various stages of child development.	HE - 5
16S06	At this stage in life, it may be wise to study evolution as it is taught in most secular schools, along with evidences which support Biblical teachings and refute evolution.	SB - 3
16S07	Use a good science book or experiment kit to study sound and sound waves.	SP - 5
16S08	Study the technology of radio, telephone, and other sound transfer equipment.	SP - 5
16S09	Direct one or more children in conducting one or more experiments from ***The Backyard Scientist***.	SP or SC - 2 each
16S10	Draw a flow chart explaining some scientific process in terms that can be easily understood by young children.	SP or SC - 5
16S11	Read and outline *The Brain and Nervous System* (46-73) in ***ABC's of the Human Body*** by Reader's Digest. Refer to *The Outline* (110-112) in ***Writers INC***.	HA - 5
16S12	Color and study about the brain and nervous system (40-45 and 116-117) in ***Gray's Anatomy Coloring Book.***	HA - 2 each section completed
16S13	Do research and write a paper on the brain and nervous system from the encyclopedia or other sources. Refer to *Writing to Learn* (473-474) in ***Writers INC***.	HA - 4 EC - 2
16S14	There is true mental illness caused by physical problems in the brain. Many times emotional problems, unconfessed sin, or harmful habits are treated as mental illness. Find out how to distinguish true Biblical counseling from standard psychology by reading ***Addicted to Recovery***.	B - 2

Health and Physical Fitness

		Points
16H01	Study the various types of learning styles and the best methods for teaching each type.	HF - 5
16H02	Using a physical education teacher's book, camp manual, material from Boy or Girl Scouts, or any of several books on recreation, learn several fitness games which are appropriate to teach to children of different ages. Prepare a file of 8-10 games for each age group.	PE - 2 per game up to 20 per age for 3 ages
16H03	Lead or direct a group of children, any age, in a sport or organized game which includes rules and the teaching of at least some skills.	PE - 5 HF - 2
16H04	Study about various handicaps and/or learning disabilities and how they affect a child's ability to learn.	HE - 4
16H05	Research ways to teach children with each of the disabilities above.	HE - 3
16H06	Use a good herb guide and/or nutrition books to determine what foods in the diet affect the brain and mental acuity.	HE - 4
16H07	Using a **Physician's Desk Reference** or medical encyclopedia study the effects and side effects of Ritalin and other drugs which are often prescribed for children with ADD and other learning disabilities.	HE - 2
16H08	Study the medical benefits of a happy, cheerful outlook on life.	HE - 3

Practical Arts

		Points
16P01	Tutor a peer or younger child in some school subject in which you excel.	HF - 3 per hour to 5
16P02	Teach or show a peer or younger person how to do some skill at which you are good.	HF - 3 per activity max. 12
16P03	Teach a child how to make something.	HM - 3
16P04	Attend one or more home school conferences and sit in on the parents' sessions.	HF - 25 each
16P05	Listen to tapes or watch videos by Greg Harris, Jonathan Lindvall, Karl Reed, Mary Pride or other Christian home educators.	HF - 3 per tape
16P06	Spend time on a regular basis with one or more young children and develop a close relationship with them.	HF - 1 per hour up to a total of 25
16P07	Organize and teach a child's Bible study class or Good News Club.	B - 10
16P08	Work as a teacher or helper in Vacation Bible school.	B - 15 per week
16P09	Serve as a counselor in a Christian summer camp or day camp.	PE - 50 per week
16P10	Study *The Christian Counselor's Manual* to find advice for specific problems which you or other young people may face and learn how to counsel someone from Scripture.	B - 8
16P11	Take a course in lay Christian counseling through your church, local counseling center, Christian college, the 700 Club, or special interest ministries such as CPC's or homeless shelters.	B - 20 HF - 10
16P12	Volunteer as a counselor for a Crisis Hotline, some Christian ministry listed above, or a similar group.	B - 5 per week
16P13	Prepare and present a Bible object lesson for young children.	HF - 2 B - 2
16P14	Volunteer to visit and read the Bible or other literature to blind or invalid patients at a hospice or nursing home.	L - 2 HF - 2 per visit
16P15	Prepare and lead a Bible study, for girls, on one of Paul's epistles.	B - 10 one lesson

	Points
16P16 Prepare a resource file and/or center of materials to use in teaching school subjects in a Biblical manner.	HM - 10
16P17 Prepare a unit study on any topic of interest to be used with a specific age of a child. Be sure to include activities for each learning style and adequately cover all needed subjects.	HF - 25 EC - 10
16P18 Develop one original educational game and teach it to someone else.	HF - 10
16P19 Teach a child some academic facts through the use of an educational song.	HF - 5
16P20 Prepare a file of catalogs and other materials from various suppliers of educational materials.	BE - 5
16P21 With your mother's plans to follow as a guide, make lesson plans for one week for a real or imaginary student from books, workbooks, and teacher's manuals of your choice.	HF - 10
16P22 Attend a workshop or class on how to use Konos, Weaver, Alta Vista, or other unit study program.	HF - 8
16P23 Attend a workshop or class to learn how to make your own unit study.	HF - 10

Creative and Performing Arts

		Points
16A01	Write an original song to use for teaching some academic fact or concept to younger children. Use an original or existing tune.	MA - 8
16A02	Draw pictures of happy family scenes.	VA - 2
16A03	Use calligraphy skills to make posters or plaques of one or more of the Scripture passages studied in this unit.	VA - 4 per poster
16A04	Draw a mural or make a collage to show the many aspects of nurturing.	VA - 4
16A05	Draw an original design for a T-shirt extolling the virtues of home education.	VA - 5
16A06	Design an original cover for your unit study.	VA - 3
16A07	Design and create one or more posters, bulletin boards, or other original visual aids to use in the Sunday school or Bible school class with which you work.	VA - 15 each bulletin board
16A08	Draw illustrations for each of the sections in your unit study.	VA - 2 each
16A09	Design and create one original craft and teach it to children in VBS or camp.	VA - 5 HF - 3
16A10	Create a poster or bulletin board display to help teach some academic subject.	HF - 3 VA - 5
16A11	Learn to play and/or sing several educational songs to be shared with young children.	MA - 3
16A12	Copy the pictures from *Bible Visual Resource Book* to make a timeline for major Bible events.	B - 1 per picture
16A13	Create a book with one of the following titles: *Education, Education Through History, Wisdom, The Brain and Nervous System, Home Schooling, or Child Training.* This can be a simple notebook that includes all the reports and art work during this unit or a bound story book written as a nonfiction book. You may include text and illustrations as you desire. Points will depend on the subject you choose and the amount of time spent on this project. Share the book with someone.	Parents Discretion

Unit 17 ❦

"She looketh well to the ways of her household and
eateth not the bread of idleness."

Proverbs 31:27

Introduction to Unit 17

This unit is the most comprehensive of all as it covers all aspects of home-making and family life not addressed in any other unit. Our studies will be aimed at identifying and meeting the needs of your family and caring for your home. Looking well to the ways of one's household implies a thorough understanding of all types of needs, including the spiritual, physical, and emotional, and a plan to meet them. We will provide the tools to prepare you for this task now and in your family of the future. We will study the need for diligence and the dangers of laziness as outlined in the Scriptures.

While studying diligence we'll have a chance to study the men and women who "looked unto the ways of their household" by traveling west during the westward movement in America. We will look at The Gold Rush, The Oregon Trail and everyday life of the settlers.

This unit takes a look at governmental and private agencies which offer services designed to help you manage and meet the various needs of your household. We will examine these programs and see which are and are not consistent with Biblical directives concerning the proper roles of government, church, and family. We will learn how to lobby and petition the government for help in those areas where it is needed but not forthcoming. We will also examine the laws and regulations which directly affect the running of your home and the well-being of your family, comparing them to the rules and commands of God to see if there are any conflicts.

We will offer you opportunities and suggestions for learning how to do all of the mundane but necessary jobs which go into running a house and caring for a family. You will learn how and when to do a wide variety of household chores and will be encouraged and given directions to organize these tasks so they will not be so easily forgotten and can be more easily accomplished. We will include some instruction in basic household plumbing, wiring, and appliance repair. We are not trying to make plumbers, repairmen, or electricians of our students, but we want you to know basic maintenance and enough about the problems to talk intelligently with a repairman.

Bible

		Points
17B01	Read your Bible daily as started in #01B01. You can read the Bible through each year by reading three chapters each day or by following the Daily Bible Reading Schedule in **The Narrated Bible.** ☺	B - 1 per 7 chapters
17B02	Examine Proverbs 31:27 in several versions, then list everything in a household you think would be included in this.	B - 2
17B03	Study the practical advice in Proverbs 18:30.	B - 1 as parent sees fit
17B04	Memorize as much of the book of Proverbs as possible.	B - 2 per week up to 20
17B05	Study what the Bible says about prayer by reading and outlining **The Kneeling Christian**. Refer to *The Outline* (110-112) in **Writers INC.**	B - 5 EC - 3
17B06	To look well to the spiritual needs of your family, do an in-depth study of the Beatitudes and look for ways you need to improve in those areas.	B - 8
17B07	Complete a study of the rest of the Sermon on the Mount following the pattern of #17B06 above.	B - 8
17B08	Study and memorize Proverbs 6:6-11.	B - 5
17B09	Begin a specific prayer list for the particular needs of your family. Pray regularly for each family member and for ways you can help meet the needs of each.	B - 4
17B10	Using a good commentary or a study guide, take an in-depth look at the Lord's Prayer as a pattern for your own talks with the Lord.	B - 5
17B11	Use a concordance to find and study all verses in Proverbs which talk about the evils of being lazy or a sluggard.	B - 2 each
17B12	Memorize one or more of the above verses.	B - 2 each
17B13	Look up the following verses: Proverbs 15:17; 17:1; 21:19; 24:3-4; 25:24. Write a paragraph explaining how important attitude is in keeping the home.	B - 2 each EC - 2
17B14	Define hospitality and make a list of ways you can show hospitality in your home.	B - 1 HF - 1

Far Above Rubies © 1995

Cultural Studies

		Points
17C01	Study city building codes, deed restrictions, noise/litter ordinances, and other local laws that directly affect your family and home, making sure you are complying with them.	CG - 10 for thorough research
17C02	Research and list all government services which directly affect your family, including such things as roads, garbage pickup, water service, etc. Try to be as thorough as possible.	CG - 5
17C03	Analyze the above services to determine which are or are not authorized in Scripture for civil government.	CG - 10
17C04	Study the career options available in your community which are of service to families. List as many jobs as possible and their duties.	CG - 6
17C05	Study the requirements for holding various public offices and how the office holders are chosen. Include such offices as tax collector, judge, and police chief as well as more visible jobs.	CG - 2
17C06	Familiarize yourself with the political system in your state and/or city and learn how to lobby on issues of importance to you and/or your family.	CG - 5
17C07	Search for and learn about groups actively involved in lobbying or providing other political support for Christian families.	CG - 3
17C08	Attend a meeting of your city council, county commission, school board, or other local governmental agencies.	CG - 2
17C09	Attend a state legislative session at which a topic of special interest to your family is being discussed.	CG - 2
17C10	List and study non-governmental agencies offering support services to families in your area.	CG - 3
17C11	Study your church programs and how they encourage or defeat family goals. Find a Biblical basis (if there is one) to justify each program.	B - 2
17C12	Attend public hearings on issues important to your family.	CG - 3
17C13	Read about westward movement and events in other countries during that time in *Kingfisher's Illustrated World History* (612-636).	H - 5
17C14	Study volume 1, chapter 2 on *Family Government* in **God and Government**.	CG - 8

	Points
17C15 Study your state's laws regarding the age of majority and parental responsibility for minor children.	CG - 3
17C16 Tour city hall and/or your county courthouse, with a guide, to explain the activities of city government.	CG - 2
17C17 Listen to the tape *History Alive Through Music: Westward Ho!*	H - 1
17C18 Find out when the Pony Express started and how long it lasted.	H - 1
17C19 Watch a video about pioneers, covered wagons or the Oregon Trail.	H - 1
17C20 Listen to the tapes about the westward movement in *America: The First 350 Years*.	H - 1
17C21 The Oregon Trail extended over 2,000 miles from Independence, Missouri, to the Columbia River in Oregon. Draw a map showing the Oregon Trail.	G -2
17C22 Play the computer game *Oregon Trail.*	H - 1 each
17C23 Read *Liberty for All*, book five of the *History of US* series. It includes the stories of: Davy Crockett, John Quincy Adams, Emily Dickenson, Sojourner Truth, John James Audubon, and Dred Scott.	H - 5
17C24 Read *Story of the Great American West* by Reader's Digest. A detailed book full of photos about 1780's to the 1870's in America. Includes: The coming of the Europeans, Encountering the Indians, the Mississippi by Foot, Wagon and Boats, Mountain Men and Fur Trappers, Louisiana Purchase, Custer's Last Stand, Yellowstone, Across the Rockies by Prairie schooner, The Gold Rush, Civil War conflicts, The Transcontinental Railroad, Cowboys and Cattle Kings, Settling the Plains, and much more. Dozens of quotes and 133 biographical sketches of men such as: Daniel Boone, Abraham Lincoln, Tecumseh, Geronimo, and John Muir.	H - 10
17C25 Do research about any of the events or people listed in #17C23 or #17C24. Write a summary paragraph about each.	H - 1 each EC - ½
17C26 Do research to find out about the Indians in the 1800's. Write a mini report about 5 different tribes.	H - 1 each
17C27 Watch a video or read a book about the life of a cowboy on a ranch in the 1800's.	H - 2
17C28 Do research and write an essay about the Lewis and Clark expedition.	H - 2

Reading and Literature

		Points
17R01	Read and outline *Sidetracked Home Executive*.	HM - 4
17R02	Read *Clutter's Last Stand* and another book by Don Aslett.	HM - 4 each
17R03	Read any remaining sections of *The Hidden Art of Homemaking* by Edith Schaeffer.	HM - 2
17R04	Read Edith Schaeffer's *What is a Family?*	HF - 4
17R05	Read for enjoyment *Cheaper by the Dozen*.	L - 4
17R06	Read and outline *The Happy Home Handbook*.	HM - 4
17R07	For help in taking control in the area of family finance, read *What Husbands Wish Their Wives Knew About Money* by Larry Burkett.	BE - 3
17R08	To spur your thinking in the area of political and social action on behalf of your family, read *A Christian Manifesto* by Francis Schaeffer, and discuss it with your parents or other Christian adults.	B - 4
17R09	Read *The California Gold Rush*.	H - 3
17R10	Read poetry by Henry David Thoreau and Ralph Waldo Emmerson.	L - 1 each
17R11	Read a biography about Lewis and Clark.	H - 3
17R12	Read *Little Women* by Lousia May Alcott.	L - 3
17R13	Read poetry by Henry Wadsworth Longfellow.	L - 1 each
17R14	Read *The Mentor Book of Major American Poets*.	L - 5
17R15	Read *Great American Short Stories*.	L - 5
17R16	Read about the Lewis and Clark Expedition in *Streams to the River, River to the Sea*.	L - 4 H - 2
17R17	Read *Custer and Crazy Horse*.	L - 3 H - 2
17R18	Read *Pioneers Go West*.	H - 3
17R19	Read a story about the early railroad.	H - 3

Composition

	Points

17W01 Continue making entries in your handwriting notebook started in #01W01. Include every Bible verse studied or memorized from this unit. ☺

EG - 1
B - 1 each page

17W02 Continue placing vocabulary words in the notebook you started in #01W02. Add at least 10 new words per week. ☺

EG - 1
per 10 words

17W03 Continue adding to your school journal started in #01W03. Review *Journal Writing* (470-471) in **Writers INC**. ☺

EC - 1
per week

17W04 Have someone dictate several paragraphs to you using passages from books used in this unit. Proofread and correct the paragraphs. Refer to *Proofreader's Guide* (600-714) in **Writers INC**.

EC - 1 per 3
paragraphs

17W05 Have someone dictate several Bible verses to you, using verses you have studied in this unit. Proofread and correct the verses.

EC - 1 per 3
verses

17W06 Write letters to lawmakers or other officials on issues affecting your life. Refer to *Writing a Business Letter* (412) in **Writers INC**.

EC - 1 each
CG - 1 each

17W07 Copy the Beatitudes several times in your best handwriting and/or calligraphy.

VA - 3 each
B - 1 each

17W08 Write a public service spot explaining some service available in your town, giving phone number and fees, if any.

EC - 2

17W09 Write a paper analyzing the services offered by government agencies in your area, giving Biblical evidence as to whether each is or is not a legitimate function of civil government.

EC - 2
CG - 2
B - 2

17W10 Write a letter to your church governing body suggesting a new program or a change to an existing one which would help meet your family's needs.

EC - 2

17W11 Write a research paper or major report on one of the professions offering service to your community. Include requirements, duties, schooling, and/or licenses needed, numbers of jobs available, etc. Review *Writing the Research Paper* (135-173) in **Writers INC**.

EC - 10
CG - 10

17W12 Outline one or more of the books in this unit. Refer to *The Outline* (110-112) in **Writers INC**.

EC - 3 each

17W13 Write letters to various agencies for information about services and fees.

EC - 1 each

	Points

17W14 Take a spelling test using words from your spelling notebook. Look up the spelling rule for each word spelled incorrectly.

EG - 1 per 10

17W15 Look up any prefixes, suffixes, and roots of new vocabulary words. Refer to section 446-448 in **Writers INC**.

EG - 1 per 10 words

17W16 Write reports on all field trips. For organization and clarifying ideas refer to *Writing About Place* (120) in **Writers INC**.

EC - 2 each

17W17 Write an essay giving what you believe to be the meaning of the verse studied in this unit. Refer to *Writing Essays* (105-118) in **Writers INC**.

EC - 3
B - 2

17W18 Proofread and correct all grammar and punctuation errors in all written work. Refer to *Proofreader's Guide* (600-714) in **Writers INC**.

EG - 1 per page

17W19 Proofread and correct spelling errors in all written work. Add any misspelled words to your spelling notebook.

EG - 1 per paper

17W20 Scan the section *Improving Sentence Style* (058-082) in **Writers INC**. Review papers you or someone else has written. Find and correct one of each of the following: sentence fragment, comma splice, run on sentence, rambling sentence, and incomplete sentence.

EG - ¼ each sentence corrected

17W21 Henry David Thoreau, James Fenimore, Henry Wadsworth Longfellow, and Ralph Waldo Emmerson were great authors during the 1800's. Write a few paragraphs about each of them.

EC - ¼ each

17W22 Write a poem about the Oregon Trail.

EC - 2

17W23 Scan the section *Using the Right Word* (715-837) in **Writers INC**. Choose 10 words. Write a paragraph using each of the words. Include affect, effect, counsel, council, desert, dessert, heard and herd. Refer to this section any time you have a usage question.

EG - 1

17W24 Write a letter to a friend as if you were a girl traveling on a prairie schooner with a wagon train on the Oregon Trail. Describe your trip in detail. Explain what you took with you on the trip.

EC - 1
H - 1

17W25 Write a newspaper advertisement for the first train ride. Remember the steamboat is your biggest competition.

EC - 1

17W26 Write a letter as if you were living in California in the 1800's trying to persuade a friend to move to California from the East.

EC - 1

Math and Personal Economics

		Points
17M01	Keep a schedule of actual activities engaged in by different members of the family for a month. At the end of that time, find what percentage of each person's time is spent in different types of activities.	M - 7 HM - 3
17M02	Chart the above activities on one or more types of graphs.	M - 3 each
17M03	Time a number of different cleaning tasks done in different ways and chart the amount of time saved by doing each in the most efficient manner.	M - 2 HM - 3
17M04	Prepare a graph showing the amount of time spent in each household chore.	M - 3
17M05	Pay your family's bills for a month. If you cannot actually write the checks, plan the payments and figure the total expenses.	M - 10 BE - 5
17M06	Keep track of your family's grocery bill for one month and find ways to reduce it.	M - 5 BE - 5
17M07	Make a budget for your family and try to keep your family's expenses within it for a minimum of six months. You will probably need to enlist your parents' involvement in this activity.	M - 7 BE - 5 CE - 5

Science

17S01 From the book *Formulas, Tips, and Household Cleaners*, learn the household uses of common chemicals.

SC - 3

17S02 From a good how-to book, learn about the makeup of your family's plumbing system and how each part operates.

SP - 3

17S03 By reading the owner's manuals, other books, or through asking someone else to teach you, learn about the appliances in your home and how each operates.

SP - 2 each

17S04 This is a good point at which to include a chemistry course if you and/or your parents wish. It is a required course if you plan on attending college.

SC - 1 Credit

17S05 Using information from the manufacturers or your local building supply store, study different types of insulation and how they work.

SP - 3

17S06 Study a good how-to guide to learn the basics of household electricity and how to avoid electrical hazards.

SP - 3

17S07 Arrange with your utility company for an energy analysis of your home and discuss their findings with your family, making arrangements to correct any problems found.

SP - 3
SE - 2

17S08 Study the landfill and/or other solid waste facilities in your community and find out what their capacity is, how close they are to it, and what alternate measures are being considered.

SE - 3

17S09 Learn about the benefits of recycling various types of products and the best procedures for doing so.

SE - 3

Health and Physical Fitness

		Points
17H01	List all prescription drugs normally taken by members of your family and find as much information as possible about the purpose, chemical contents, and effects of each.	SC - 3 HE - 3
17H02	Study any allergies and/or chronic illnesses which affect members of your family and all preventive and/or treatment measures you can take at home.	HE - 5
17H03	Study immunizations, pro and con, by reading books and articles on both sides of the issue. Make a decision about whether or not you plan to have them given to your children.	HE - 2
17H04	Take a first aid or basic nursing or home health care course through the Red Cross, a hospital, or an adult continuing education program.	HE - 1/2 credit
17H05	Learn about home remedies and over-the-counter measures which can be used for common illnesses and ailments.	HE - 1 per illness up to 10
17H06	Investigate homeopathy, chiropractic, and other alternatives to traditional medical care. You can find information on these at health food stores, the Seventh Day Adventist Church, or other groups. Members of your home school support group may have information on these topics.	HE - 8
17H07	Look well to your family's health by monitoring nutrition and exercise needs of each member and working with others to correct deficiencies.	HE - 3 per family member

Practical Arts

		Points
17P01	Learn to clean and maintain any and all appliances in your home.	CR - 2 each
17P02	Learn to clean out and defrost (if needed) your refrigerator and freezer and/or dump and clean the drip pan.	HM - 3
17P03	Learn to clean a refrigerator and/or freezer coils.	HM - 1
17P04	Learn to sweep, mop, and scrub all tile or vinyl floors in your home, using the right materials and cleaning products.	HM - 3 each type
17P05	Learn to strip and apply wax on all wood floors in your home.	HM - 5
17P06	Learn to spot clean various types of stains on your carpet and/or upholstery using the recommended products for each type of fabric.	HM - 2 each type
17P07	Learn the correct way to repair and/or re-cover upholstered furniture by using a good book on the subject or taking a course at a community college, adult education class or through a local upholsterer.	CR - 25
17P08	Learn to wash dishes by hand, including special care required for crystal, china, cast iron, etc.	HM - 1
17P09	Learn to use and clean a vacuum cleaner.	HM - 1
17P10	Learn to load, unload, use, and care for a dishwasher.	HM - 1
17P11	Learn to change sheets and make beds.	HM - 2
17P12	Learn the correct way to sweep and/or dust mop wood floors.	HM - 1
17P13	Using a book on the subject or user instructions from the flooring manufacturer or installer, learn to refinish and care for wood floors, paneling, and furniture.	HM - 8
17P14	Read *File Don't Pile*.	HM - 5
17P15	Read *Organize Yourself*.	HM - 5
17P16	Become adept at doing family laundry, learning to sort garments, pre-treat spots, and choose correct temperature for each type of garment.	HM - 5
17P17	Learn how and when to use bleach, fabric softener, etc. and what types to use for different garments.	HM - 1 each type
17P18	Learn to mend rips, tears, and pulled out seams on your family's clothing.	HM - 3

		Points
17P19	Learn to replace broken zippers in all types of garments.	HM - 3
17P20	Develop a system for your family to see that mending gets done on a regular schedule as needed.	HM - 1
17P21	Arrange and organize the drawers in your dresser in a way which will make it easier and faster for you to put away your things and to find an item you need.	HM - 3
17P22	Arrange and organize one or more cabinets or cupboards in your kitchen in a way which will make it easier and faster for you to put away your things and to find an item you need.	HM - 3
17P23	Arrange and organize your family's storage area in a way which will make it easier and faster to put away things and to find an item you need.	HM - 5
17P24	Learn to iron all garments worn regularly by members of your family.	HM - 1 each
17P25	Learn to oil, maintain, and properly care for your sewing machine.	CR - 4
17P26	Work with each family member to organize his or her time in a more productive manner for the following month. If some family members protest, skip theirs. Your own is the most important.	BE - 2 HM - 2 per person
17P27	Learn to replace buttons on clothing.	HM - 2
17P28	Learn to alter hem lengths on pants, skirts, and dresses and to replace pulled out hems.	HM - 3

Creative and Performing Arts

		Points
17A01	Use calligraphy to create a poster or plaque from one or more of the verses you have memorized in this unit.	VA - 5
17A02	Use calligraphy to make a poster of the Beatitudes.	VA - 5
17A03	Use any decorative art or art medium of your choice to illustrate your poster of the Beatitudes.	VA - 5
17A04	Draw pictures to illustrate your reports on field trips.	VA - 3 each
17A05	Make a collage showing all the variety of activities included in this verse this unit is based on.	VA - 5
17A06	Create and direct or perform a skit to go with your public service announcement.	DR - 10
17A07	Write a cowboy song.	MA - 1
17A08	John Audubon was an artist that lived from 1785 to 1851. He drew portraits of American nature. Do research to see some of his paintings. Write a report about him.	VA - 1 EC - 1
17A09	Create a book with one of the following titles: *Westward Movement, Government,* or *Home Making.* This can be a simple notebook that includes all the reports and art work during this unit or a bound story book written as a nonfiction book. You may include text and illustrations as you desire. Points will depend on the subject you choose the amount of time spent on this project. Share the book with someone.	Parents Discretion

Unit 18

"Her children arise and call her blessed;"

Proverbs 31:28a

Introduction to Unit 18

This unit deals with a mother's relationship and responsibility toward her children. We will look at Biblical examples of good mothers and the effects they had on their offspring. We will study Proverbs and other passages of Scripture which address this issue, from both the mother's and child's viewpoint. We will look at instructions to parents for training and nurturing children and commands to children with regard to their attitude toward and treatment of parents.

This unit covers state regulations and local ordinances relating to child abuse, adoption, and child care. Birth certificates and standards for medical personnel who deliver babies will also be discussed. We will deal with abortion, strictly from a Christian perspective, as the sin we believe the Bible teaches it to be. Also studied in this unit are the various governmental and para-governmental agencies which offer services to families with children.

We will read a number of books about families, family life, and children in various eras and situations. Our reading will include a number of instruction or self-improvement type books on child rearing, teaching, and childbirth.

Health and practical arts will deal with a wide variety of materials and activities relating to child rearing and child development. We also discuss the medical issues relating to pregnancy and childbirth as well as mother and infant nutrition.

Bible

		Points
18B01	Read your Bible daily as started in #01B01. You can read the Bible through each year by reading three chapters each day or by following the Daily Bible Reading Schedule in *The Narrated Bible.* ☺	B - 1 per 7 chapters
18B02	Study the lives of Hannah and her son Samuel from the book of First Samuel.	B - 3
18B03	Study all Biblical references to Lois and Eunice and their influences on Timothy.	B - 2
18B04	Study Biblical references to Mary, the mother of Jesus, and try to develop a picture of the kind of mother she was.	B - 4
18B05	Research other Biblical mothers and show the ways in which they helped or hindered the spiritual development of their children.	B - 1 each up to 10
18B06	Use a concordance to find and read all verses in Proverbs which refer to things which are a blessing or a source of joy or pride to a mother.	B - 5
18B07	Write a summary paragraph about God's hand in childbirth using the following verses: Job 10:8-12, Ps 71:6, 139:13-16, Eccles 11:5 and Jer 1:5.	B - 5 EC - 3
18B08	Read the following verses about parents praying for their children: Gen 17, 18-20, II Sam 12:16, and Job 1:5.	B - 5
18B09	Use the concordance to cross-reference each of the traits referred to in #18B05 to find instructions for instilling them in a child.	B - 8
18B10	Study all passages of Scripture which refer to children as a blessing of the Lord.	B - 8
18B11	Memorize one or more of the verses in #18B07 or #18B08.	B - 2 each
18B12	Study Jochebed the mother of Moses, Aaron, and Miriam.	B - 2
18B13	Read and outline *What the Bible Says about Child Training*.	B - 3
18B14	Memorize Proverbs 22:6 and Proverbs 29:15-17.	B - 2 each
18B15	Compare Hannah's prayer: I Sam 2:1-10 and Mary's song: Luke 1:46.	B - 2

Cultural Studies

		Points
18C01	Continue adding to the timeline started in Unit 1. Prepare an entry for each person or event studied in this unit. ☺	H - 1 VA - 1 each
18C02	Learn about your state's regulation of home births, birth certificates, mid-wifery, and other things relating to childbirth.	CG - 3
18C03	Study your state's laws regulating or otherwise related to daycare facilities.	CG - 3
18C04	Investigate your state's child abuse laws, giving close attention to what kind of things constitute abuse, what evidence is needed to bring charges, who has jurisdiction in such cases, what sentences are given for offenses, and how cases are handled.	CG - 3
18C05	Study your state's laws concerning adoptions and foster care.	CG - 3
18C06	Study the court cases of Roe v. Wade, Webster v. Reproductive Health, and others which have had an impact on the availability of abortions in this country.	CG - 2
18C07	Investigate and study any laws in your state which restrict or regulate abortions or the abortion industry.	CG - 3
18C08	Interview your state legislator or one of his or her staff members for information on any current bills relating to any of the above areas. Discuss the issues and find out how he or she stands on each one. Determine your own stand on each, based on Biblical principles.	CG - 5
18C09	Lobby your legislators and/or Congressmen on behalf of any bills you favor relating to abortions, child abuse, and other issues with regard to children or family relationships.	CG - 3 each issue and effort up to 12 total
18C10	Study the various services offered by your state's Human Services, Human Resources, or similar department. Analyze each service in light of the Scriptural role of government.	CG - 5
18C11	Study the increase of crime, abortion, drug use, and immorality since this nation began separating religious practices from public affairs in 1962 by reading *America: To Pray or Not to Pray*.	CG - 5
18C12	Interview a case worker from your state's agency which deals with child abuse and family welfare. Find out how they perceive their jobs and what they do.	CG - 3

		Points
18C13	Study foster care agencies operating in your area and the programs they offer.	CG - 3
18C14	Investigate all adoption agencies that operate in your area. Contrast and compare them with regard to philosophy, attitude toward children and birth parents, and procedures used.	CG - 3
18C15	Interview several working parents who use different types of child care. Find out what parents like and dislike about each.	CG - 1 per family
18C16	Study the history and social effects of abortion on demand in this country.	H - 3
18C17	Study the lives of famous adopted children.	H - 2 each
18C18	As you study people or events in this unit, write each item on a 3 x 5 card along with the corresponding date or time period, illustrate appropriately, and add to timeline in chronological order.	H - 1 each VA - 1 each
18C19	Study the historical period of each event or person in this unit and add to the timeline all major events from each era.	H - 1 each VA - 1 each
18C20	Make timeline entries for any major historical event mentioned in any of the books used in this study.	H - 1 each VA - 1 each
18C21	Investigate and list the various types of child care services in your community. Find out eligibility requirements, standards, and fees of each type.	CG - 3
18C22	Read **Birth Customs.**	H - 2
18C23	Do research or read **Child Influencers**. Make a chart showing the drastic change of the amount of time children spent with parents, reading, religious instruction, peers, chores, and television. in the 17th century and today.	H - 2 HM - 4

Reading and Literature

		Points

18R01   Study ***The Joy of Natural Childbirth*** with your parents. Includes: Physical, and spiritual aspects of childbirth, common fears and misconceptions, prenatal nutrition, preparation, contemporary birthing practices, breast feeding advice, family centered child care, husbands role in pregnancy, birth and parenting, childbirth through the ages, childbirth in the Bible, and extensive bibliography. **PARENTS**: see note on page 26.
     HA - 4

18R02   Read ***Under the Apple Tree***. It includes a wealth of information about marriage, natural childbirth, natural family planning, breastfeeding and parenting from a Christian perspective.
     HE - 2
     HA - 2
     HF - 2

18R03   Read ***Susanna Wesley*** and biographies of other women who are famous primarily because of their children.
     H - 4 per book

18R04   Study the godly principles in child rearing by reading ***Child Training in the Home School: A Legacy of Grace*** by Jeff and Mary Barth.
     HF - 5

18R05   Read ***Abortion and the Conscience of a Nation*** by Ronald Reagan.
     CG - 4

18R06   Read the novel ***Weeping in Ramah***, which presents a logical future for a nation which encourages abortion on demand. (Contains some graphic material and may be objectionable to some parents.)
     L - 4

18R07   Read ***Abortion Letters I, II, and III***.
     CG - 2 each volume

18R08   Read and memorize poems totaling 50-60 lines written to or in honor of mothers.
     L - 5

18R09   Read and memorize poems totaling at least 50-60 lines about children or childhood.
     L - 5

18R10   Read ***A Full Quiver: Family Planning and the Lordship of Christ***. Discuss this book with your parents.
     HF - 5
     B - 2

18R11   Read ***Letting God Plan Your Family***. Discuss the book with your parents.
     HF - 5
     B - 2

18R12   Read biographies of famous people who were adopted children.
     L - 4

	Points
18R13 Study the influence of television on children by reading ***Saturday Morning Mind Control***.	HF - 5
18R14 Read biographies about Mother Teresa and other women who "mothered" homeless orphaned children. Do not duplicate any books used in other units.	L - 1 H - 3 per book
18R15 Read ***The Shaping of a Christian Family***.	HF - 5
18R16 Study the occult dangers, through media and other influences, on children in today's world by reading ***Lambs To the Slaughter***.	HF - 5
18R17 Read how God miraculously provided for the orphaned children in the ***Autobiography of George Muller***.	L - 2 H - 3
18R18 Study the influence of television, peers, parents and schools on children by reading ***The Child Influencers***. Copy or make your own charts from the charts and illustrations in the book showing the drastic change of the amount of time children spent with parents in the 17th century and today.	HF - 5
18R19 Read a variety of short stories written and set in different countries and depicting mothers and mother/child relationships in those areas.	L - 1 each
18R20 Read ***Little Women***, paying special attention to the relationship of the mother with each of her daughters.	L - 5
18R21 Read ***Five Little Peppers and How They Grew***, looking at the various family relationships.	L - 5
18R22 Read ***Parents' Rights*** by John Whitehead.	CG - 4
18R23 Read ***The Child Abuse Industry***.	CG - 4
18R24 Read ***Home By Choice*** by Brenda Hunter.	HF - 4
18R25 Read and thoroughly study ***The Way Home*** and its sequel ***All the Way Home***.	HF - 5 each book
18R26 Read ***A Chance to Die: The Biography of Amy Carmichael***.	L - 1 H - 3
18R27 Read the novel written by a pro-life activist that sounds the call for the return to righteousness in our nation, ***A Haunt of Jackals***. Based on Jer 9:7,11a.	L - 4

Composition

	Points
18W01 Continue making entries in your handwriting notebook started in #01W01. Include every Bible verse studied or memorized from this unit. ☺	EG - 1 B - 1 each page
18W02 Continue placing vocabulary words in the notebook you started in #01W02. Add at least 10 new words per week. ☺	EG - 1 per 10 words
18W03 Continue adding to your school journal started in #01W03. Review *Journal Writing* (470-471) in *Writers INC*. ☺	EC - 1 per week
18W04 Have someone dictate several paragraphs to you using passages from books used in this unit. Proofread and correct the paragraphs. Refer to *Proofreader's Guide* (600-714) in *Writers INC*.	EC - 1 per 3 paragraphs
18W05 Have someone dictate several Bible verses, to you, using verses you have studied in this unit. Proofread and correct the verses.	EC - 1 per 3 verses
18W06 Look up and mark pronunciation, accent, syllables, etc. for all vocabulary.	EG - 1 per 10 words
18W07 Take a spelling test using words from your spelling notebook. Look up the spelling rule for each word spelled incorrectly.	EG - 1 per 10
18W08 Take a spelling test using words from your spelling notebook. Look up the spelling rule for each word spelled incorrectly.	EG - 1 per 10
18W09 Write a newspaper or magazine article on the selection of the lady described in Proverbs 31 as "Woman of the Year." Give her a name and personal data so you can write as if she is a real person.	EC - 2
18W10 Write a job recommendation for your mother or another godly homemaker, applying the skills acquired and used in the home to a job situation.	EC - 1
18W11 Write a paper on *What the Bible Says About Working Mothers*. Substantiate all your statements or conclusions with actual Scripture references. For organization and clarifying ideas refer to *Writing to Persuade* (125) in *Writers INC*.	EC - 4
18W12 Write a poem in honor of your mother or grandmother, recognizing the virtues and skills mentioned in Scripture.	EC - 2
18W13 Write a letter to your mother praising her godly virtues and expressing your love and admiration for her. Give it as a gift for Mother's Day or some other special occasion.	EC - 2

		Points

18W14   Write a fictional story in which the main female character is patterned after your own mother. Refer to *Writing the Short Story* (218-227) in **Writers INC**.   EC - 5

18W15   Proofread and correct all grammar and punctuation errors in all written work. Refer to *Proofreader's Guide* (600-714) in **Writers INC**.   EG - 1 each page

18W16   Rewrite Proverbs 31:10-31 in modern English to reflect activities and lifestyles more common to our modern world.   B - 2 / EC - 2

18W17   Write an essay on specific ways in which your mother has been a blessing to you. Refer to *Writing Essays* (105-118) in **Writers INC**.   EC - 3

18W18   Proofread and correct spelling errors in all written work. Add any misspelled words to your spelling notebook.   EC - 1 per paper

18W19   Use the library inter loan system to get several books about Susanna Wesley. Write a research paper about her, include a bibliography. Refer to *Writing the Research Paper* (135-173) in **Writers INC**.   EC - 1 per week

18W20   Interview several mothers. Ask how they encourage positive character qualities in their children. Record the answers and write a paper entitled *Encouraging Positive Character Qualities in Children*. Refer to *Interviewing* (238) in **Writers INC**.   EC - 3

18W21   Write an essay on what you believe is meant by "her children rise up and bless her."   EC - 3

18W22   Write a short story about a fictional family in which children are blessed by their mother and are a blessing to her. Refer to *Writing the Short Story* (218-227) in **Writers INC**.   EC - 5

18W23   Find and list the seven suggestions in **Writers INC** for writing an opening or lead paragraph.   EC - ¼

18W24   Read *Writing to Learn* (473) in **Writers INC**. Focus on activity #9. Write a sentence stating what you think an ideal mother would be like. On the next line answer the question "Why?" in a complete sentence. On the next line answer the question "Why?" Again, answer in a complete sentence. Keep going until you can't write anymore. Then re-read what you have written and write a paragraph about what you were thinking while you were writing.   EC - 2

Math and Personal Economics

18M01 Compare prices charged by month, week, day, and hour at various child care facilities using two or more different types of graphs.

M - 3 each graph

18M02 Compute mean, mode, and median weekly, monthly, and hourly rates for child care using figures in # 18M01.

M - 1

18M03 Find the amount per day or per hour parents are paying facility in # 18M01. FInd out what percentage of their paycheck pays for child care.

M - 3

18M04 Use the information in # 18M01 to compute percentage of differences in price between different facilities.

M - 2

18M05 Collect necessary statistics and prepare line graphs comparing level of live births, still births, and abortions in your state or locality.

M - 3 each graph

18M06 Prepare a line or pie graph showing the infant mortality rate in your state or locality and comparing the major causes of infant death.

M - 3

18M07 Prepare a bar graph to compare the birth rate and rate of infant deaths for mothers of different ages and social-economic groups.

M - 3

18M08 Prepare a bar graph to compare infant mortality rate in your state with several others in the country.

M - 3

18M09 Use any or all of the statistics from the above activities to compute ranges, averages, percentages, and proportion for as much practice as you and your parents feel you need.

Parents' discretion

Science

		Points
18S01	Study the anatomical and physiological development of babies from conception to birth.	HA - 5
18S02	Study a good basic guide to infant and child development.	HA - 5
18S03	Study the maternal instinct of a variety of animals and compare the amount of nurturing baby animals get and the time periods during which they are under the mother's care.	SB - 3
18S04	Watch the birth of one or more baby animals of different types.	SB - 2 each type
18S05	Incubate and hatch one or more eggs from a chicken, duck, or other bird.	SB - 2
18S06	Tour a zoo nursery and learn as much as you can about the way they care for the babies there.	SB - 2
18S07	Study the behavior of various animals with regard to their young and prepare a list of those animals in which the parents stay together and raise the young as a family.	SB - 5
18S08	Study books on child psychology to find studies and statistics to show the importance of snuggling, touching, and other forms of nurturing in the development of a baby.	HF - 5
18S09	Watch a documentary about animals and their young.	SB - 3
18S10	Read the ***Apple Tree Guide for Expectant Parents.*** This guide is to be used with a notebook, a Bible, a copy of ***Under the Apple Tree*** and ***The Joy of Natural Childbirth***. Its purpose is to guide the reader into a deeper relationship with Jesus Christ in all areas of her life as she prepares for the birth of a child.	HE - 1 HA -1 B - 1

Health and Physical Fitness

		Points
18H01	Study the physical and emotional effects of abortion on the mother.	HE - 3
18H02	Study pre-natal care from a good medical encyclopedia or a publication given by doctors to their pregnant patients.	HE - 3
18H03	Interview a midwife and an obstetrician and compare their views of the childbirth process and the care needed by the mother during pregnancy, labor, and delivery.	HE - 2 per interview
18H04	If it interests you, study further on the subject of midwifery.	Parents' discretion
18H05	Learn about common drugs used during labor and delivery, their uses, and dangers.	HE - 3
18H06	Study the medical problems often connected with childbirth and learn the best way to deal with each.	HE - 3
18H07	Study the advantages and disadvantages of breast feeding for both infant and mother.	HE - 3
18H08	Study childhood nutrition and diseases which may be related to food or nutrition or inadequacies thereof.	HE - 3
18H09	Study the nutritional needs of pregnant and nursing mothers.	HE - 3
18H10	Learn about common childhood diseases and their prevention and treatment.	HE - 3
18H11	Study both sides of the controversy on childhood immunizations and make an informed decision as to whether or not you will have your children immunized.	HE - 4
18H12	Take infant and child CPR at your local fire department, hospital, or Red Cross.	HE - 4
18H13	Learn to take the temperature of children of different ages.	HE - 2
18H14	Learn about different medication often given to babies and children and how to give them. (NEVER give any child medicine without his parent's or doctor's directions.)	HE - 3

Practical Arts

		Points
18P01	Learn to hold, feed, burp, change, dress, and bathe babies from newborn to toddler.	HM - 2
18P02	Baby-sit or play with at least one child of each age from infant to age ten.	HM - 1 per child
18P03	If you don't know children for #18P01 or #18P02, take a baby-sitting course through the Red Cross, 4-H, or local hospital.	HM - 10
18P04	Learn first aid for common childhood accidents and injuries.	HE - 1
18P05	Practice feeding an infant from a bottle.	HM - 1
18P06	Practice feeding an infant or toddler strained or pureed food with a spoon.	HM - 1
18P07	Learn to puree an assortment of foods so they can be eaten by babies or invalids.	HM - 1
18P08	Volunteer regularly in the church nursery or another children's program.	HE - 3
18P09	Learn several games for children of all ages and teach some to younger children.	PE - 2 per game
18P10	Using file cards or a loose leaf binder, make a file of children's games divided by age, skills needed or taught, where played, how many players, etc. Cross reference the various categories. Include directions and list of needed materials.	PE - 1 per card
18P11	Use throw-away materials to create a toy, game, or other craft for a young child and teach him or her how to use it.	CR - 3
18P12	Decorate and furnish a nursery or child's room in a home, doll house, or room box.	CR - 25
18P13	Knit, crochet, or sew blankets, quilts, afghans or similar items for a child's room.	HM - 10 each item
18P14	Make one or more items of baby clothing. If there are no babies in your family, give them as gifts, donate them to a children's ministry or Crisis Pregnancy Center.	HM - 5 each item

 Far Above Rubies © 1995

Creative and Performing Arts

		Points
18A01	Design and/or paint a mural or other wall decoration for a nursery or child's room.	VA - 25
18A02	Use calligraphy or other stencil painting to make a plaque or poster from this scripture verse or one of the ones you are memorizing.	VA - 5
18A03	Draw or paint one or more pictures that would be appropriate to hang in a child's room.	VA - 5
18A04	Create a special picture for your mother to express your love for her. Use the style, theme, and medium of your choice.	VA - 5
18A05	Use the poem you wrote or any suitable one to make a poster or plaque using calligraphy or another art form.	VA - 5
18A06	Compose a tune for the poem you wrote in honor of your mother or another poem of the same type.	MA - 5
18A07	Learn to sing one or more of your mother's favorite hymns and sing it for her at some special occasion or activity.	MA - 5
18A08	Learn to play any or all of the above songs on the musical instrument of your choice.	MA - 5 each
18A09	Create a book with one of the following titles: *Mothering, Parenting, Children, Child Training, Abortion, Bible Mothers,* or *Birth Through History*. This can be a simple notebook that includes all the reports and art work during this unit or a bound story book written as a nonfiction book. You may include text and illustrations as you desire. Points will depend on the subject you choose and the amount of time spent on this project. Share the book with someone.	Parents Discretion

Unit 19 ❦

.. her husband also, and he praiseth her. Many daughters have done virtuously, but thou excellest them all. Favour is deceitful, and beauty is vain: but a woman that feareth the LORD, she shall be praised.

Proverbs 31:28b-30

Introduction to Unit 19

In this unit, we will learn about praise as it applies to God and to the accomplishments of others. We will look at the importance of praising God in the life of a believer. We will also consider the effects of genuine praise offered to others for worthy endeavors and accomplishments, and the importance of giving such praise when it is deserved. We will also study the meaning of fearing the Lord and its value in the life of a Christian.

The content of the verse necessitates that we take another look at husband/wife relationships and especially at wives who created the aforementioned response in their husbands. We will look at the lives of women from the Bible and other historical periods who could be said to have done nobly. In doing so, we will examine the difference between the Biblical and secular connotations of that phrase.

We'll take this opportunity to study the heart and circulatory system. We will look at circulatory network, blood, blood cells, immunity, blood pressure and heart disorders.

We will look at a variety of tests and other methods by which our society measures excellence. In this context we will look at and learn whatever we can from the various tests and measuring instruments often used to compare people. We do not agree with some of the common uses made of these instruments and do not encourage parents to make routine use of them. However, we believe that future parents need to know how these instruments work and how they are scored, so they can make wise decisions concerning their use in their own families.

We will look at people whom our society considers beautiful and compare their lives to the standards of God's Word. We will examine the proper role of physical attractiveness for the believer and how a godly woman can make the most of her own appearance without making it an issue of too much importance.

In the area of excellence, we will also study works of art, music, and drama by those who are commonly considered to be the masters of their crafts. We will look for those qualities in the works of each which make them distinct and cause people to consider them better than the works of others. We will study the importance of striving for excellence in everything as we work unto the Lord.

		Points
19B01	Continue your daily Bible reading started in #01B01. Read three chapters each day or use a Bible study plan. ☺	B - 1 per 7 chapters
19B02	Use a concordance to study the word "praise". Find out the different ways it is used in Scripture and what it means in each context.	B - 12
19B03	Study I Peter 3:1-6 as the standard for godly wives, following Sarah's example.	B - 3
19B04	Study the life of Sarah (Sarai) from Genesis 12, 15-18, and 20-23. Compare and contrast her with the ideal set forth in Proverbs 31 and I Peter 3.	B - 8
19B05	Study the life of Esther from the Old Testament book of that name.	B - 8
19B06	Study the life of Ruth from the Old Testament book of that name.	B - 5
19B07	Study the story of Abigail in I Samuel 25 and list ways her life would have been altered if Nabal had been a godly man.	B - 3
19B08	Most of the above Bible stories are available on cassette — word for word or dramatized. These are good for non-visual learners, to include younger siblings in the study, and/or to make double use of travel or chore time.	B - 3 each
19B09	Complete the Bible study book, ***Becoming a Woman of Excellence***.	B - 10
19B10	Memorize I Peter 3:1-6.	B - 3
19B11	Study the Biblical accounts of Delilah, Herodias, Michal, and Salome, all of whom were beautiful but ungodly.	B - 3
19B12	Use all appropriate reference works to find the exact meaning of the phrase "fears the Lord" as used in this verse.	B - 5
19B13	Use resources at hand to conduct a word study of all Greek and/or Hebrew words translated as "fear". Analyze all possible meanings of each word found.	B - 10
19B14	Study Matthew 10:27-31 and determine which of the above words meaning "fear" is meant in each usage.	B - 2

Cultural Studies

		Points
19C01	Continue adding to the timeline started in Unit 1. Prepare entries for each woman studied in this unit and the important events in the life of each. ☺	H - 1 VA - 1 each
19C02	Continue adding reports to the geography notebook started in #01C04. Write a report on any country studied this unit. ☺	G - 2 EC - 1 each
19C03	Study the marriage vows used in your church group and discuss them with your parents and/or clergyman to learn their Biblical and/or doctrinal basis.	B - 1
19C04	From publications, and polls of your own, compile a list of 10 popular and/or highly-respected women of today along with a list of their accomplishments.	HF - 2
19C05	Study the lives of well-known queens throughout history who ascended to the throne themselves, not through marriage.	H - 2 each woman
19C06	Study the lives of women who did nobly as missionaries or in other Christian work.	H - 2 each
19C07	Study the lives of women who have served as elected national leaders anywhere.	H - 2 each
19C08	Study women who have been prominent in the political arena in this country.	H - 2 each
19C09	Study Christian women martyrs, using one of the books in the next section.	H - 2 each
19C10	Watch video biographies of godly women who lived at different times in history.	H - 2 each
19C11	Prepare timeline entries for all major historical events mentioned in the studies, books, or videos in this unit.	H - 1 VA - 1 each card
19C12	Interview five adult acquaintances about the one woman they admire most. Find out as much as you can about the appearance and character traits of each woman, and what caused her to be admired.	H - 1 VA - 1 each interview

Reading and Literature

		Points
19R01	Study both husband's and wife's Scriptural roles and responsibilities and life together in oneness of spirit in ***Becoming Heirs Together of the Grace of Life: A Study on Christian Marriage***.	HF - 4 B - 2
19R02	Read the life stories of faithful women in ***Light in the North***, ***Foxe's Book of Martyrs,*** or similar books.	L - 1 each
19R03	Read one or more biographies of Christian women whom you believe have "done nobly".	L - 2 each H - 2 each
19R04	Read one or more biographies of queens, or similar female rulers.	L - 2 each H - 2 each
19R05	Read biographies of women who have been elected to high political offices in this country or abroad.	L - 2 each H - 2 each
19R06	Read biographies of painters and other artisans who are considered to excel in their craft.	H - 2 each AA - 2 each
19R07	Read biographies of composers who are considered to excel in their work.	H - 2 each MA - 2 each
19R08	Read and analyze magazine articles about any or all of the women in #19C02.	L - 1 each
19R09	Read a variety of poems written by men to, or in honor or memory of, their wives.	L - 1 each
19R10	Memorize 40-50 lines of the above poetry.	L - 3
19R11	Continue to read a minimum of one book per week, from these studies or another approved list, to use for a book report.	L - 2
19R12	Read ***Christian Excellence*** by Jon Johnston.	B - 2 L - 2
19R13	Read and/or see the play ***Esther the Queen***, or one of the movies made from it. Compare to the Scriptural account.	B - 2
19R14	Add book reviews of any or all of the books read in this unit to a reading log. Refer to *Reading Log* (257) in ***Writers INC.***	EC - ½ each book

Composition

		Points
19W01	Continue making entries in your handwriting notebook started in #01W01. Include every Bible verse studied or memorized from this unit. ☺	EG - 1 B - 1 each page
19W02	Continue placing vocabulary words in the notebook you started in #01W02. Add at least 10 new words per week. ☺	EG - 1 per 10 words
19W03	Continue adding to your school journal started in #01W03. Review *Journal Writing* (470-471) in **Writers INC**. ☺	EC - 1 per week
19W04	Have someone dictate several paragraphs to you, using passages from books used in this unit. Proofread and correct the paragraphs Refer to *Proofreader's Guide* (600-714) in **Writers INC**.	EC - 1 per 3 paragraphs
19W05	Have someone dictate several Bible verses, to you, using verses you have studied this unit. Proofread and correct the verses.	EC - 1 per 3 verses
19W06	Read about outward appearance in I Sam 16:7, Prov 11:22, Matt 6:28-29, 23:28, and John 7:24. Write a paragraph explaining how God feels about outward appearance.	B - 2 EC - 2
19W07	Take a spelling test using words from your spelling notebook. Look up the spelling rule for each word spelled incorrectly.	EG - 1 per 10
19W08	Write one book report per week on a book related to this unit or another approved by parents. Refer to *Writing About Literature* (250-256) in **Writers INC**.	EC - 2 each
19W09	Write a play or puppet show based on the book of Ruth.	EC - 4
19W10	Write a biography of Esther based on that book in the Bible.	EC - 4
19W11	Write letters of proposal and acceptance as you believe Ruth and Boaz might have.	EC - 2
19W12	Using a dictionary, mark syllables and pronunciation of all vocabulary words.	EG - 1 per 10 words
19W13	Proofread and correct all grammar and punctuation errors in all written work. Refer to *Proofreader's Guide* (600-714) in **Writers INC**.	EG - 1 per 10 words
19W14	Proofread and correct spelling errors in all written work. Add any misspelled words to your spelling notebook.	EG - 1 per paper

		Points
19W15	Write a diary as if it had been kept by one of the women studied in this unit. Refer to *Journal Writing* (470-471) in **Writers INC**.	EC - 5 per week
19W16	Summarize in writing every article in the women's magazine you read in this unit. Refer to *Writing Summaries* (180-182) in **Writer's INC**.	EC - 1 each
19W17	Write a Scriptural analysis of one or more of the magazines you read.	EC - 3 each
19W18	Write a report on the results of your interviews, telling the type of people who are most admired.	EC - 3
19W19	Write a character sketch of each of the women named and described in response to your interviews.	EC - 2 per person
19W20	Use Webster's 1828 dictionary to define charm, beauty, and excellence.	EG - 1
19W21	Write a paper comparing the three words above.	EC - 2
19W22	Prepare a 15 minute acceptance speech for receiving the Mother of the Year Award. Refer to *Speech Skills* (490-524) in **Writer's INC**.	EC - 2
19W23	Review some of your writings with your parents. Find occurrences that lack detail or examples. Read *Showing Verses Telling* (051) in **Writers INC**. Rewrite these sentences into paragraphs adding substance and depth. .	EC - ½ per paragraph
19W24	Read *The Writing Process* (002) in **Writer's INC**. Write a few paragraphs explaining the stage of the process that gives you the most trouble.	EC - ½
19W25	William Harvey discovered how blood circulates through the body. Write a report on his findings.	EC - 2 HA - 2
19W26	Look up any prefixes, suffixes, and roots of new vocabulary words. Refer to section 446-448 in **Writers INC**. Include the root words card, cord, and vent as in coronary, cardiac, and ventricle.	EG - 1 per 10 words
19W27	The words "vain," "vane," and "vein" are frequently confused. Scan the section *Using the Right Word* (715-837) in **Writers INC.** Choose 10 words. Write a paragraph using each of the words.	EG - 1

Math and Personal Economics

		Points
19M01	Compile test scores on various types of tests taken by different sets of students and find the mean and median of each to see which scores are rated excellent.	M - 2
19M02	Obtain and analyze a readout of your own scores on the most recent standardized test you have taken and learn what each of those numbers mean.	M - 1
19M03	Compare the percentage of questions you got right on each section of the above test with your percentile score.	M - 2
19M04	Consult with a professional tester to learn how percentiles and grade level scores are computed and what their significance is.	M - 1
19M05	Interview 12-15 men and their wives separately. Ask each man what he considers praiseworthy about his wife. Ask each wife what she believes her husband would consider most important. Make a graph to show this information.	M - 5 HF - 3
19M06	Use statistical and mathematical analyses to show the result of the above interviews.	M - 5

Science

		Points

19S01 Study the works of well-known women who have "done nobly" in the area of science or research. — H - 2 each

19S02 Study the scientific evidence on the effects of praise and pleasant talk on the growth of plants. — SB - 2

19S03 Conduct your own experiment to see if the above findings are true. Plant three identical plants in pots placed in different rooms. Feed, water, and otherwise treat them identically. Talk kindly and softly to one, scream and yell at one, and make no sounds around the other. After a month, check and chart differences in growth. — SB - 3

19S04 Talk to veterinarians and animal trainers about how praise affects the ability and willingness of animals to obey. — SB - 2

19S05 Read the labels of various beauty products you use and investigate the chemical properties of the ingredients, especially any known to cause side effects. — SC - 4 / HE - 2

19S06 Read and outline *The Heart and Circulatory System* (88-111) in **ABC's of the Human Body** by Reader's Digest. Refer to *The Outline* (110-112) in **Writers INC.** — HA - 5

19S07 Color and study pages 72-73, 102-103, and 110-111 in **Gray's Anatomy Coloring Book**. — HA - 2 each section completed

19S08 Do research and write a paper on the *heart and circulatory* system from the encyclopedia or other source. Refer to *Writing to Learn* (473-474) in **Writers INC**. — HA - 4 / EC - 2

19S09 Do research to find out what happens to the heart when you are under stress, when you age, and when you don't exercise. — HA - 3

19S10 William Harvey discovered how blood circulates through the body in the 16th century. Do research and add to your timeline all the medical discoveries to do with the heart since then. Include the discovery of capillaries, the first demonstration of blood pressure, invention of the stethoscope, the first pacemaker and heart implants. — HA - 1 each

19S11 Read about the heart and circulatory system in **Fearfully and Wonderfully Made.** Draw and label a diagram of the heart. — HA - 3

19S12 Do research and study the circulatory system of an earthworm, a fish and a snail. Draw a diagram of each. — SB - 3

19S13 Interview a cardiologist or other doctor. Find out the symptoms, causes and prevention of heart disease. — HA - 2

Health and Physical Fitness

		Points
19H01	Study the psychological tests and findings of Pavlov and others concerning the place of praise in conditioning.	HE - 2
19H02	Investigate the psychological tool of behavior modification to determine its usefulness and appropriateness, if any for Christians.	HE - 2
19H03	Read *Hide or Seek* by James Dobson for a Christian look at the issue of self-esteem and the importance of praise in the life of a child.	HE - 4
19H04	Investigate psychological studies on the effects of praise on the attitudes, emotions, and physical performance of individuals.	HE - 2
19H05	Check *Prevention Magazine*, medical journals or other reference works to find information on skin cancer and other negative results from tanning and intentional exposure to sun.	HE - 4
19H06	Check Prevention magazine, medical journals or other reference works to find information on negative affects to skin of overuse of certain cosmetic products.	HE - 4
19H07	Study anorexia, bulimia, and other eating disorders which are often connected with obsessive concern about appearance.	HE - 2 each

Practical Arts

		Points
19P01	Make the necessary scenery, and/or props for producing the play you wrote about the book of Ruth.	CR - 10
19P02	Make costumes for the play you wrote about Ruth or for your performance of Esther the Queen.	HM - 5 each complete garment
19P03	Make the puppets and/or puppet stage for the puppet show in #19A01.	DR - 10
19P04	Use this or another verse in honor of godly wives to woodburn onto a plaque, poster, or wall hanging.	VA - 5
19P05	Frame and mat one or more of the pictures or posters you created in the creative arts section.	CR - 5
19P06	Use the video play of Ruth as a chance to learn to operate a video camera if you don't already know.	CR - 1
19P07	Learn to administer and grade one or more of the tests used in math section of this unit.	HF - 2 each

Creative and Performing Arts

		Points
19A01	Write and perform a puppet show based on the life of someone studied in this unit. Recruit some friends to help with the performance if needed.	EC - 5 DR - 5
19A02	Work with friends to perform and video tape the play you wrote about Ruth.	DR - 10
19A03	Work with friends or family to tape Esther the Queen as a radio play.	DR - 10
19A04	Listen to and learn a variety of songs of praise.	MA - 2
19A05	Listen to several songs extolling the virtues of women and list those things for which each subject is praised. Compare to the list in Proverbs 31.	MA - 2 B - 1
19A06	Learn to sing one or more of the above songs.	MA - 5 each
19A07	Learn to play one or more of the above songs on your instrument of choice.	MA - 5 each
19A08	Compose a tune for one of the poems you memorized in this unit and learn to sing the song.	MA - 5
19A09	View artwork produced by those who are considered "masters" and compare them to other works to determine why they are considered superior. (You will have to use prints and copies unless you are able to travel to the museums which house the originals.)	AA - 2
19A10	Write and set to music a song expressing your love for the Lord.	MA - 5
19A11	Learn to sing a hymn which speaks of love and fear of the Lord.	MA - 5
19A12	Set one of the Scripture passages in this unit to music with an original tune.	MA - 5
19A13	Listen to tapes or CD's of classical music composed by some of the people who are considered "masters." Determine what causes them to be considered superior.	MA - 2
19A14	Do research to find out why the heart is a symbol for love.	MA - 1

Unit 20 &

Give her of the fruit of her hands;
and let her own works praise her in the gates.

Proverbs 31:31

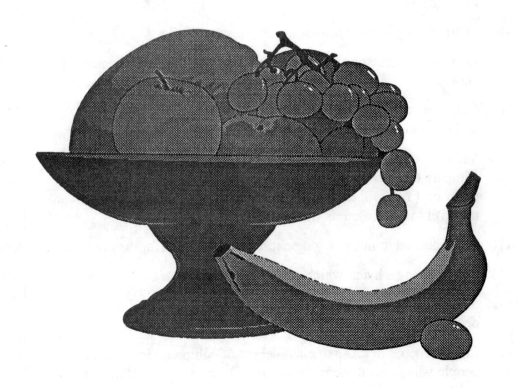

Introduction to Unit 20

Since this unit is the culmination of our entire course it is the only one which really must be done in a particular order. It is to be last, at the end of the student's high school career. The emphasis in this unit, as in the verse on which it is based on, is the "fruit of her labors." We also deal with the fruit of the Spirit as in Scripture and with the growing of real fruit.

You will have the opportunity to analyze and evaluate your own progress and what you have learned throughout this course. One method of such evaluation is to take a standardized achievement test. Though we don't necessarily endorse these tests and definitely do not consider them necessary, we offer them as a way of achieving the goals of the course. Other tests which may be taken as a part of this course include the GED or one of the popular college entrance exams. If you plan to continue your education in a formal manner you should check with the college or university you wish to attend for their recommendation concerning entrance exams. If you wish to use one or more of these tests for self-evaluation, but don't need the results for any other purpose, we recommend taking the sample test which can be found in the study manual for each of these.

This unit involves you in several projects in which you demonstrate your accumulated knowledge and/or skills. These range from papers to write and music recitals to sewing and handcraft projects. Many activities in this unit are related to preparations for receiving a high school diploma and attending a graduation ceremony. If you are not a part of a home school group which offers such things, please have your parents get in touch with us for help in holding one just for you. We will issue you a diploma for a reasonable fee whether you are in a group which holds a graduation or not. If you design your own diploma as suggested herein, you can have it printed at any local copy shop. Then just have your parent or homeschool group leader sign it and fill in the necessary information.

We will also study famous people and movements from history, looking at the "fruits" of their efforts and how well they have stood the test of time. Much of this study is left for you to do on your own as you apply the research and study skills you have learned during this course.

Bible

	Points

20B01 Read your Bible daily as started in #01B01. You can read the Bible through each year by reading three chapters each day or by following the Daily Bible Reading Schedule in *The Narrated Bible.* Share what you are learning with a parent or other adult. ⊕ — **B - 1** per 7 chapters

20B02 Maintain the list of prayers and answers you have been keeping for the last several units. Examine it to see how God has blessed you and others through your prayer life. — **B - 5**

20B03 Read the following verses and write a summary of each hindrance to prayer: *Anxiety*: Phil 4:6. *Disobedience*: Deut 1:43-45, 3:26, II Sam 22:27, Jer 11:10-11, Lam 3:8, and Mic 3:4. *Doubt*: James 1:5-7. *Failure to heed God's law:* Prov 28:9 and Zech 7:12. *Faithlessness*: Heb 11:6. *Haughtiness*: Job 35:12-13 and James 4:6, 10. Hypocrisy: Ps 78:36, Ezek 33:31, Matt 15:1-9, and Mark 12: 38-40. *Improper husband/wife relationship*: I Pet 3:7. *Refusal to help the poor*: Prov 21:20. *Selfishness*: James 4:3. *Self righteousness*: Luke 18:9-14. *Unconfessed sin*: Ps 66:18, Isa 59:1, John 9:31, and James 4:8. *Wickedness*: Prov 1:24, 27-31, 15:8, 29, Isa 1:15, and 59:1. — **B - 10** / **EC - 3**

20B04 Read the following verses about the value of prayer. Write a summary of each topic. *Assures God's presence*: Ps 145:18, and James 4:8. *Brings blessings from God*: Ps 86:5, Matt 7:11, Luke 11:9-10, and Rom 10:12. *Brings help in time of need:* Heb 4:16. *Brings joy*: John 16:24. *Brings physical and spiritual healing*: James 5:15, 7:16. *Brings understanding*: Jer 33:3. *Is powerful and effective:* James 5:16. *Pleases God:* Prov 15:8. *Strengthens us against temptation*: Matt 26:41. — **B - 6** / **EC - 3**

20B05 Memorize Proverbs 11:30. — **B - 2**

20B06 Study and memorize Colossians 1:9-12. — **B - 4**

20B07 Study Matthew 7:15-21 and analyze it's meaning. — **B - 5**

20B08 Memorize Galatians 6:7-10. — **B - 3**

20B09 Study II Corinthians 13:5-7 and apply the tests given to your own spiritual life. — **B - 2**

20B10 Study and memorize Galatians 5:22-23. — **B - 3**

		Points

| | | Points |

20B11 Identify and study one person from the Bible who exhibited each of the fruits of the spirit. — B - 5

20B12 Make a chart showing another specific scripture reference relating to each of the fruits of the Spirit listed in Galatians 5:22-23. — B - 3

20B13 Attend the *Institute in Basic Life Principles* by Bill Gothard with the Advanced Training Institute International. — HF - 25, B-10

20B14 Attend the *Advanced Institute in Basic Life Principles* by Bill Gothard with the Advanced Training Institute of America. — HF - 25, B - 10

20B15 Listen to the tape *The Scriptural Role of a Godly Wife* by Jonathan Lindvall. as a guide along the path toward Christian womanhood. — HF - 3

Cultural Studies

		Points
20C01	Continue adding to the timeline started in Unit 1. Prepare an entry for each person or event studied in this unit. ☺	H - 1 VA - 1 each
20C02	Complete the geography notebook started in #01C04. ☺	G - 2 EC - 1 each
20C03	Study the **Christian History of the United States Constitution** to see the fruit of the labors of our Christian forefathers in this land.	H - 5
20C04	For a more thorough understanding of the seed sown which resulted in the fruits of our nation, read **The Light and the Glory** and study it with the accompanying study guide.	H - 5
20C05	Listen to the tapes you have not listened to and complete the workbook **America 350 Years**.	H - 50
20C06	Study the major missionary efforts over the years and the results achieved. Judge the effectiveness of each method by God's blessing upon it.	H - 4
20C07	Study the origins and history of your own church or denomination and subject it to the standards used in #20C06.	H - 3
20C08	Study the life and ministry of several famous preachers in various periods of history. Look at their message, their lifestyles, and the fruits of their labor.	H - 3 each
20C09	Apply the standard of God's word to all the cultures and societies we have studied in this curriculum. Look for and study more closely those which appear to be godly.	H - 2 B - 4
20C10	Analyze the Reformation, the Great Awakening, the Massachusetts Bay, Plymouth Colonies, and the Confederate States of America, to see how well each of them lived up to their goal of bringing God's kingdom to the Earth.	H - 10 each
20C11	Complete any unused lessons in any volume of **God and Government**.	CG - 3 per chapter
20C12	Study the Biblical guidelines for restoring Christian principles to society and public affairs in America by listening to the tape **Eight Principles of the Reformation**.	H - 3
20C13	Read the extraordinary collection of inspiring character traits in **Gaining Favor with God and Man**.	H - 5 B - 3

Reading and Literature

		Points
20R01	Read **L'Abri** by Edith Schaeffer, noting especially the fruit God produced through that ministry.	L - 4
20R02	Read the inspiring biography **Jim Elliot,** about a missionary killed by Auca Indians in Latin America.	H - 3
20R03	Read **A Gardner Looks at the Fruits**.	L - 4
20R04	Read the biography about a godly man who took the gospel to China and the secret of his strength in **Hudson Taylor's Spiritual Secret**.	L - 4
20R05	Read about the dedicated life and tragic death of William Borden in the biography **Borden of Yale**.	H - 3
20R06	Read biographies of leaders of the Reformation or any of the other great Christian movements you have studied.	H - 4 per person
20R07	Read **What Happens When Women Pray**.	L - 4
20R08	Read **The Kneeling Christian**.	B - 5
20R09	Read some of the best stories about missionaries and miracles in **Stories Worth Rereading**.	L - 4
20R10	Read 3-5 other novels about Christian families and make note of examples of children who grew to bear good fruit from their childhood training.	L - 4 each book
20R11	Read biographies of C.H. Spurgeon, John Knox, George Whitefield, the Wesleys and other "fruitful" ministers.	H - 4 each book
20R12	Take and score well on reading and all related sections of ACT, SAT, GED or similar standardized test if needed or desired.	L - 6 per test battery
20R13	Continue to read at least one book per week from the approved list for book reports.	L - 2 each book
20R14	If you plan on going to college read *College Prep Skills* (485-488) in **Writers INC.**	

Composition

	Points
20W01 Complete your handwriting notebook started in #01W01. You now have a record of every Bible verse studied or memorized from this course. ☺	EG - 1 B - 1 each page
20W02 Complete the vocabulary notebook you started in #01W02. Continue adding at least 10 new words per week. ☺	EG - 1 per 10 words
20W03 Complete your school journal started at the beginning of this course in Unit 1.☺	EC - 1 per week
20W04 Have someone dictate several paragraphs to you using passages from books used in this unit. Proofread and correct the paragraphs. Refer to *Proofreader's Guide* (600-714) in ***Writers INC***.	EC - 2 per 3 paragraphs
20W05 Have someone dictate several Bible verses, to you, using verses you have studied this unit. Proofread and correct the verses.	EC - 1 per 3 verses
20W06 Using commentaries and other references, write a paper giving a thorough description of what can be included in the fruit of righteousness.	EC - 5 B - 5
20W07 Using the list of skills and traits to be learned at the beginning of this course, analyze your own progress and write a paper detailing what you have learned and how the course has been useful to you.	EC - 5
20W08 Prepare a commencement address summing up your high school career and outlining God's calling for your future. Refer to *Speech Skills* (493-495) in ***Writers INC***.	EC - 5
20W09 Write an evaluation of this course with ideas for improvements. Mail to us at the address in the book. We will pay for suggestions used.	EC - 4
20W10 Proofread this course manual and send us a list of any errors, with page numbers.	EG - 5
20W11 Using any necessary references, write a Biblical analysis of Matthew 7:15-21.	EC - 2 B - 2
20W12 Write a research paper on one or more of the people studied in this unit. Refer to *Writing the Research Paper* (135-173) in ***Writers INC***.	EC - 10
20W13 Write one book report per week on a book related to this unit or another approved by parents. Refer to *Writing About Literature* (250-256) in ***Writers INC***.	EC - 2 each report

Far Above Rubies © 1995

20W14 Enter any essays or speeches written for this course in any appropriate contest and keep a record of any prizes won.

20W15 Write a paraphrase of Col. 1:9-12.

EC - 2

20W16 Review and pass quiz on the spelling and definitions of all words in notebook.

EG - 1 per 10 words

20W17 Proofread and correct spelling errors in all written work. Take a spelling test from the record of your frequently misspelled words from other units.

EG - 2 per paper

20W18 Take and score well on language arts sections of ACT, SAT, or GED if needed or necessary.

EG - 5 per test

20W19 Proofread and correct all grammar and punctuation errors in all written work. Refer to *Proofreader's Guide* (600-714) in **Writers INC**.

EG - 1 each page

20W20 Reminisce your experiences in the last few years. Write a paper explaining how you think your studies in *Far Above Rubies* have prepared you for life. Please send us a copy.

EC - 1 each page

20W21 Write a news article, with headline, which reports your own graduation as a newsworthy event. Refer to Writing the News Story (230-238) in **Writers INC**.

EC - 1

20W22 If you plan on going to college read *College Prep Skills* (485-488) in **Writers INC.** Write a college entrance essay. Here are some examples of questions you may receive: How has your experience as a teenager significantly differed from those of your friends? Which of your talents, interest or activities mean the most to you? Refer to *Writing Essays* (105-118) in **Writers INC**.

EC - 3

Math and Personal Economics

		Points
20M01	Get all your test scores or grades on standardized or other tests and average them.	M - 2
20M02	Plot all the above grades on a line graph.	M - 3
20M03	If your family gives number and/or letter grades at the end of a reporting period, get your parents to let you do the averaging and compile your report card grades for the last semester.	M - 2
20M04	Assign the appropriate number to each letter grade (A=4, B=3, C=2, D=1) on your transcript and use them to find your GPA for each year and overall.	M - 2
20M05	Complete and score well on the math sections of ACT, SAT, GED or another standardized test if needed or desired.	M - 7
20M06	Compute all the money you have earned and/or won as a direct result of this course. Include the monetary value of goods and/or services received in exchange or barter arrangements.	A - 3
20M07	Prepare a detailed spreadsheet of income, expenses, and overall profit or loss for the business you ran during this course.	A - 10
20M08	Compute the points allotted for each of the items you have done in this course and determine your total credits in each subject. Your parents may have kept up with this throughout the course, but you should do it now as a math project.	M - 10

Far Above Rubies © 1995

Science

		Points
20S01	Study fruit trees and the production of fruit, especially concentrating on the varieties that grow well in your area.	SB - 3
20S02	Catalog all common fruits according to their scientific genus, species, etc.	SB - 2
20S03	Using a good management training guide, study the relationship between feedback and performance.	HF - 5
20S04	Study **Spirit-Controlled Temperament** by Tim LaHaye or a similar book to analyze your own personality type and how it influences who and what you are. Be on the lookout for areas you need to yield more and more to God.	HE - 3 B - 2
20S05	Read about the spiritual and physical fruits produced by reading the biography **George Washington Carver**.	H - 5

Health and Physical Fitness

		Points
20H01	Analyze your own physical condition and how it has improved during this course. Look back at the goals you set for your physical fitness in unit 7 and compare your current situation to them.	PE - 4
20H02	Study the nutritional value of various kinds of fruit.	HE - 2
20H03	Prepare a booklet containing basic information on the various health care topics you have studied.	HE - 20
20H04	Prepare a chart or poster showing the correct first aid or home health care procedure for as many of the conditions you have studied as possible.	HE - 10
20H05	Demonstrate before some group or teach others the basic first aid techniques you have learned in this course.	HF - 10
20H06	Contact your local YMCA, recreation department, or a fitness center and take a nationally-normed fitness test to see how you rate in that area.	PE - 10

Practical Arts

		Points
20P01	Prepare and type a resume for yourself, highlighting all the skills learned, jobs held, and experiences acquired during this course.	BE - 10
20P02	Learn how to plant, grow, and harvest several different kinds of fruit.	PA - 2
20P03	Plant, nurture, and harvest one or more fast-producing fruits (strawberries, blackberries, grapes).	PA - 2
20P04	Plant and care for one or more dwarf fruit trees.	PA - 2
20P05	Run your entire household for one week, caring for all aspects of it as if you were the mother. This might be scheduled when (and if) your mother becomes ill or is out of town for some reason.	HM - 25
20P06	Prepare yourself a hope chest (dowry) consisting of household things you have made and/or decorated.	HM - 2
20P07	Design and fill out (with your mother's approval) a transcript of your high school work.	BE - 3
20P08	Make your own trousseau or work wardrobe consisting of a wide variety of garments.	HM - 10 per outfit
20P09	Compile a book or file of recipes you have used and learned to like during this course.	HM - 5
20P10	If your home school offers a graduation ceremony and they will allow you to do so, make your own cap and gown for it.	HM - 10
20P11	Build a cabinet or wooden box in which to house items for your hope chest.	CR - 5
20P12	Attend the seminar (or listen to the tapes) *Apprenticeship Plus* by Inge Cannon. This course will help you if your goal is college or apprenticeship.	BE - 8

Creative and Performing Arts

		Points
20A01	Using calligraphy and/or other artistic skills, design and make a high school diploma for your home school. Have it printed or copied so it will look official.	VA - 5
20A02	Design a certificate for our company to issue to the young ladies who complete this course. All those sending in final documents will receive some type of certificate, but we would like to change it often to reflect ideas from our students. Designers of those used will receive a cash reward.	VA - 5
20A03	Design your own personal graduation announcements to be printed and mailed.	VA - 3
20A04	If you are able to have a graduation ceremony, you may wish to create the flower arrangements and other decorations.	VA - 5
20A05	Perform a recital of the songs you have learned to sing during this course.	MA - 2 per song
20A06	Perform a recital of the songs you have learned to play in this course.	MA - 2 per song
20A07	Perform at a recital or for some group one or more of the songs you have written during this course.	MA - 2 per song
20A08	Choose one or more appropriate songs or tunes and see if you can have it played or sung at your graduation ceremony.	MA - 2
20A09	Create a book with one of the following titles: *Fruit, Graduation, My Home School Experience* or *Famous Fruit Bearers*. This can be a simple notebook that includes all the reports and art work during this unit or a bound story book written as a nonfiction book. You may include text and illustrations as you desire. Points will depend on the subject you choose and the amount of time spent on this project. Share the book with someone.	Parents Discretion

Appendix Foreword to Students and Parents

The following material is offered for your convenience in locating the resources suggested for use with *Far Above Rubies* curriculum. You will notice that the guide is not done in bibliographical form, as we preferred a more informal listing. We hope this will meet your needs.

1. **Appendix I** — list of suggested resources and suppliers. Reference materials may, of course, be used as often as needed in any or all units.

2. **Appendix II** — specifically recommended items listed by unit and referenced to activities, with title, author, publisher, suggested sources. All items are listed in alphabetical order in each unit and are referenced to the activity number for which they are recommended. Items recommended for use in more than one unit will be listed separately for each applicable unit. Some items (marked with ♦) can be used in several sections.

If the dealer from whom you purchased this curriculum manual or any local Christian business carries any of these resources, we encourage you to patronize his/her company. Addresses for sources are listed on page 293 for those items that cannot be found in your area. If you have trouble finding certain materials in your area, or if those suggested do not fit your family's beliefs, please feel free to find and use other materials for the same purpose.

You may find idea substitutions in Mary Pride's *Big Book of Home Learning,* Cathy Duffy's *Christian Home Educator's Curriculum Manual for Junior/Senior High*, your local Christian bookstore, or from other home educators. Most activities are not essential to successful completion of this course. Feel free to skip any project for which you are unable to find adequate resources. If you cannot find resources and still strongly desire to do the activity, please write us. We will try to assist you in your search.

Far Above Rubies Companion
Teacher Tips, Lesson Planning, and Record Keeping

The *Far Above Rubies Companion* is a valuable guide/planner/record keeper. It thoroughly explains the Christian and educational philosophy used in *Far Above Rubies*. Over 300 pages divided into the following sections:

♥ Teaching philosophies, ideas, supplemental resources and remedial help in each of the nine subject categories as well as book list of novels, biographies and other books for further reading in each unit.
♥ Book reviews on the favorite selected books in each unit, making it much easier to decide on which books to use.
♥ Lesson planning, record planning and goal planning sheets for each of the twenty units to make it easy to keep track of points and credits earned during each unit.

Order from any of the suppliers listed in the Appendix on page 293.

Appendix I

Bible

All scripture is given by inspiration of God, and is profitable for doctrine, for reproof, for correction, for instruction in righteousness: That the man of God may be perfect, thoroughly furnished unto all good works. 2 Tim 3:16-17

The Bible is the world's greatest literature. It is the living Word that changes lives. Students should read the Bible through at least once each year, not just during this study but for the rest of their lives. Students may also find the following helpful throughout the course, in addition to those books named in the curriculum:

The Narrated Bible presents the Bible in a chronological order. It is neither a translation nor a paraphrase. The central text is composed entirely of scripture, using the NIV. This very easy to read book reads like a beautiful, exciting story. ✝☆❋

The Bible Mapbook is brightly illustrated and full of 3-D graphics, charts, names, and locations all in chronological order. ✝

Konos makes an excellent *Bible Timeline* of colorful laminated Bible figures to cut out and affix to a wall time line. P

The Bible Overview Chart is a 25½ x 11 full color Bible timeline. Extremely durable, its laminated and printed on card stock. Easy to understand and very inexpensive. ✝

The Bible Visual Resource Book is a timeline in a book. Illustrations tell the chronological story of the Bible. You can make a wall time line from it because it is reproducible. Also includes charts and maps. ✝

The Principle Thing: A Daily Guide to Godly Wisdom, Morals and Manners is a wonderful Bible study on the book of Proverbs. Proverbs is the most practical book in Scripture, establishing God's universal moral code. God Himself said in Proverbs that it was written to: know wisdom and instruction; to perceive the words of understanding; to receive the instruction of wisdom, justice, judgment, and equity; to give subtlety to the simple, to the young man knowledge and discretion. Proverbs 1:2-4. ✝

The Narrow Way: Character Curriculum is a character curriculum/Bible study for all ages! *The Narrow Way* is a curriculum devoted solely to building Godly characters in children. It is a simple tool, with love and just a few minutes each day you can mold your children after 1 Peter 1:5-8. An excellent Bible study. The lessons use the first 8 Pearable books including: Faith, Virtue, Knowledge, Temperance, Patience, Godliness, Brotherly Kindness, and Charity. ✝

♦ - Suggested in several units ✝- Family Christian Academy ❋- Elijah Company

☆- Lifetime Gifts and Books P- Order from publisher (see page 292 for addresses)

Composition

A general knowledge of grammar is assumed for any of the activities in the composition section. Knowledge of the definitions and rules of grammar does *not*, itself, improve student writing. If you wanted to learn to ride a bike, you would not go to the library and find pictures of bikes then circle the handle bars or underline the tires twice! You would get on a bike to learn to ride. In the same way, that is how students learn to write—by writing.

The composition section of each *Far Above Rubies* unit is full of writing assignments. To make an excellent writer, require daily writing from your student. When you encourage your daughter to become a better writer, the grammar improves too, even if she is not diagramming sentences or using grammatical terms. Additional or remedial grammar suggestions:

Learning Language Arts Through Literature is an excellent language program using portions of great literature and the dictation method. Every language art skill is included: spelling, writing, vocabulary, mechanics, penmanship and thinking skills. Supplemental books are needed for each level. **The Green Book** is designed for seventh and eighth grade. It includes grammar, diagramming sentences, poetry, speech making, and the research paper.
The Gray Book is designed for eighth and ninth grade. It includes research assignments, paraphrasing, notetaking, poetry, grammar review and more.
The Gold Book is designed for high school. It takes an in-depth look at American poetry, short stories and novels. Emphasis is on the elements of poetry and fiction as well as how to read and interpret the selections. A section of the book is devoted to the essay. The composition skills are intended for college preparation. ✝☆✸

Wordsmith is a writing course for young people designed to get them excited about getting their thoughts on paper. It covers all the writing steps in a clear concise manner and in an easy and fun way with no busy work. Created by a freelance writer, not a text book company. Designed for sixth grade and up. ✝

Jensen's Grammar is a workbook approach series designed for seventh grade and up. Jensen is called the Saxon of grammar. Students learn grammar by studying sentences in a interesting story format rather than sentences that do not relate to each other. Spaced repetition, constant review, and information given incrementally causes a natural progression of detail and concept. ✝

Italic Handwriting

Write Now is a self teaching program for middle grades through adults who want to develop elegant italic handwriting. Includes basic handwriting, cursive italic, and introduces calligraphy. ✝☆✸

History Sources

For studying general history, historical people, events, and specific periods, try any of these as well as items from Appendix II:

Also check your state archives, which are probably located in your state capital. Timelines can be purchased from Konos Curriculum or most school supply stores or use *World History Dates* or *The Junior Wall Chart of History*.

Title	Source
Cultural Atlas for Young People	✝☆✳
Streams of Civilization	✝☆✳
The Junior Wall Chart of History	❦
Timetables of History	☆
History Timeline	Konos

For more historical fiction, check one or more of the following bibliographies:

Title	Author	Source
A Family Program for Reading Aloud	Rosalie J. Slater	✝
America in Story (historical fiction)	Elizabeth Howard	📖
American History Through Historical Novels	Walter Spearman	📖
American Historical Fiction	A.T. Dickinson Jr	📖
Books Children Love	Elizabeth Wilson	✝☆✳
European Historical Fiction	Jeanette Hotchkiss	📖
Let the Authors Speak: A Guide to Worthy Books Based on Historical Settings	Carolyn Hatcher	✝☆✳

Additional historical fictions are listed chronologically in the **Far Above Rubies Companion**.

Science and Technology

Check the science section of your library for books on the individual subject. Try one or more good encyclopedias. Use *Guide to Periodicals* for recent information. For gems, minerals, etc. obtain information from the United States Geological Survey. County Extension Offices and/or your state's land grant college will have material free to the public on a variety of Earth and life sciences, especially as related to animals, agriculture or horticulture. For help in finding projects to enhance any science coursessee *Science Experiments on File* (3 vol.) published by Facts on File · 460 Park Ave. ·New York, NY 10016.

Practical and Creative Arts

The Agricultural Extension Service in your county (See government listings in phone book.), and/or the county 4-H club office will have booklets and pamphlets on homemaking as well as many other how-to topics.

Health Education

Use *Gray's Anatomy*, any good college anatomy book, or any good medical encyclopedia. (See if your doctor or a nurse will recommend one for you.)

Reading and Literature

Remember that you cannot get credit for reading the same book twice, even if it is appropriate, or even suggested, for more than one unit. Parents can give credit for books not listed in this curriculum.

Classic Novels

Students may use any of the classics which meet parental approval. See the *Far Above Rubies Companion* for a extensive list of the classics.

Biographies of Men and Women of Faith

Choose any titles from the Sower Series or the Men and Women of Faith Series. Also try individual titles listed in the *Far above Rubies Companion*.

Biblical Fiction

The Biblical Biographies series (reading level 4-8) by Ethel Barrett are available in Christian bookstores and church libraries. The books by Lois Henderson and Marjorie Holmes are in many public libraries. (These books feature people and stories from the Bible and are reverent and respectful, but they do add some material about which the Bible doesn't speak but which may have happened. They are true to the culture and customs of the place and time and adhere to Biblical standards of behavior. Read them as novels, not as Bible stories.) Available at most Christian bookstores. By Lois Henderson: *Hagar, Miriam, Aquila and Priscilla, Abigail, Lydia,* and *Ruth,* By Marjorie Holmes: *Two from Galilee, Mary and Joseph,* and *Martha of Bethany.*

Home School Suppliers

There are dozens of home school suppliers. We could not possibly list them all here. If the dealer from whom you purchased this curriculum manual carries any of these resources, we encourage you to patronize his/her company.

All Around Education ▲
1147 Freemont Drive
Montogomery, AL 36111

The Elijah Company ✳
Rt 2 Box 100
Crossville, TN 38555
(615) 456-6284

Family Christian Academy ✝
The Unit Study & Teaching Materials Catalog
487 Myatt Drive
Madison, Tn 37115
(615) 860-3000 •Fax 615-860-9788
Credit Card Orders: 1-800-788-0840

Greenleaf Press 🍎
1570 Old Laguardo Road
Lebanon, TN 37087
(615) 449-1617

Lifetime Books and Gifts ☆
The Always Incomplete
Resource Guide and Catalog
3900 Chalet Suzzane Drive
Lake Whales, FL
(813) 676-6311 •1-800-377-0390

Most materails can be ordered from the home school suppliers on the previous page. Materials not carried by those on the previous page can be ordered directly from one of these other book sellers or publishers:

Bible Memory Association
PO Box 12000
Ringgold, LA 71068-2000

Bob Jones
Customer Service
Greenville, SC 29614
1-800-845-5731

Chalcedon Audio-Visual Productions
P.O. Box 188
Vallecito, CA 95251

Christian Life Workshops
PO Box 250
Gresham, OR 97030

Education Plus
PO Box 1591
Sterling, Virginia 20167

Foundation for American Christian Education
PO Box 27035
San Francisco, CA 94127

Geneva Media
708 Hamvasy Lane
Tyler, TX 75701.

Good Apple
1204 Buchanan St
Carthage, IL 62321-0299

Good News Broadcasting
Lincoln, NE 68501

Home School Digest
Wisdom Publications
PO Box 3154
La Vale, MD 21502

Konos
PO Box 1534
Richardson, TX 91007

Maxis Computer Software
2 Thetre Square
Suite 230
Orinda, Ca 94563-3346

National Geographic Society
PO Box 2895
Washington DC 20077-9960

Software Labs
100 Corporate Point Suite 195
Culver City, CA 90230

Southern Living Magazine
OxmoreHouse Publishing
PO Box 2463
Birmingham, AL 35201

Paternoster Press
3 Redford Crescant
Exeter, Devon,
London, England

Pilgrim Tape Ministry
739 E. Lincoln Avenue
Myerstown, PA 17067

Practical Home Schooling
PO Box 1250
Fenton, MO 63026

Teaching Home Magazine
PO Box 20219
Portland, OR 97220

Specialized Encyclopedias

Each of the following are multi volume sets:

Dictionary of Scientific Biography
Charles C. Gillispie, ed.
American Council of Learned Societies

Dictionary of American Biography
Scribner's

Dictionary of Literary Biography
Gale Research Co.

Great Lives from History
(several series, on different time periods and areas of activity, ask for the one
you need)

International Encyclopedia of Education
Pergamon Press

Index listings

Periodical articles are listed by topic or type. These are all reference periodicals which
may be on file at your library or through a college or state government research facility.

Index to How-to-Do-It Information
Norman Lathrop Ent. (annually)
P.O. Box 198
Wooster, OH 44691-0198

Master Index to Poetry

Index on General Science

Index of the Humanities

Index on Education

Index of Biography

Unit	Title	Activity #	Author	Publisher	Source
1	Abigail Adams	01R01	Evelyn Witter	Sower Series	✝☆✱
1	Advanced Institute in Basic Life Principles Seminar	01P12	Bill Gothard	Advanced Train Institute Internation	Seminar
1	Antiquities of the Jews	01C07	Josephus, Flavius		📚✝
1	Baker's Bible Atlas ◆	01C14	Charles F. Pfeiffer	Baker Book House	✝†
1	Beautiful Girlhood ◆	01R03	reprint by Karen Anderola	Great Expectations	✝✱†☆
1	Book of the Centuries ◆	01C08	Bonnie Dettmer	Small Ventures	✝
1	Christian Character: A Course for Training Young People to Have Habits that will Lead to Godly Character	01B13	Maldaner, Gary	Plain Path Publishers	✝☆
1	Dear Princess	01R13	Mary M. Landis	Rod and Staff	✝
1	Diary of Anne Frank, The (book or video)	01R08	Anne Frank		📚✝
1	Dictionary of Chemistry	01S16	Usborne	Usborne	✝▲✱☆
1	Gem Hunter's Kit	01S12	Tim Lutz	Running Press	✝✱☆
1	Geode Kit, The	01S13	Running Press	Running Press	✝✱☆
1	God's Priceless Woman	01B03	Sanseri, Wanda	Back Home Ind.	✝
1	Institute in Basic Life Principles Seminar	01P11	Bill Gothard	Advanced Train Institute Internation	Seminar
1	Jewish Wars, The	01C05	Josephus, Flavius		✝
1	Kingfisher's Illustrated History of the World ◆	01C06		Kingfisher	✝✱†
1	Manners and Customs of Bible Lands	01B26	Wright, Fred H.	Moody Press	✝†
1	Mysteries of the Bible	01B01		Reader's Digest	✝📚
1	Narrated Bible: In Chronological Order ©	01M11	F. LaGuard Smith	Harvest House	✝
1	Oh, Euclid (game)	01M13	Aristoplay	Aristoplay	✱
1	Old Fashioned Crafts	01B24			📚
1	Personal Holiness	01H08	Greg Bahnsen	Geneva Media	P
1	Physicians Desk Reference	01B08			📚
1	Saga Begins, The Book 1 Bible Log Series	01B08	Bible Log Series	Victor Books	✝
1	Scriptural Role of a Godly Wife	01P13	Jonathan Lindvall	Bold Parenting	✝
1	Streams of Civilization ◆	01C08		Christian Liberty Press	✝☆✱🌿

◆ - Suggested in several units   ✝- Family Christian Academy   ✱- Elijah Company   ☆- Lifetime Gifts and Books   ⌨- Computer store,   🌿- Greenleaf Press

P- Order from publisher (see page 292 for addresses), † Most Christian book stores, ▲ All Around Education, 📚 Library   V Video rental

Far Above Rubies Appendix II

Unit	Title	Code	Author / Source	Publisher	Availability
1	Time Traveler Books (Four Usborne Books in One) ◆	01C09	Usborne	Usborne	▲ ✛ ✷ ☆
1	Woman and the Church: Earthly Images of the Heavenly Bride	01R11	Vernon S. Grieger	Luther Rose	✛
1	Women of the Bible	01B04	Vander Velde	Kregel	✛
1	World History: A Christian Survey	01C16	R. J. Rushdoony	Chalcedon Audio-Visual Productions	P
1	World History Dates ◆	01C05	Usborne	Usborne	✛ ▲ ✷ ☆
1	Write Now	01W14		Italic Handwriting Series	✛ ✷
1	Writers INC ◆	several	Write Source	Write Source	✛
2	All the Way Home	02R07	Mary Pride	Crossway	✛ ✷ ☆
2	Apple Tree Guide for Expectant Parents ◆ (need Under the Apple Tree)	02H10	Helen Wessel & Kathy Nesper	Bookmates International	✛
2	Apple Tree Ministries Newsletter ◆	02P03	Helen Wessel Nickle	Apple Tree Ministries	P
2	Apple Tree Personal Study Guide (need Under the Apple Tree)	02B09	Helen Wessel Nickle	Apple Tree Ministries	P
2	Aquila and Priscilla	02R13	Lois Henderson	Walker and Co.	✛
2	Bankers Confession, A	02M04	Gary Sanseri	Back Home Industries	✛
2	Becoming Heirs Together of the Grace of Life	02R03	Jeff and Marge Barth	Parable Publishing House	✛
2	Bible and Birth Control	02H04	Charles D Provan	Zimmer Printing	✛
2	Bold Christian Youth Seminar	02P17	Jonathan Lindvall	Bold Parenting Seminars	✛
2	Born in Zion ◆	02S01	Carol Balizet	Christ Centered Publishing	✛
2	Choices and Consequences	02H01	New Vision Press	Right to Life Advocate	☆
2	Christian Family, The	02B07	Larry Christenson	Bethany House	✛ ✛
2	Christy	02R02	Catherine Marshall	Avon	✛ ✛ 📖
2	Creative Counterpart	02R09	Linda Dillow	Nelson	🐌
2	Financial Management Calendar	02M01	Agricultural Extension Office in your county	contact agriculture department for address of nearest extension office	agriculture department
2	Full Quiver: Family Planning and the Lordship of Christ, A ◆	02H08	Rick and Jan Hess	Family Christian Academy	✛
2	Get a Grip on Your Money ◆	02M02	Larry Burkett		✛
2	God and Government, volumes 1 - 3	02C04	Gary Demar	Wolgemuth and Hyatt	✛
2	Godly Homes in America (free audio tape from publisher)	02B15	Martian Freed	Pilgrim Tape Ministry	P
2	Gray's Anatomy Coloring Book	02S07	Freddy Stark Ph.D.	Running Press	✛
2	Joy of Natural Childbirth	several	Helen Wessel & Kathy Nesper	Bookmates International	✛

◆ - Suggested in several units   ✛- Family Christian Academy   ✷- Elijah Company   ☆- Lifetime Gifts and Books   🖥- Computer store,   🐌- Greenleaf Press
P- Order from publisher (see page 292 for addresses),   ✝ Most Christian book stores,   ▲ All Around Education,   📖 Library V Video rental

Far Above Rubies Appendix II

Unit	Title	Code	Author	Publisher	Source
2	Kingfisher's Illustrated History of the World ◆	02C13	Kingfisher	Kingfisher	✢
2	Letting God Plan Your Family ◆	02H04	Samuel Owen	Crossway	✢
2	MacBeth	02R16	William Shakespeare		📖
2	Narrated Bible: In Chronological Order ◆	01B01	F. LaGuard Smith	Harvest House	✢
2	Passion and Purity ◆	02R01	Elisabeth Elliot	Revell	✢
2	Passion and Purity (audio tape)	02B16	Elisabeth Elliot	Good News Broadcasting	P
2	Preparing for Romance (audio tape) ◆	02P01	Jonathan Lindvall	Bold Parenting	✢☆✳
2	Pursuing Christian Womanhood, The (tape series)	02B18			✢
2	Rejoicing in Truth	02B13	The Looking Glass series	Christian Liberty press	P
2	Scriptural Role of a Godly Wife (tape)	02P16	Jonathan Lindvall	many editions available	✢
2	Shaping of a Christian Family	02B17	Elisabeth Elliot	Good News Broadcasting	✢☆
2	Sketches from Church History ◆	02C06	S M Houghton	Family Christian Academy	✢✳
2	Streams of Civilization ◆	02C08		Christian Liberty press	✢☆📖
2	Talk to Godly Teens about Sex and Romance, A ◆	02P02	Jonathan Lindvall	Bold Parenting	✢☆✳
2	Taming of the Shrew, The	02R06	William Shakespeare		📖
2	Under the Apple Tree	02H09	Helen Wessel	Bookmates International	✢
2	Wedding Covenant	02R08	Institute in Basic Life Principles	Advanced Training Institute of Am	P
2	What Ever Happened to Penny Candy?	02M03	Richard Marbury	Bluestocking Press	✢☆
2	What Every Christian Should Know About the Aids Epidemic	02H06	Franklin Payne	Covenant	✢
2	What is a Family?	02R12	Edith Schaeffer		✢
2	What's a Smart Woman Like You Doing in a Place Like This?	02R07			✝
2	World History Dates ◆	02C13	Usborne	Usborne	✢▲✳☆
2	Writers INC ◆	several	Write Source	Write Source	✢
2	Writers INC ◆	several	Write Source	Write Source	🐢
2	Youthful Romance: Scriptural Patterns	02P18	Jonathan Lindvall	Bold Parenting Seminars	P
3	Beggar to King: All the Occupations of the Bible ◆	03B15	Walter B. Duckat	(out of print) Doubleday	📖
3	Foxfire Books, The ◆	03P06	Elliot Wigginton	Doubleday	✢
3	Gaining Favor With God and Man	03B08	author unknown	Mantle Ministries (re-printed)	✢

◆ - Suggested in several units ✢ - Family Christian Academy ✳ - Elijah Company ☆ - Lifetime Gifts and Books 📖 Computer store, 🐢 Greenleaf Press

◆ - Order from publisher (see page 292 for addresses), ✝ Most Christian book stores, ▲ All Around Education, 📖 Library V Video rental

Far Above Rubies Appendix II

#	Title	Code	Author	Publisher	Availability
3	Kingfisher's Illustrated History of the World ◆	03C13		Kingfisher	⇗
3	Lessons from a Sheep Dog	03R10	Philip Keller	Family Christian Academy	⇗
3	Narrated Bible: In Chronological Order ◆	01B01	F. LaGuard Smith	Harvest House	⇗
3	Shepherd Looks at Psalm 23, A	03R03	Philip Keller	Family Christian Academy	⇗
3	Willingness to Work	03B07		Christ-Centered Curriculum	†
4	America 350 Years (audio tape set and workbook) ◆	04C04	Steve Wilkins	Covenant	⇗
4	American Heritage (audio tapes) ◆	04C02	Richard "Little Bear" Wheeler	Mantle Ministries	⇗
4	Ancient World, The	04C32		Usborne	⇗▲✻☆
4	Audubon Bird Field Guide	04S10	Audubon	Audubon	✻☆🐢
4	Baker's Bible Atlas Study Guide for Baker's Bible Atlas	04C11	Charles F. Pfeiffer	Baker Book House	⇗
4	Bird Watching for All Ages	04S15	Globe Pequot	Family Christian Academy	⇗
4	Church Hits the Road, The	04B01	Bible Log Series	Bible Log Series	⇗
4	Christopher Columbus	04R06	reprint by "Little Bear" Wheeler	Mantle Ministries	⇗
4	Columbus and the New World (republished)	04R04		Good Apple Books	⇗
4	Explorers	04C18	Good Apple Books	Good Apple Books	⇗
4	Explorers: from Columbus to Armstrong	04R02	Usborne	Usborne	⇗▲✻
4	Global Pursuit	04C25		National Geographic Society	P
4	Illustrated History of the World	04C39	Kingfisher	Kingfisher	⇗
4	Isaac Newton	04S10	John Hudson Tiner	Sower Series	⇗
4	Kingfisher's Illustrated History of the World ◆	04C39		Kingfisher	⇗
4	Make this Viking Settlement	04A11	Usborne	Usborne	⇗▲✻🐢
4	Magnetism and Electricity	04S04	Usborne	Usborne	⇗▲✻
4	Messianic Music and Blessings Tape (come in Haggadi Package)	04B14		Lederer	⇗
4	Messianic Passover Haggadah Package (tape, book, preparation guide)	04B13	Barry Rubin	Lederer Foundation	⇗
4	Narrated Bible: In Chronological Order ◆	01B01	F. LaGuard Smith	Harvest House	⇗
4	Once a Month Cooking ◆	04P01	Mimi Wilson	Family Christian Academy	⇗
4	Ornithology	04S12	Usborne	Usborne	▲☆
4	Picture World History	04C36	Usborne	Usborne	⇗▲✻

◆ - Suggested in several units ⇗ - Family Christian Academy ✻ - Elijah Company ☆ - Lifetime Gifts and Books 🖥 Computer store, 🐢 Greenleaf Press P- Order from publisher (see page 292 for addresses), † Most Christian book stores, ▲ All Around Education, 📖 Library 🎦 Video rental

Far Above Rubies Appendix II

	Title	Code	Author/Publisher	Store/Source	Symbol
4	Ring of the Nebulung, The	04A02	Richard Wagner	video rental stores	V
4	Rome (computer game)	04C35	Maxis 1-800-33-Maxis	software retailer	💻
4	Sailing Ships and How to Draw Them	04A03	Dover Publications	Dover Publications	P
4	Sailor Through History	04C41	Thompson Learning	Thompson Learning	✝
4	Sea Explorers (computer game)	04C19	software retailer	software retailer	💻
4	Seas and Oceans	04R07	Usborne	Usborne	✝⭐💻
4	SIM Farm (computer game) ◆	04S08	Maxis 1-800-33-Maxis	software retailer	💻
4	Spices of the World, The (game)	04C29	Avalon Hill Game Company	toy stores	✝⭐💻
4	Spotters Guide to Birds of North America	04S10	Usborne	Usborne	✝⭐💻
4	Story of Rolf and the Viking Bow, The	04R08	Allen French	Allen French	✝⭐💻
4	Streams of Civilization ◆	04C03	Christian Liberty Press	Christian Liberty Press	✝☆⭐
4	Vikings, The	04R03	Usborne	Usborne	✝▲⭐💻
4	War Terrible War	05C39	Joy Hakan	A History of US	✝
4	What is a Family	04R13	Edith Schaeffer		✝⭐⭐
4	Where in the World is Carmen Sandiego?	04C26		software retailer	💻
4	Where in the World	04C16	Aristoplay	Aristoplay	⭐☆
4	World History Dates	04C39	Usborne	Usborne	✝▲⭐☆
4	World History: A Christian Survey (audio tapes)	04C33	R. J. Rushdoony	Chalcedon Audio-Visual Productions	P
4	Writers INC ◆	03W04	Write Source	Write Source	✝
4	Writers INC ◆	03W04	Write Source	Write Source	✝
4	Writers INC ◆	03W04	Write Source	Write Source	✝
5	ABC's of the Human Body ◆	several	Reader's Digest	Reder's Digest	✝
5	Abraham Lincoln	05R15	Sower Series	Family Christian Academy	✝⭐☆
5	America 350 Years (audio tapes) ◆	05C18	Steve Wilkins	Covenant Publications	✝
5	Battle of Gettysburg.	05C17	Neil Johnson	FRWI	✝☆
5	Ben Hur	05R03	Lew Wallace	Pendulum Press	✝
5	Christ in the Camp	05R25	Jones		P
5	Confederate Trilogy for Young Readers.	05R26	Williamson		P

◆ - Suggested in several units   ✝- Family Christian Academy   ✳- Elijah Company   ☆- Lifetime Gifts and Books   💻 Computer store, ☕ Greenleaf Press

P- Order from publisher (see page 292 for addresses), ✝ Most Christian book stores, ▲ All Around Education, 📖 Library V Video rental

Far Above Rubies Appendix II

Unit	Title	Code	Author	Publisher	Source
5	Devil on Deck	05R19	Lois Hoadley Dick	Revell	📖
5	Dinner's in the Freezer	05P02			✤
5	Facts the Historians Leave Out: A Confederate Primer	05C33	Tilley		P
5	Fearfully and Wonderfully Made	05S01	Dr. Paul Brand	Zondervan	✤✱☆
5	Food, Fitness and Health	05S11	Usborne	Usborne	✤▲✱☆
5	Gone with the Wind	05R02	Margaret Mitchell	many editions available	🖳✱
5	Golden Goblet, The	05R28	Eloise Jarvis McGraw		🖳✱
5	Gray's Anatomy Coloring Book	05S14		Running Press	✤
5	Greenleaf's Guide to Ancient Egypt	05C04	Freddy Stark Ph.D.	Greenleaf Press	✤✱☆🖐
5	Hagar and/or Miriam	05R05	Lois Henderson	Walker & Co	✤
5	Hidden Art of Homemaking ◆	05R21	Edith Schaeffer	Tyndal House	✤☆
5	Home Made Health	05H17	Raymond Moore		✱☆
5	How to Live on Practically Nothing and Have Plenty	05R22	Janet Chadwick	Knopf	📖
5	In His Image	05S01	Dr. Paul Brand	Zondervan	✤📖
5	John Brown's Body	05R10	Steven Vincent Benet	Elephant	📖
5	Joseph	05R06	Philip Keller		✝✤
5	Killer Angles	05R27	Shaara		☆
5	Kingfisher's Illustrated History of the World ◆	05C38	Charles Dickens	Kingfisher	✤
5	Little Dorrit	05C36		many editions available	🖐
5	Long Walk Home, The	05R20		video rental stores	V
5	Myra, Daughter of the Nile	05R01	Eloise Jarvis McGraw		✤🖐✱
5	Narrated Bible: In Chronological Order ◆	01B01	F. LaGuard Smith	Harvest House	✤
5	Once a Month Cooking ◆	05P02	Mimi Wilson	Family Christian Academy	✤
5	Pharaohs of Ancient Egypt	05C05	Elizabeth Payne	Landmark	✤✱☆🖐
5	Price of Liberty, The	05C03	reprint by "Little Bear" Wheeler	Mantle Ministries	✤
5	Red Badge of Courage	05C09	Stephen Crane	many editions available	📖
5	Robe, The	05C03	Lloyd Douglas	many editions available	📖
5	Robert E Lee	05R23	Lee Roody / Sower Series	Family Christian Academy	✤✱☆

◆ - Suggested in several units ✤ - Family Christian Academy ✱ - Elijah Company ☆ - Lifetime Gifts and Books 🖳 Computer store 🖐 Greenleaf Press
P - Order from publisher (see page 292 for addresses), ✝ Most Christian book stores, ▲ All Around Education, 📖 Library V Video rental

Far Above Rubies Appendix II

	Title				V
5	Roots	05R18	Howard Fast	Buccaneer Books	📖 †
5	Spartacus	05C04	Howard Fast	many editions available	📖 ▲ ✻ ☆
5	Stonewall Jackson	05R24	Charles Ludwig / Sower Series	Family Christian Books	💻 💻 ✻ ☆
5	Uncle Tom's Cabin	05R14	Harriet Beecher Stowe	Airmont	💻 📖
5	Up From Slavery	05R11	Booker T. Washington	Airmont	†
5	Walking in Divine Health	05H01	Dr. Ted and Sharon Broer	NCS Nutrition	†
5	World History Dates	several	Usborne	Usborne	† ◆ 📖 ✻ ☆
5	Writers INC ◆	03W04	Write Source	Write Source	†
5	Writers INC ◆	03W04	Write Source	Write Source	†
6	ABC's of the Human Body	several	Reader's Digest	Reader's Digest	†
6	Audubon Pocket Guide to Familiar Wildflowers	06S15	Audubon Society	Audubon	✻ ☆
6	Audubon Pocket Guide to Familiar Trees	06S15	Audubon Society	Audubon	✻ ☆
6	Botany Coloring Book	06S40&41			†
6	Botany for All Ages	06A01	Jorie Hunkin	Globe Pequot	†
6	Drawing from Nature	06S42	Jim Arnosky		✻ 💻 ☆
6	Fall and Winter in North Carolina Forest	06R03	Rod and Staff	Family Christian Academy	†
6	Farmer Through the History	06C13		Thomson Learning	†
6	Gardener Looks at the Fruits, A	06R01	Philip Keller	Family Christian Academy	†
6	George Washington Carver	06R04	David Collins/ Sower Series	Family Christian Academy	†
6	God and Government, volumes 1 - 3	06C15	Gary Demar	Wolgemuth and Hyatt	†
6	Grapes of Wrath, The	06R02	John Steinbeck	out of print	📖
6	Hidden Art of Homemaking, The	06R13	Edith Schaeffer	Tyndale House	†
6	Kingfisher's Illustrated History of the World ◆	06C27		Kingfisher	†
6	Mysteries and Marvels of Plant Life	06S13	Usborne	Usborne	† ◆ ▲ ✻
6	Narrated Bible: In Chronological Order ◆	01B01	F. LaGuard Smith	Harvest House	† ▲ ✻
6	Secret Garden, The	06R12	Frances Hodgson Burnett	many editions available	† 📖
6	SIM Farm (computer game) ◆	06S18	Maxis 1-800-33-Maxis	software retailer	📖
6	Spring and Summer in North Carolina Forest	06R03	Rod and Staff	Family Christian Academy	†

◆ - Suggested in several units   ✝- Family Christian Academy   ✻- Elijah Company   ☆- Lifetime Gifts and Books   💻 Computer store,   🐚 Greenleaf Press

P- Order from publisher (see page 292 for addresses),   † Most Christian book stores,   ▲ All Around Education,   📖 Library   V Video rental

Far Above Rubies Appendix II

Unit	Title	Code	Author	Publisher	Sources
6	Thinking Christianly	06S19	Dr. Albert Green	Alta Vista College	✝
6	Way Things Work, The (also available for the computer)	06S41	David Macaulay		✝▲✳☆
6	Writers INC ◆	03W04	Write Source	Write Source	✝
6	Writers INC ◆	03W04	Write Source	Write Source	✝✳☆
7	Basic Greek in 30 Minutes a Day	07P01			✝✳☆🐾
7	Beautiful Girlhood ◆	07H01	Revised by Karen Andreola	Great Expectations	✝☆
7	Blood and Guts	07S01	Linda Allison	LB	✝✳☆🐾
7	Chariots of Fire (book or video)	07R05		out of print	📖 V
7	Child's Homer (The Iliad and the Odyssey -easier reading level)	07R02	Homer		✝✳☆🐾
7	Christian in Complete Armor, The	07B06	William Gurnall	Banner of Truth	✝✝
7	Coloring Book of the Olympics	07A08	Bellerophon	Bellerophon	🐾
7	Dave Dravecky	07R15	Dave Dravecky		✝
7	Fearfully and Wonderfully Made	07R16	Dr. Paul Brand	Zondervan	✝✳☆
7	Gray's Anatomy Coloring Book ◆	07S02	Gray		✝☆
7	Greeks, The	07C06	Usborne	Usborne	✝✳☆🐾
7	Greenleaf's Famous Men of Greece	07C04	Rob and Cyndy Shearer	Greenleaf Press	✝✳☆🐾
7	Greenleaf's Guide to Famous Men of Greece	07C05	Rob and Cyndy Shearer	Greenleaf Press	✝✳☆🐾
7	How Your Body Works	07S12	Usborne	Usborne	✝▲✳
7	Human Body Pop up Book, The	07S13	Jonathan Miller	Viking	✝☆
7	Iliad, The	07R01	Homer retold by Rieu		✝✳☆
7	In His Image	07R04	Dr. Paul Brand	Zondervan	✝✳☆
7	Joni	07R12		Zondervan	✝
7	Kingfisher's Illustrated History of the World ◆	07C18-19		Kingfisher	✝
7	Last Days of Socrates	07R03	Plato		✝✳☆🐾
7	Ludi at the Circus Maximus	07P02		Aristoplay	✝✳☆🐾
7	Narrated Bible: In Chronological Order ◆	01B01	F. LaGuard Smith	Harvest House	✝✳☆🐾
7	Odyssey, The	07R01	Homer retold by Rieu	Harvest House	✝
7	Rummy Roots (card game)	07W08			✝✳☆🐾

◆ - Suggested in several units ✝- Family Christian Academy ✱- Elijah Company ✩- Lifetime Gifts and Books ☐ Computer store, 🐾 Greenleaf Press
P- Order from publisher (see page 292 for addresses), ✝ Most Christian book stores, ▲ All Around Education, 📖 Library V Video rental

Far Above Rubies Appendix II

	Title	Code	Author/Source	Publisher	
7	Sportworks	07R14	Ontario Science Center	Addison-Wesley	📖☆
7	Streams of Civilization ◆	07C07		Christian Liberty Press	✝✱☆
7	Visible Man and Visible Woman	07S12		plastic models of human anatomy	toy store
7	Walking in Divine Health ◆	07S03	Dr. Ted and Sharon Broer	NCS Nutritious Ministry	✝
7	World History Dates	07C19	Usborne	Usborne	✝✱☆
7	World History Dates	09C14	Usborne	Usborne	✝▲✱☆
8	ABC's of the Human Body	several	Reader's Digest	Reader's Digest	✝
8	Astronomy and the Bible	08S01	Donald Deyoung	Baker Book House	✝☆
8	Christian Character	09B10			✝
8	Constellation Station	08S02	Aristoplay	Aristoplay	✱
8	Energy and Power	08S18	Usborne	Usborne	✝▲✱
8	Energy and Fuels	08S17	Usborne	Usborne	✝▲✱
8	Glow in the Dark, Night Sky Book, The	08S07	Hatchet	Running Press	✝
8	Gray's Anatomy Coloring Book	08S14	Freddy Stark Ph.D.	Running Press	✝
8	Johannes Kepler	08R03	John Hudson Tiner	Sower Series	✝☆
8	Kingfisher's Illustrated History of the World ◆	08C24		Kingfisher	✝
8	Magnetism and Electricity	08S19	Usborne	Usborne	✝☆✱
8	Men of Science, Men of God ◆	08R01	Henry Morris	Master	✝☆✱
8	Miracle Worker	08R04	William Gibson	Bantam	✝
8	Moby Dick	08R10	Herman Melville	several sources	✍💻
8	Narrated Bible: In Chronological Order ◆	01B01	F. LaGuard Smith	Harvest House	✝
8	Scientists from Archimedes to Einstein	08R02	Usborne	Usborne	✝▲✱
8	Sources of Energy	08S35	Good Apple workbook	Good Apple	P
8	Way Things Work, The ◆	08S16	Macaulay	Houghton Mifflin	✝✱☆
9	ABC's of the Human Body	09S09	Reader's Digest	Reader's Digest	✝
9	Age of Extremes	09C15	Joy Hakim	A History of US	✝
9	Age of Revolutions	09C04	Usborne	Usborne	✝▲✱
9	Back to Basics	09P03	Reader's Digest	Reader's Digest	P

◆ - Suggested in several units   ✝- Family Christian Academy   ✱- Elijah Company   ☆- Lifetime Gifts and Books   💻 Computer store, ✍ Greenleaf Press
P- Order from publisher (see page 292 for addresses), ✝ Most Christian book stores, ▲ All Around Education, 📖 Library V Video rental

Far Above Rubies Appendix II

	Title	Code	Author	Publisher	
9	Beggar to King: All the Occupations of the Bible ◆	09B06	Walter B. Duckat	out of print Doubleday	rare 🕮
9	Blue Willow	09R04			✳
9	Fearfully and Wonderfully Made ◆	09S15	Dr. Paul Brand	Zondervan	✥ ✳ ☆
9	Foxfire Books (volumes 1-9), The ◆	09R07	Elliot Wigginton	Doubleday	✥ 🕮
9	Gray's Anatomy Coloring Book	09S10	Freddy Stark Ph.D.	Running Press	✥
9	Hidden Art of Homemaking, The ◆	09R01	Edith Schaeffer	Tyndale House	✥ ☆
9	Invention and Discovery	09S03	Usborne	Usborne	✥ ▲ ✳
9	John Brown's Body	09R06	Steven Vincent Benet	Elephant	🕮 ✥
9	Key to Geometry	09M09		Key Curriculum Press	✥
9	Kingfisher's Illustrated History of the World ◆	09C14		Kingfisher	✥
9	Machines	09S08	Usborne	Usborne	✥
9	Narrated Bible: In Chronological Order ◆	01B01	F. LaGuard Smith	Harvest House	✥
9	Quilt in a Day, A	09P04	Eleanor Burns	Quilt in a Day Inc.	✥
9	Seven Men Who Rule the World from the Grave	09R11	D. Breese	Houghton Mifflin	✥ ☆
9	Way Things Work, The ◆	09S07	Macaulay	Houghton Mifflin	✥ ✳
9	Writers INC ◆	03W04	Write Source	Write Source	✥
10	Age of Extremes	10C25	Joy Hakim	A History of US	✥
10	Autobiography of George Muller	10R02	George Muller	Family Christian Academy	✥
10	Biblical Economics in Comics	10M09	Vic Lockman	Lockman Inc.	✥
10	Bringing in the Sheaves	10R13	George Grant	Crossway Books	✝
10	Chance to Die: The Life and Legacy of Amy Carmichael ◆	10R03	Elizabeth Elliot	Revell	✥
10	Dispossessed	10R04	George Grant	Crossway Books	rare ✥
10	George Muller, The Autobiography of ◆	10R02	George Muller	Family Christian Academy	✥
10	Get a Grip on Your Money ◆	02M11	Larry Burkett		✥
10	God Made them Great ◆	10R05	John Tallach	Family Christian Academy	✥ ✳ ☆
10	God and Government, volumes 1 - 3 ◆	10C03	Gary Demar	Wolgemuth and Hyatt	✥
10	Hidden Art of Homemaking, The ◆	10R09	Edith Schaeffer	Tyndale House	✥ P

◆ - Suggested in several units ✥ - Family Christian Academy ✳ - Elijah Company ☆ - Lifetime Gifts and Books 🖳 Computer store, 🐦 Greenleaf Press
P - Order from publisher (see page 292 for addresses), ✝ Most Christian book stores, ▲ All Around Education, 🕮 Library V Video rental

Far Above Rubies Appendix II

	Title	Code	Author	Publisher	
10	In the Shadow of Plenty	10R04	George Grant	American Bureau of Economic Restoration	rare 📖
10	Invention and Discovery	10S10	Usborne	Usborne	✝▲✶☆
✓10	Kingfisher's Illustrated History of the World ◆	10C23	Kingfisher	Kingfisher	✝
10	Machines	10S11	Usborne	Usborne	✝▲✶☆
10	Major Barbara	10R06	George Bernard Shaw	college bookstores	📖
10	Narrated Bible: In Chronological Order ◆	01B01	F. LaGuard Smith	Harvest House	✝
10	Oliver Twist	10R10	Charles Dickens	many versions available	📖
10	What Ever Happened to Penny Candy? ◆	10M10	Richard Maybury	Bluestocking Press	✝
10	Way Things Work, The ◆ (also available on CD ROM)	10S11	Macaulay	Houghton Mifflin	✝✶☆
✓10	World History Dates ◆	10C23	Usborne	Usborne	✝▲✶☆
10	Writers INC ◆	03W04	Write Source	Write Source	✝
✓11	Beggar to King: All the Occupations of the Bible ◆	11B12	Walter B. Duckat	Doubleday	rare 📖
11	Discovered Noah's Ark	11R02	Ron Wyatt	World Bible Society	✝
✓11	Foxfire Books (1-9), The	11R11	Elliot Wigginton	Doubleday	✝
✓11	Genesis Flood, The	11R12	Henry Morris	Master Books	✝✶☆
11	Global Pursuit	11C08		National Geographic Society	P
✓11	Hidden Art of Homemaking, The	11R04	Edith Schaeffer	Tyndale House	✝
11	Narrated Bible: In Chronological Order ◆	01B01	F. LaGuard Smith	Harvest House	✝
11	Noah's Ark and the Lost World	11R01		Master Books	✝✶☆
11	Spotters Guide to the Weather	11S17	Usborne	Usborne	✝▲✶
11	Weather and Climate	11R13	Usborne	Usborne	✝▲✶
11	Weather and the Bible	11S01	Young		✝
11	Weather Source Book	11S02		Globe Pequot	✝
✓11	Writers INC	03W04	Write Source	Write Source	✝
12	ABC's of the Human Body	12S12	Reader's Digest	Reader's Digest	✝
12	Beggar to King: All the Occupations of the Bible ◆	12B10	Walter B. Duckat	Doubleday	rare 📖
12	Bible Smuggler	12R16	Louise Vernon	Doubleday	✝✶☆📖🖥

◆ - Suggested in several units   ✝- Family Christian Academy   ✶- Elijah Company   ☆- Lifetime Gifts and Books   🖥 Computer store,   🖐 Greenleaf Press
P- Order from publisher (see page 292 for addresses),   ✝ Most Christian book stores,   ▲ All Around Education,   📖 Library   V Video rental

Far Above Rubies Appendix II

	Title	Code	Author	Publisher	
12	Builder Through History	12C18		Thompson Learning	⊹
12	Castle (video or book)	12C19	David Macaulay		📖✓🎥🐚
12	Cathedral (video or book)	12C19	David Macaulay		📖✓🎥🐚
12	City (video or book)	12C19	David Macaulay		📖✓🎥🐚
12	Discovered: Sodom and Gomora	12C19	Ron Wyatt		⊹
12	Everyday Life in Old Testament Times	12C03	E. W. Heaton	MacMillan	📖
12	Fearfully and Wonderfully Made	12S11	Dr. Paul Brand	Zondervan	⊹✳☆
12	Foxes Book of Mayters	12R08			
12	Foxfire Books (1-9), The ◆	12R06	Elliot Wigginton	Doubleday	📖
12	Gray's Anatomy Coloring Book	12S13	Freddy Stark Ph.D.	Running Press	⊹
12	Greenleaf's Guide to Famous Men of the Renias. and Reformation	12C11	Rob and Cyndy Shearer	Greenleaf Press	⊹✳☆🐚
12	Greenleaf's Famous Men of the Renaissance and Reformation	12C11	Rob and Cyndy Shearer	Greenleaf Press	⊹✳☆🐚
12	Heart Strangely Warmed	12R05	Louise Vernon	Greenleaf Press	⊹✳☆🐚
12	Hidden Art of Homemaking, The ◆	12R02	Edith Schaeffer	Tyndale House	⊹
12	Kingfisher's Illustrated History of the World ◆	12R13	Kingfisher	Kingfisher	⊹✳
12	Manners and Customs of Bible Lands ◆	12C03	Fred Wight	Moody Press	P
12	Narrated Bible: In Chronological Order ◆	01B01	F. LaGuard Smith	Harvest House	⊹
12	Odyssey, The	12R07	Homer	see The Child's Homer	🖥🐚
12	Renaissance: History of Everything, The	12C23			
12	Sketches from Church History ◆	12C14	S M Houghton	Family Christian Academy	⊹✳
12	Streams of Civilization	12C09	Christian Liberty Press	Christian Liberty Press	⊹✳☆🐚
12	Teaching From the Tabernacle	12B03	Roy Lee Dwitt	Baker	⊹
12	The Man Who Laid the Egg	12R14	Louise Vernon	Greenleaf Press	⊹✳☆🐚
12	Thunderstorm in Church	12R14	Louise Vernon	Greenleaf Press	⊹✳☆🐚
12	World History Dates	12C17	Usborne	Usborne	⊹▲✳
12	Writers INC ◆	03W04	Write Source	Write Source	⊹
13	America: 350 Years (audio tapes and workbook) ◆	13C03	Steve Wilkins	Covenant	⊹
13	America's Godly Heritage (video or cassette)	13C25	David Barton	Wallbuilders	⊹

◆ - Suggested in several units ⊹- Family Christian Academy ✳- Elijah Company ☆- Lifetime Gifts and Books 🖥 Computer store, 🐚 Greenleaf Press

P- Order from publisher (see page 292 for addresses), ✝ Most Christian book stores, ▲ All Around Education, 📖 Library V Video rental

Far Above Rubies Appendix II

13	Title	Code	Author	Publisher	Source
13	Basic History of the United States, A	13C24	Clarence Carson	American Textbook Committee	rare 📖
13	Bulletproof George Washington	13C03	David Barton	Wallbuilders	✝
13	Christian Leadership in the Home (free audio tape)	13B09	Pilgrim Tape Ministry	Pilgrim Tape Ministry	P
13	Daniel Webster	13R12	Robert Allen	Sower Series	✝✱☆
13	From Sea to Shining Sea (available in child's version for jr high)	13R02	D Manuel and Peter Marshall	Revell	✝
13	George Washington	13R18	Norma Camp /Sower Series	Family Christian Academy	✝
13	God and Government, volumes 1 - 3 ◆	13C12	Gary Demar	Wolgemuth and Hyatt	📖
13	Great Americans and their Noble Deeds ◆	13C05	reprint by "Little Bear" Wheeler	Mantle Ministries	✝
13	Hail to the Chief (game)	13C25		Aristoplay	✱☆
13	Hawk that Dare not Hunt by Day, The ◆	13R17		Bob Jones Press	✝
13	History Alive Through Music: America	13A09	Dianna Waring		✝
13	Kingfisher's Illustrated History of the World ◆	13C07		Kingfisher	📖
13	Kings and Queens of England	13R13			✝
13	Light and the Glory, The (available in child's version for jr high)	13R01	D Manuel and Peter Marshall	Revell	✝
13	Making of the 13 Colonies	13C17	Joy Hakam	A History of the US	✝
13	Narrated Bible: In Chronological Order ◆	01B01	F. LaGuard Smith	Harvest House	✝
13	Noah Webster	13R19	David Collins /Sower Series	Family Christian Academy	✝✱☆
13	One Nation Under God	13R20	reprint by "Little Bear" Wheeler	Mantle Ministries	✝
13	Open Church, The ◆	13R14	James Rutz	Seed Sower	✝✝
13	Plymouth Settlement	13C04	reprint by "Little Bear" Wheeler	Mantle Ministries	✝
13	Political Sermons of the American Founding Era	13B10	Ellis Sandoz	Liberty Press	✝
13	Politics and Government	13C24	Usborne	Usborne	✝
13	Preparing for Romance	13P01	Jonathan Lindvall	Bold Parenting	✝✱☆
13	Rebirth of a Nation	13R03	various authors	DeMoss Associates	✝✱☆
13	Rewriting of America's History	13C07	Catherine Millard		▲✱
13	Talk to Godly Teens about Sex and Romance	13P02	Jonathan Lindvall	Bold Parenting	✝✱☆
13	Toliver's Secret	13R16	Ester Wood Brady		✝✱☆📖
13	United States Constitution, The	13C15	most U.S. history textbooks	free from your Congressman's office	📖

◆ - Suggested in several units   ✝ - Family Christian Academy   ✱ - Elijah Company   ☆ - Lifetime Gifts and Books   📖 Computer store,   🎅 Greenleaf Press

P - Order from publisher (see page 292 for addresses),   ✝ Most Christian book stores,   ▲ All Around Education,   📚 Library V Video rental

Far Above Rubies Appendix II

Unit	Title	Code	Author	Publisher	
13	What the Founding Fathers Really Meant by Separation of Church and State (video, audio and book notes available)	13C08	David Barton	Wallbuilders	✝
13	Witch of Blackbird Pond, The	13R15	Elizabeth George Spear	Note: Not about witchcraft	✝
14	Writers INC ◆	03W04	Write Source	Write Source	✝
14	All the Way Home	14R10	Mary Pride	—	✝✶☆
14	Apprenticeship Plus	14P13	Inge Cannon	Education Plus	P
14	Beggar to King: All the Occupations in the Bible	14B07			rare📖
14	Bronze Bow, The	14R06			✶☆🐌
14	Business by the Book	14B09	Larry Burkett	Moody Press	✝
14	City	14C06	David Macauley		📖✶☆🐌
14	Disciplined Life, The	14B11	Richard Shelly Taylor		✝✶
14	Drawing on the Right Side of the Brain	14A06	Betty Edwards	Tarcher	✝
14	Everyday Life Through the Ages	14B07	Readers Digest	Readers Digest	✝
14	Forbidden Gates	14R06		out of print - rare	✶☆🐌
14	Found Money	14R14			📖
14	Gaining Favor with God and Man ◆	14B03	reprint by "Little Bear" Wheeler		✝
14	God's Principles for Operating a Business	14C18	Larry Burkett	Christian Financial Concepts	✝
14	Greenleaf's Guide to Famous Men of Rome	14C05	Rob and Cyndy Shearer	Greenleaf Press	✝✶☆🐌
14	Greenleaf's Famous Men of Rome	14C04	Rob and Cyndy Shearer	Greenleaf Press	✝✶☆🐌
14	How Should We Then Live ◆	14C10	Frances Schaeffer	Crossway	✝
14	If I Made a Million	14R16	David Schwartz	Scholastic	P
14	In Jesus' Times	14C08	Kathryn Merrill		✶
14	Kingfisher's Illustrated History of the World ◆	14C25		Kingfisher	✝
14	Knowing God	14B10	J I Packard	Intervarsity	✝✶
14	Last Days of Pompeii, The (video)	14C09		local video store	V
14	Living History: Classical Rome	14R08			✝▲✶☆🐌
14	Living History: Ancient Greece	14A01	Usborne	Usborne	✝▲✶☆🐌
14	Make this Roman Fort	14R08			✝▲✶☆🐌

◆ - Suggested in several units ✝ - Family Christian Academy ✶ - Elijah Company ☆ - Lifetime Gifts and Books 📖 Computer store, 🐌 Greenleaf Press

P - Order from publisher (see page 292 for addresses), ✝ Most Christian book stores, ▲ All Around Education, 📖 Library V Video rental

Far Above Rubies Appendix II

Unit	Title	Code	Author	Publisher	Symbols
14	Make this Roman Villa	14A01	Usborne	Usborne	✝▲✻☆🐘
14	Merchant of Venice, The	14R09	William Shakespeare		📖🐘
14	Minding Your Own Business	14R15	Raymond and Dorothy Moore		✻
14	Money in My Cookie Jar	14R14		out of print	📖
14	Narrated Bible: In Chronological Order ◆	01B01	F. LaGuard Smith	Harvest House	✝
14	Quo Vadis	14R02	Henry Sienkiewicz		✝✻🐘
14	Richest Christian, The	14M05		Christian Life Workshops	P
14	Robe, The	14R04	Lloyd Douglas		✻📖
14	Romans, The	14C03	Usborne	Usborne	✝▲✻☆🐘
14	Rome (computer game)	14P12	Maxis 1-800-33-Maxis	software retailer	📖
14	Rome and Romans	14C07	Usborne	Usborne	✝▲✻☆🐘
14	Runaway	14R05	Patrica St. John		✻☆🐘
14	Stories of Jesus: Our Lord and Saviour	04R01	reprint by "Little Bear" Wheeler	Mantle Ministries	✝
14	Streams of Civilization ◆	14C11	Stanon & Hyma	Christian Liberty Press	✝✻☆🐘
14	Teenage Entrepreneurs' Guide	14R13	Sarah Riehm	Surrey	P
14	Wealth of Nations	14C23	Adam Smith		📖
14	World History Dates	14C25	Usborne	Usborne	✝▲✻☆
14	Writers INC ◆	03W04	Write Source	Write Source	✝
14	Writing Resumes for Teen	14W09	Inge Cannon	Education Plus	P
15	ABC's of the Human Body	15H09	Reader's Digest	Reader's Digest	✝
15	All the Way Home	15R19	Mary Pride		✝✻☆
15	Arthur and the Knights of the Round Table	15R06		several versions available	📖🐘
15	Backyard Scientist	16S09	Jane Hoffman		✝☆
15	Beowulf	15R12	Frederick Rebsamen		🐘
15	Caring for Planet Earth	15S10		Lion	✝
15	Castle (video)	15C06	David Macauley		🐘
15	Castle	15C06	David Macauley		✝✻🐘
15	Cathedral	15C07	David Macauley		✝✻🐘

◆ - Suggested in several units   ✝- Family Christian Academy   ✻- Elijah Company   ☆- Lifetime Gifts and Books   📖 Computer store,   🐘 Greenleaf Press

P- Order from publisher (see page 292 for addresses),   ✝ Most Christian book stores,   ▲ All Around Education,   📖 Library V Video rental

Far Above Rubies Appendix II

	Title	Code	Author	Publisher	
15	Cathedral (video)	15C07	David Macauley	Revell	📹
15	Chance to Die: The Life and Legacy of Amy Carmichael ◆	15R07	Elizabeth Elliot	Revell	✝
15	Christian Charm Course, The	15B19	Emily Hunter	Harvest House	✝
15	Christian Legal Advisor, The	15C16	John Eidsmoe	Baker Book House	✝
15	City of Bees	15S01	Bob Jones	Bob Jones	P
15	Coming Economic Earthquake, The	15R14	Larry Burkett	Moody Press	✝
15	Cultural Atlas of the Middle Ages	15C09			✳☆📹
15	Days of Vengeance	15R15	David Chilton	Dominion Press	✝
15	Disciplines of a Beautiful Woman, The ◆	15B07	Ann Ortlund	Word Books	✝
15	Door in the Wall, The	15R01	Marguerite De Angeli		✝✳☆
15	Everyday Life Through the Ages	15C25	Reader's Digest	Reader's Digest	✝
15	Florence Nightingale	15R15	David Collins	Sower Series	✝✳☆
15	God Made Them Great ◆	15R08			✝
15	Gray's Anatomy Coloring Book	15H10	Freddy Stark Ph.D.	Running Press	✝
15	Green Leaf's Guide to Famous Men of the Middle Ages	15C04	Rob and Cyndy Shearer	Greenleaf Press	✝✳☆
15	Green Leaf's Famous Men of the Middle Ages	15C03	Rob and Cyndy Shearer	Greenleaf Press	✝✳☆📹
15	Hawk and the Dove, The	15R02	Penelope Wilcock		✝✳
15	History Alive Through Music	15C23	Diana Waring		✝
15	How Should We then Live ◆	15C15	Francis Schaeffer		✝✳☆
15	Ivenhoe	15R04	Sir Walter Scott		✝✳☆
15	Jackaroo	15R03	Cynthia Voigt		✝
15	John Brown's Body ◆	15W09	Steven Vincent Benet	Elephant	📖✝
15	Kingfisher's Illustrated History of the World ◆	15C24		Kingfisher	✝
15	Knights and Castles	15C08	Usborne	Usborne	✝▲✳📹
15	Knowing God ◆	15B06	J I Packard	Intervarsity	✝
15	Late, Great Planet Earth, The	15R16	Hal Lindsey	Harp	✝
15	Make this Model Castle	15A01	Usborne	Usborne	✝▲✳📹
15	Otto of the Silver Hand	15R16	Howard Plye	Dover	✝📹

◆ - Suggested in several units ✝- Family Christian Academy ✳- Elijah Company ☆- Lifetime Gifts and Books 📖 Computer store, 📹 Greenleaf Press
P- Order from publisher (see page 292 for addresses), † Most Christian book stores, ▲ All Around Education, 📖 Library V Video rental

Far Above Rubies Appendix II

Unit	Title	Code	Author	Publisher	
15	Parousia, The	15R16	J. Stuart Russell	Baker Book House	✞
15	Piercing the Darkness	15R17	Frank Peretti	Crossway Books	✞
15	Putting Food By	15P01	R Hertzberg, B Vaughan, and J Greene	Stephen Greene Press	📖
15	Sketches from Church History ◆	15C13	S M Houghton	Family Christian Academy	✞✶
15	Story of King Arthur and His Knights	15R05	Howard Plye	Dover	✞☆🐚
15	Streams of Civilization ◆	15C03		Christian Liberty Press	✞☆✶
15	This Present Darkness	15R17	Frank Peretti	Crossway Books	✞✞
15	Tristan	15R06			📖
15	Trumpeter of Krakow	15R15	Eric P. Kelly		
15	World History Dates	15C26	Usborne	Usborne	✞☆✶▲✶☆
15	Writers INC ◆	03W04	Write Source	Write Source	✞
15	Writing Resumes for Teens	14W04	Inge Cannon		P
16	America 350 Years (audio tape set and workbook) ◆	16C05	Steve Wilkins	Convent Publishing	✞☆
16	Bible Visual Resource Book ◆	16A12			✞
16	Bible, Home Schooling, and the Law, The	16C09	Karl Reed	Christian Home Ministries	P
16	Child Training and the Home School	16R03	Jeff and Marge Barth	Parable Publishing House	✞
16	Christian Home Educator's Curriculum Manual, The	16R18	Cathy Duffy	Home Run Enterprises	✞✶☆
16	Christian Manifesto, A	16C06	Frances Schaeffer	Crossway	✞✶☆
16	Competent to Counsel	16R11	Jay Adams	Presbyterian & Reformed	✞
16	Daily Words of Wisdom	16B13	Bible Memory Association	Bible Memory Association	P
16	Dare to Discipline	16R10	James Dobson	Tyndale	✞
16	Dinosaurs: Those Terrible Lizards	16S01	Duane Gish	Master Books	✞
16	Dumbing Us Down	16R04	John Taylor Gatto	Wolgemuth & Hyatt	✞✶☆
16	Education and the Founding Fathers (video, audio and notes available)	16C04	David Barton	Wallbuilders	✞✶☆🐚
16	Fine Art of Mentoring	16R15	Ted Engstrom	Wolgemuth & Hyatt	✞
16	For the Children's Sake	16R08	Susan Schaeffer Macauley	Crossway Books	✞✶☆🐚
16	Foundation for Excellence (video)	16R01	HSLDA	HSLDA	✞

◆ - Suggested in several units ✞- Family Christian Academy ✶- Elijah Company ☆- Lifetime Gifts and Books 📖 Computer store, 🐚 Greenleaf Press

P- Order from publisher (see page 292 for addresses), ✞ Most Christian book stores, ▲ All Around Education, 📖 Library V Video rental

Far Above Rubies Appendix II

	Title	Code	Author	Publisher	
16	Government Nannies	16C08	Cathy Duffy	Home Run Enterprise	✦
16	Hard Times in Paradise	16R25	Colfax		✦
16	Home Schooling for Excellence	16R24	David and Micki Colfax	Warner Books	✦✱
16	Home Education and Constitutional Liberties	16C12	John Whitehead and W Bird	Crossway Books	✦
16	Home-Grown Kids	16R12	Dr. Raymond Moore	Word	✦✱
16	Home-Spun Schools	16R12	Dr. Raymond Moore	Word	✦✱
16	Home-style Teaching	16R12	Dr. Raymond Moore	Word	✦✱
16	How the Bible Came to us	16B14	Meryl Doney	Lion	✦☛
16	How to Create Your Own Unit Study	16R16	Valerie Bendt	Common Sense Press	✦✱☆☛
16	How to Lead a Child to Christ	16B19		Child Evangelism Fellowship	P
16	Kneeling Christian, The	16B07	anonymous		✦
16	Learning Styles and Tools ◆	16R06	Alta Vista College	Family Christian Press	✦✱☆
16	Lifestyle Evangelism	16B20	Joseph Aldrich	Multnomah Productions	✝
16	Light and the Glory, The (also in child's version for jr high)	16B17	D Manuel and Peter Marshall	Revell	✦✱☆
16	Messianic Character of American Education, The	16C07	Rousas John Rushdooney	Craig Press	✱
16	Muggins Math, Knock-Out, and nine other games	16M07	Allan Schuller	Hazelden	✱
16	Never Too Early	16R13	Doreen Claggett		✦
16	Our Reeds Grow Free	16R19	Karl Reed	Christian Home Ministries	✦✱
16	Peanut Butter Family Home Schools, The	16R20	Bill Butterworth	Revell	✦
16	Physician's Desk Reference	16H07	E.R. Barnhart	Medical Economics	📖
16	Principle Thing, The	16B23			✦
16	Right Choice: Home Schooling, The	16R02	Christopher Klicka	Noble Press	✦✱
16	Thieves of Innocence	16R04	John Ankerburg & C Branch		✦
16	Training Children in Godliness	16R24	Jacob Abbot	Christian Liberty Press	✦✱
16	Webster's 1828 dictionary ◆	16W19	Noah Webster	FACE	✦
16	What the Bible Says about Child Training ◆	16R07	Richard Fugate	Alpha Omega	✦
16	What the Founding Fathers Really Meant by Separation of Church and State (video, audio or notes available)	16C18	David Barton	Wallbuilders	✦

◆ - Suggested in several units   ⇩- Family Christian Academy   ✱- Elijah Company   ☆- Lifetime Gifts and Books   💻 Computer store,   🐍 Greenleaf Press
P- Order from publisher (see page 292 for addresses),   ✝ Most Christian book stores,   ▲ All Around Education,   📖 Library   V Video rental

Far Above Rubies Appendix II

	Title	Code	Author	Publisher	
16	Why Christians are Going Home to School	16C03	Llewellyn Davis	Elijah Co	✝❋☆🖙
16	Wisdom Hunter	16R24	Randall Arthur	Questar	✝❋☆🖙
16	Writers INC ◆	03W04	Write Source	Write Source	✝
17	California Gold Rush	17R09	May McNear	Landmark	✝❋☆🖙📖
17	Cheaper by the Dozen	17R04	Frank Gilbreth/ E Carey	Bantam	✝
17	Christian Manifesto, The	17R08	Francis Schaeffer	Crossway	✝
17	Clutter's Last Stand	17R02	Don Aslett	Writer's Digest Books	✝❋
17	File Don't Pile	17P14	Pat Dorff	St Martin Press	✝
17	Formulas, Tips, and Data for the Home	17S01	Kenneth Swezey	Harper & Row	📖
17	God and Government ◆	17C14	Gary Demar	Wolgemuth and Hyatt	✝
17	Great American Short Stories ◆	17R15			✝❋☆
17	History Alive Through Music	17C17	Dianna Waring	Kingfisher	✝
17	Hidden Art of Homemaking, The ◆	17R03	Edith Schaeffer	Tyndale House	✝
17	Happy Home Handbook, The	17R06	Jo Berry	Fleming H. Revell	📖
17	Kingfisher's Illustrated History of the World ◆	17C13	author unknown	Kingfisher	✝❋☆
17	Kneeling Christian, The	17B05	author unknown	Mantle Ministries	✝
17	Liberty for All	17C24	Richard "Little Bear" Wheeler	Mantle Ministries	✝❋☆📖
17	Little Women	17R12	Lousia May Alcott	several available	✝❋☆
17	Mentor Book of Major Poets	17R14	various		✝❋☆
17	Oregon Trail	17C22			📖
17	Organize Yourself	17P15	Ronni Eisenberg	Collier Books	✝
17	Sidetracked Home Executives	17R01	Pam Young and Peggy Jones	Warner Books	📖
17	Story of the Great American West	17C24	Reader's Digest	Reader's Digest	✝📖
17	The Pioneers Go West	17R09	George Stewart	Landmark	✝
17	What is a Family?	17R04	Edith Schaeffer	Tyndale House	✝❋☆📖
17	What Husbands Wish Their Wives Knew About Money	17R07	Larry Burkett	Victor Books	✝
17	Writers INC ◆	03W04	Write Source	Write Source	✝
18	Abortion and the Conscience of a Nation	18R09	Ronald Reagan	Nelson	✝

◆ - Suggested in several units   ✝- Family Christian Academy   ❋- Elijah Company   ☆- Lifetime Gifts and Books   ⌨ Computer store,   🖙 Greenleaf Press

P- Order from publisher (see page 292 for addresses),   † Most Christian book stores,   ▲ All Around Education,   📖 Library   V Video rental

Far Above Rubies Appendix II

18	Title	Code	Author	Publisher	
18	Abortion Letters (I, II, and III)	18R07	Karl Reed	Family Christian Academy	✞
18	All the Way Home ◆	18R25	Mary Pride	Crossway	✞✳
18	America: To Pray or not to Pray	18C10	David Barton	Wallbuilders	✞
18	Apple Tree Guide for Expectant Parents ◆ (need Under the Apple Tree)	18R02	Helen Wessel & Kathy Nesper	Bookmates International	✞
18	Apple Tree Personal Study Guide (need Under the Apple Tree)	18S10	Helen Wessel Nickle	Apple Tree Ministries	P
18	Autobiography of George Muller, The ◆	18R17	George Muller		✞✞
18	Born in Zion	18R02	Carol Balizet	Family Christian Academy	✞
18	Chance to Die: The Life and Legacy of Amy Carmichael ◆	18R26	Elizabeth Elliot	Revell	✞
18	Child Influencers, The	18R18	Don Adams (home school dad)		✞
18	Child Training and the Home School ◆	18R04	Jeff and Marge Barth	Parable Publishing House	✞
18	Child Abuse Industry	18R23	Mary Pride	Good News	
18	Children: Blessing or Burden?	18R13			✞
18	Five Little Peppers and How They Grew	18R21	Margaret Sydney	Grossett & Dunlap	✞✞🕮
18	Full Quiver: Family Planning and the Lordship of Christ, A ◆	18R10	Rick and Jan Hess		✞✞
18	Haunt of Jackals, A	18R27	Paul DeParrie		✞
18	Home By Choice	18R24	Brenda Hunter	Multnomah	✞
18	Husband Coached Childbirth	18S10	Dr. Robert Bradley	Harper and Row	✞🕮
18	Lambs to the Slaughter	18R17	Johanna Michaelson	Harvest House	✞✞
18	Letting God Plan Your Family ◆	18R12	Samuel Owen	Crossway	✞
18	Little Women	18R21	Louisa May Alcott	Grossett & Dunlap	🖳✞∪
18	Parents' Rights	18R24	John W. Whitehead	Crossway	✞
18	Roses for Mama	18R23	Janette Oke	Bethany House	✞
18	Saturday Morning Mind Control	18R14	Phil Phillips		✞
18	Shaping of a Christian Family, The ◆	18R16	Elizabeth Elliot		✞
18	Susanna Wesley	18R04	Charles Ludwig	Sower Series	✞✳☆
18	Way Home, The	18R27	Mary Pride	Crossway	✞
18	Weeping in Ramah	18R07			✞
18	What the Bible Says about Child Training	18B13	Richard Fugate	Alpha Omega	✞

◆ - Suggested in several units ✞ - Family Christian Academy ✳ - Elijah Company ☆ - Lifetime Gifts and Books 🖳 Computer store, 🕮 Greenleaf Press
P- Order from publisher (see page 292 for addresses), ✞ Most Christian book stores, ▲ All Around Education, 🕮 Library V Video rental

Far Above Rubies Appendix II

	Title	Code	Author	Publisher	
18	Writers INC ◆	03W04	Write Source	Write Source	✝
19	Becoming a Woman of Excellence	03W04	Cynthia Heald	Navpress	✝
19	Christian Excellence	19R12	Jon Johnston	Baker House	✝
19	Esther the Queen		Gilbert Aberg	Carnation	✝
19	Foxes' Book of Martyrs	19R02	John Foxe	Whitaker House	✝✱☆
19	Hide or Seek	19H03	James Dobson	Revell	✝
19	Light in the North	19R02	J D Douglas	Paternoster Press	✝☆
19	Writers INC ◆	03W04	Write Source	Write Source	✝
20	8 Principles of the Reformation (audio)	20C12	David Barton	Wallbuilders	✝
20	America: 350 Years (audio tape and workbook) ◆	20C05	Steve Wilkins	Covenant	✝
20	Bordan of Yale	20R05	Taylor	Taylor	✝✱☆
20	Christian History of the Constitution of the U. S. A., The	20C03	Verna M. Hall	Foundation Am Christian Education	P
20	Gaining Favor With God and Man ◆	20C13	author unknown	Mantle Ministries (re-printed)	✝
20	Gardener Looks at the Fruits, A	20R03	Philip Keller		✝
20	George Washington Carver	20S05	Charels Ludwig	Sower Series	✝✱☆
20	God and Government ◆	20C11	Gary Demar	Wolgemuth and Hyatt	✝
20	Hudson Taylor's Spiritual Secret	20R14	Dr. Howard Taylor	Moody	✝
20	Jim Elliot	20R02	White		✝✝☆
20	Kneeling Christian, The	20R08	anonymous		✝
20	L'Abri	20R01	Edith Schaeffer	Tyndale House	✝
20	Light and the Glory and study guide, The	20C04	Peter Marshall and D Manuel	Revell	✝
20	Spirit-Controlled Temperament	20S04	Tim LaHaye	Tyndale	✝
20	Stories Worth Rereading	20R09	various	Review and Herald	✝✝☆
20	What Happens When Women Pray	20R07	Evenlin Christianson		✝
20	Writers INC ◆	03W04	Write Source	Write Source	✝

◆ - Suggested in several units ✝- Family Christian Academy ✱- Elijah Company ☆- Lifetime Gifts and Books 🖳 Computer store, ☏ Greenleaf Press
P- Order from publisher (see page 292 for addresses), ✝ Most Christian book stores, ▲ All Around Education, 📖 Library V Video rental

Far Above Rubies Appendix II

	Title	Code	Author	Publisher	
18	Writers INC ◆	03 W04	Write Source	Write Source	✧
19	Becoming a Woman of Excellence		Cynthia Heald	Navpress	✧
19	Christian Excellence	19R12	Jon Johnston	Baker House	✧
19	Esther the Queen		Gilbert Aberg	Carnation	†
19	Foxes' Book of Martyrs	19R02	John Foxe	Whitaker House	✧ ✱ ☆
19	Hide or Seek	19H03	James Dobson	Revell	✧
19	Light in the North	19R02	J D Douglas	Paternoster Press	†✧ ☆
19	Writers INC ◆	19W02	Write Source	Write Source	✧
20	America: 350 Years (audio tape and workbook) ◆	20C05	Steve Wilkins	Covenant	✧
20	8 Principles of the Reformation (audio)	20C12	David Barton	Wallbuilders	✧
20	Bordan of Yale	20R05	Taylor	Foundation Am Christian Education	✧ ✱ ☆
20	Christian History of the Constitution of the U. S. A., The	20C03	Verna M. Hall	Foundation Am Christian Education	P
20	Gaining Favor With God and Man ◆	20C13	author unknown	Mantle Ministries (re-printed)	✧
20	Gardener Looks at the Fruits, A	20R03	Philip Keller		✧
20	George Washington Carver	20S05	Charels Ludwig	Sower Series	✧ ✱ ☆
20	God and Government ◆	20C11	Gary Demar	Wolgemuth and Hyatt	✧
20	Hudson Taylor's Spiritual Secret	20R14	Dr. Howard Taylor	Moody	✧
20	Jim Elliot	20R02	White		✧ ☆
20	Kneeling Christian, The	20R08	anonymous		✧
20	L'Abri	20R01	Edith Schaeffer	Tyndale House	✧
20	Light and the Glory and study guide, The	20C04	Peter Marshall and D Manuel	Revell	✧
20	Spirit-Controlled Temperament	20S04	Tim LaHaye	Tyndale	✧
20	Stories Worth Rereading	20R09	various	Review and Herald	✧
20	What Happens When Women Pray	20R07	Evenlin Christianson		✧
20	Writers INC ◆	03 W04	Write Source	Write Source	✧

◆ - Suggested in several units ✧ - Family Christian Academy ✱ - Elijah Company ☆ - Lifetime Gifts and Books 🖳 Computer store, Greenleaf Press

P - Order from publisher (see page 292 for addresses), † Most Christian book stores, ▲ All Around Education, 📖 Library V Video rental